P9-CQM-567

ALSO BY JOAN PEYSER

BERNSTEIN: A BIOGRAPHY

THE ORCHESTRA: ORIGINS AND TRANSFORMATIONS (editor)

BOULEZ: COMPOSER, CONDUCTOR, ENIGMA

20TH CENTURY MUSIC: THE SENSE BEHIND THE SOUND

SIMON & SCHUSTER

NEW YORK LONDON TORONTO SYDNEY TOKYO SINGAPORE

THE MEMORY OF ALL THAT

•

THE LIFE OF GEORGE GERSHWIN

•

JOAN PEYSER

SIMON & SCHUSTER
SIMON & SCHUSTER BUILDING
ROCKEFELLER CENTER
1230 AVENUE OF THE AMERICAS
NEW YORK, NEW YORK 10020

DESIGNED BY KAROLINA HARRIS
PICTURE SECTION DESIGNED BY BARBARA BACHMAN
MANUFACTURED IN THE UNITED STATES OF AMERICA

1 3 5 7 9 10 8 6 4 2

LIBRARY OF CONGRESS
CATALOGING-IN-PUBLICATION DATA

PEYSER, JOAN.
THE MEMORY OF ALL THAT: THE LIFE OF
GEORGE GERSHWIN/JOAN PEYSER.
P. CM.
INCLUDES INDEX.
1. GERSHWIN, GEORGE, 1898–1937.
2. COMPOSERS—UNITED STATES—BIOGRAPHY. I. TITLE.
ML410.G288P5 1993
780'.92—DC20
[B] 92-44272 CIP MN
ISBN 0-671-70948-8

TO MY MOTHER

1902–1945

ACKNOWLEDGMENTS

Other writers have devoted books to George Gershwin and I am indebted to them, particularly to Edward Jablonski, Robert Kimball and the late Alfred Simon who provided readers with a first-rate working knowledge of the songs and shows. I tried to do something different: give insight into Gershwin's character and temperament. I am grateful to Frances Gershwin Godowsky, George's only sister and youngest of the siblings, who spoke frequently and candidly to me about her parents. She also shared recollections of her brothers—Ira, the oldest, George, and Arthur. I thank Leopold Godowsky, her son, and Marc George Gershwin, Arthur's son, for giving me permission to quote from letters and use photographs and other materials.

I am also indebted to Charles Schwartz, author of a biography of Gershwin published in 1973 in which he reports a claim made by a man who calls himself Alan Gershwin that he is the composer's son. He writes that he brings the matter up "solely because it touches on an important, though little known, aspect of George's life and deserves further clarification."

Schwartz's words moved me to seek such clarification. That I succeeded is due in large measure to Joel Honig whose research proved meticulous and indefatigable.

At the start of my work on this book, virtually no Gershwin

performances were available on records. Robert Israel, a composer and president of Score Productions, a company providing original music for television and film, is a lifelong fan and had collected privately recorded sessions of Gershwin at the piano and conducting his concert works. Israel made copies of everything for me. His was an invaluable gift because most subsequent performances of these songs and compositions lack the lilt, the undulating rhythm, the sense of refusal to linger over anything that charaterizes Gershwin's own interpretations.

Libraries helped: Wayne Shirley, Elizabeth Auman, and Raymond A. White, The George and Ira Gershwin Collection at the Library of Congress; Martin Jacobs, The Theater Collection at the Museum of the City of New York; Lisa Brower, Rare Books and Manuscripts Division, The New York Public Library; The Rodgers & Hammerstein Archives of Recorded Sound, The New York Public Library at Lincoln Center.

Several authors provided overviews of complicated subjects: Eileen Southern, *The Music of Black Americans*; Russell Sanjek, *American Popular Music and Its Business*; Gunther Schuller, *Early Jazz* and *The Swing Era*. Other specialists who provided information in their respective fields are Randolph Herr, piano rolls; James T. Maher, American popular music, particularly the development of the dance band; Maurice Peress, the conductor who has performed a re-creation of Paul Whiteman's Aeolian Hall concert throughout the United States. Peress told me about certain details in Gershwin's works and emphasized the importance of exploring the influence of black music on the young Gershwin.

Through conservations and correspondence, the following people made important contributions: Stanley Adams, Carl Ashby, Milton Babbitt, Ben Bagley, Ethel Berle, Angela Boone, Victoria Bond, Mario Braggioti, Dr. Paul Brauer, Daniel Brewbaker, Irving Caesar, Rosalie Calabrese, Kitty Carlisle, Larry Charlestein, Murray Charleston, Judith Cimaglia, Robbie Cohen, Sidney Cowell, David Diamond, Kurt Dieterle, David Ehrenstein, Stephen Ellis, Judy Gershwin, Marc George Gershwin, Nancy Gershwin, Steven Gilbert, Leopold Godowsky,

Morton Gould, Lois Granato, Zena Hanenfeldt, Bill Harris, Al Hirschfeld, Paul J. Hoeffler, Dick Hyman, Leslie Hyman, Delilah Jackson, Eva Jessye, Donald Kahn, Constance Keene, Anna Koch, Paul Kresh, Miles Kreuger, Paul Laviano, Vera Lawrence, June Levant, Harris Lewine, Mitch Miller, Dr. Robert Miller, Evelyn Charleston Morris, Dr. Raj Murali, Paul Mueller, Emily Paley, Laura Pallay, Stephan Peskin, Marilyn Putnam, David Raksin, Bill Reed, Emil Renan, Dr. Ruth Richards, Ginger Rogers, Ann Ronell, Frances Schillinger, Mabel Schirmer, Murray Schneider, Wayne Schneider, Gunther Schuller, Mrs. Vladimir Selinsky, Margaret Sevo, Alfred Simon, Barry Singer, Nicolas Slonimsky, Anna Sosenko, Judith Anne Still, English Strunsky, Lucy Strunsky, Richard Sudhalter, Kay Swift, Michael Tilson Thomas, Horace Van Norman, Julia Van Norman, Artis Wodehouse, Kate Wolpin, Robert Wyatt, and William Youngren.

Three women, descendents of central figures in Gershwin's romantic life, deserve special mention.

Anne Chotzinoff Grossman, daughter of Pauline Heifetz and Samuel Chotzinoff, lent me old photographs and gave me unrestricted access to her mother's appointment books, which turned out to be virtual diaries.

Nancy Bloomer Deussen, a composer living in San Francisco and the daughter of Julia Van Norman, whose ties to Gershwin began in 1927 and lasted until his death ten years later, was equally generous.

Katharine Weber, named for her grandmother Kay Swift, shared the most personal material with me. She divulged the nature of the relationship between her grandmother and Gregory Zilboorg, Swift's and Gershwin's psychoanalyst, and made available to me unpublished pictures.

One area of Gershwin's life continues to remain mysterious. That is the character and extent of the aid he received from William Daly, his closest friend and a Harvard educated musician. My information leads me to believe that Daly helped orchestrate the concert works composed after *Raposdy in Blue* and also gave those compositions their final shape through skillful and intelligent editing. The musical ideas were Gershwin's; the form and many details owe a debt to Daly.

Stanley H. Brown, writer, editor, and my good friend for thirty years, did for me what I believe Daly did for Gershwin. To say I find him irreplaceable is not an exaggeration. We shall never know if Daly was irreplaceable to Gershwin. He died in December 1936, and Gershwin died seven months later.

Frank Driggs, jazz historian, photo archivist, and the man most central to my life, contributed the photographs from his collection and helped select and prepare the others here, making this photo section remarkable. He also led me to his many friends in the jazz world and all of them proved generous with their help. Driggs and I spent countless hours in New York's jazz clubs. We listened, in particular, to the great trumpeter Doc Cheatham, who played as far back as Gershwin's own time, and to Vince Giordano, whose band, The Nighthawks, recreates the arrangements of the music of that period.

I thank my good friends Myrna Lamb, Liza Redfield and Richard Goldstone for the ways they continue to nourish me. I am grateful to my brother, Robert Gilbert, both for his friendship and the photographs he took that appear in this volume. My profound gratitude goes to my children—Dr. Karen Seligman, Tony Peyser, and Monica Peyser. Now that all of them are engaged in professional lives that, incidentally, mesh with my own needs, their gifts are more than the emotional sustenance they have always extended to me. They are specialized, concrete, and invaluable.

Roslyn Targ, my agent and friend, not only gives me the support for which every writer longs; in this instance she intuitively led me to exactly the right publisher. Gershwin's biography was first published in 1931 by Simon & Schuster. Gershwin was so pleased with it that he not only wrote to at least one friend of his positive reaction; the following year he entrusted Simon & Schuster with the publication of his now famous *Songbook*.

It gives me great satisfaction, then, that *The Memory of All That* is appearing under the same imprint. I want to thank all the people at Simon & Schuster for their fine work, most particularly Bob Bender, the book's editor, Gypsy da Silva, production editor, and Bruce Macomber, who closely edited the manuscript.

Joan Peyser

December 1, 1992

INTRODUCTION

The picture most of us have of George Gershwin is that of a vigorous young man, jutting jaw, big nose, hair combed back, cigar in his mouth, in profile at a piano much like the Hirschfeld image in the photo section of this book. Always nattily dressed, often sporting a cane, Gershwin—in this version—projected an air of being at one with post–World War I New York, a self-involved, cocky Manhattanite who monopolized the piano at parties from Fifth and Park avenues to Long Island's grand estates.

But Gershwin's version of himself, in the photo section, is a vastly different image. Based on an Edward Steichen photograph of 1927, this picture—long owned by Paul Mueller, Gershwin's valet for the last seven years of his life—suggests quite another person. Gershwin's Gershwin is melancholy, thoughtful, a man very different from Steichen's and the popular view of the composer.

In 1988, Mueller gave the picture to Alan Gershwin, who, as a small boy, used to accompany his mother to the Gershwin apartments on Riverside Drive, and on East Seventy-second Street. The visits, Mueller said, were hurried and secretive, but there was never any doubt among those present that the boy was Gershwin's. When Alan Gershwin visited Mueller in the spring of 1988, the old man gave Gershwin's self-portrait to him and said that, although it was his most valuable possession, it belonged to the artist's son.

The difference between the two conceptions of Gershwin strongly suggests that the body of writing that has been published about the composer thus far is inadequate in its portrayal of the man. Gershwin knew he was not that man in the Hirschfeld cartoon; he must certainly have believed he was the man in his own painting.

Why then have we been subjected to a vision of Gershwin as limited in its dimensions as a caricature? Perhaps the most important reason is that much of what we were allowed to know about him came from the woman who was closest to him, Leonore Strunsky Gershwin, his brother Ira's wife. She has been the primary source of information about the composer for more than fifty years. A mixture of love, envy, and rage characterized her connection to him while he lived. When he was mortally sick, she dismissed his complaints as a relentless effort to call attention to himself.

We have many books about Gershwin that articulate their authors' indebtedness to Leonore and reduce this complex man to a two-dimensional figure. The consequence is that our picture of Gershwin bears no resemblance at all to the sad, unfocused portrait he gave his valet.

This book is not a diary. I have made no effort to be encyclopedic, to note all of the songs, or every song that appeared in more than one show, or George's itinerary on his European trips, or all the people he would have identified as his friends. What I have tried to do is convey to the reader how Gershwin himself might have viewed the trajectory of his life from its end, with those who were crucial to him emphasized.

A major tool in recreating the memory of all that comes from Ira's lyrics. An indefatigable diarist on his own, Ira also provided information about George. When he became his brother's primary lyricist in 1924, Ira began giving us a diary of the major events in his brother's life, which have been shrouded in secrecy.

WHAT goes on in a man's life derives from what went on when he was a boy. Patterns established in childhood become fixed; people repeat them again and again, hoping the outcome will be different at least once.

Where Gershwin is concerned, my primary source of information on the character and temperament of his parents comes from Frances Gershwin Godowsky, the youngest child of Rose and Morris, the only sister of Ira, George, and Arthur, and the only survivor of the four as this book is written.

At a Gershwin song recital in New York's Merkin Hall during the spring of 1991, Mark Grant, the producer, asked Frances Godowsky to speak. At first she told of a time she entered George's studio and found him playing "a catchy tune" for Ira. It was only four measures and was limited in pitch range, moving less than four whole notes, from F up to B-flat. Its appeal lay in the idiosyncratic offbeat accents worked into the traditional 4/4 meter. Ira listened, she said, and walked out of the room with an expression of "despair and disgust. 'How do you expect me,' he asked, 'to find a lyric for something like that?' Then he solved the problem with the lyric 'Fascinating Rhythm.' "

She sat back in her seat, apparently finished. Suddenly she reclaimed the microphone: "I just thought of another anecdote."

She told how when her brother George was ten he wanted to see a particular movie. When his mother refused him the price of admission, he went out on the street, took off his shoes, and, barefoot, begged money from strangers, saying, "I am a very poor boy." The audience laughed. Their image of Gershwin, like most people's, was in such conflict with this tale that a chuckle seemed appropriate. But the story is not funny; it is bizarre.

Afterward, her son, Leopold Godowsky, Jr., said that he had never heard that story before.

On some level Frances Godowsky must have known she was telling the public something dangerous; she presented this story as an afterthought. Her behavior echoed what had been going on between us in perhaps a dozen interviews. She frequently would offer something relatively innocuous before recalling something insightful and perhaps painful.

Before she would offer revelations about her mother, she would repeatedly insist that she not be made to appear disloyal. The portrait of Rose presented by her only daughter is crucial to our understanding of George. One of her revelations was that her mother was so self-absorbed, so narcissistic that, until Frances actually received a proposal of marriage, nothing in her relationship with her mother led her to believe that anyone would ever want to marry her. She said that she had no idea of how to be a wife or mother. "I had no role model," she explained. "There was no relationship," she said, "between the parents and children in my family. My mother made no relationship with any of us, not even with George. She was not mean, just a very bad mother who did not give herself to anyone. Everyone always had to do for her." When she did marry, Frances reported that she entered psychoanalysis on the advice of the psychiatrist Lawrence Kubie.

A vain woman, one of the first in the United States to undergo cosmetic surgery, Rose Gershwin seems to have radiated a kind of mesmerizing charm. But she was so protective of her own interests, her own privacy, that, according to Kate Wolpin, her younger sister, after their mother died, Rose refused to care for her own father for even one day.

In 1990, when Kate Wolpin was almost a hundred years old, she recounted some of the vicissitudes surrounding her older sister's will. Initially, she said, because her husband was not doing well, Rose arranged to leave her $10,000. Later, when his financial lot improved, Rose took Kate out of her will. Then, on her deathbed, Rose apparently felt remorse and instructed Ira, in the presence of Kate, to give her two diamond bracelets. After Rose died, Ira's wife, Leonore, ordered Kate to leave the bracelets in Rose's estate. Kate obeyed, and Leonore bought the bracelets from the estate. Leonore frequently told Ira that she was a replica of his mother. Her observation may have been correct. The most striking similarity between Rose and Leonore—apart from an imperious, demanding manner—was an obsession with diamonds. Truman Capote, in his *The Muses Are Heard*, an account of the first U.S. production of *Porgy and Bess* in Russia, introduced Leonore as "a woman devoted to diamonds, who wears them, quite a few, at both breakfast and dinner."

The point of illustrating the rapaciousness of Rose and Leonore is not to suggest that creativity derives from the character defects of an artist's relatives. Rather it is to observe that Gershwin's achievements—the quantity and even the form of his output—are directly related to his frequent need to please someone other than himself. In *They Went That-a-Way*, Malcolm Forbes's 1988 book about the deaths of famous people, Forbes quotes a Gershwin letter written at the end of the composer's life: "I am 38, famous, and rich, but profoundly unhappy. Why?" Forbes does not identify the recipient of the letter, but Paul Mueller reports that one sunny afternoon in his employer's last year, while Mueller was lying under an apple tree, Gershwin asked him precisely the same question.

Isaac Goldberg's biography, published in 1931 after Gershwin had already enjoyed a phenomenally successful decade, is the only book on Gershwin written by anyone who spent time with him. Goldberg writes of the composer's sadness: "Laughter comes easily to him, but so does a certain half-puzzled solemnity. . . . In these moments . . . he is prone to regard himself as a rather sad young man, adrift in a universe foredoomed to unhappiness." Goldberg quotes Gershwin: "If I cared for the ballad type of song I could write reams of them now, full of sad sobs and moony languors. But it wouldn't be me. And later, when I'd get over my blues, I'd play them through and feel that they were written by somebody else. When I'm in my normal mood, the tunes come dripping off my fingers. And they're lively tunes, full of outdoor pep." Goldberg suggests that what we get from the music is "from a Gershwin who may be over the blues, but a Gershwin who still feels them vibrating through his being."

One need not excerpt passages from *Mourning and Melancholia* to make Freud's point that he invariably finds in sad people the same impossible longing for the mother. One need go no further than to Frances Godowsky's description of her mother and consider it in light of a remark by George quoted in Goldberg's biography: "As for my mother," he told Goldberg, "she is what the mammy writers write about and what the mammy singers sing about. But they don't mean it and I do."

George was thirty-two when he said that. By that time he had written music for more than a dozen Broadway shows; composed *Rhapsody in Blue*, Concerto in F, and *An American in Paris;* and seen his face on the cover of *Time* magazine. He had made enough money to buy a house on 103d Street off Riverside Drive and move his entire family into it. A few years later, when he decided to move out and set up quarters with Ira and Leonore in adjoining apartments a mile and a half away, Rose went to bed with what she said was an attack of asthma and threatened that, in moving out, George would bring about her death. At that time, his father asked him why he had taken so long to get away from home.

In 1945 Warner Brothers produced the movie *Rhapsody in Blue*, a biography of Gershwin starring Robert Alda. Though it was for the most part a typical Hollywood version of life, it was nevertheless perceptive in some ways. The original screenplay was by Sonya Levien, who had worked with Gershwin in Hollywood and had become a good friend at the end. Even so, the writer did not show Rose as she was. Mothers then were expected to be the kind of women portrayed in the movie by actress Rosemary DeCamp—sweet, self-denying, supportive, domestic. Even so, Rose objected to one aspect of this fiction: "I never wore an apron in my life," she said. But the omnipresent apron on DeCamp does not begin to suggest the degree of distortion of Rose's character.

The real Rose was a woman who moved her face away when her son tried to kiss her; who, periodically—according to her sister Kate Wolpin—asked George if he didn't think she deserved a new mink coat—then, when he answered yes, bought a sable; who took every opportunity to point out that other composers were getting more favorable reviews than he; and who, at the end of his life, when Ira called her from California to say that George was dying and that she should get on the next plane, asked, "What good could I do then?"

George seems to have inherited his mother's looks; he also possessed her energy, gregariousness, and ambition, and her inability to connect to others. Was that a liability when it came to his work? The Russian novelist Ivan Turgenev described a writer in one of his books this way: "Like most writers, he was a cold man." The personalities of artists vary, of course, but most seem to have in common a certain self-absorbed concentration bordering on secrecy. Stories proliferate about how George invariably went to the piano on entering a room and played until it was time to leave.

Observers have said that Rose criticized her son for monopolizing the piano this way. He answered that if he did not play, he couldn't possibly have a good time. Almost every biographer has told the story of Gershwin at a party, sitting with a showgirl on his lap. When he is invited to play, he jumps up so quickly the girl falls to the floor. His behavior calls to mind Adrian Leverkuhn, the composer in Thomas Mann's *Doktor Faustus*, who, on entering a brothel, always went straight to the piano because it was, he said, the only friend in the room.

Relatives and friends agree that Rose never showed any emotion when George died. They say that it was she who would not let him marry, that no woman ever met her standards for him. Judy Gershwin, his brother Arthur's widow, agreed and added, "No wonder. Can you imagine what would have happened if George *had* married, what a difference that would have made to the family with royalties, ASCAP payments and so on?"

Artists do not need loving or supportive parents in order to succeed. Supportive parents, in fact, may even interfere with a child's success in art. Arnold Schoenberg, Igor Stravinsky, Edgard Varèse, Leonard Bernstein, and Pierre Boulez all had harsh fathers who humiliated their sons and told them that they would never succeed if they went into music. Maybe that is the combination needed to become a creative force: one hostile and destructive parent and the force that pushes an artist to triumph over a prediction he refuses to tolerate.

This creative force, call it drive, does not recognize a division between mind and body. It characterized Gershwin's fierce competing at Ping-Pong and tennis and his "playing" throughout his adult life as well as his remarkable capacity for inventiveness. "It is always possible," Gershwin wrote in an introduction to *Tin Pan Alley: A Chronicle of the Popular Music Scene*, a 1930 book by Isaac Goldberg, who would become his first biographer, "to invent something original."

Before George, the Gershwin family produced no musicians. In answer to a request for information on his background from biographer Goldberg, Gershwin was brief but emphasized invention. "My mother's father was a furrier," he wrote. "My paternal grandfather was some sort of inventor; his ingenuity had to do with the Czar's guns."

According to Kate Wolpin, their parents were born in Vilna

and moved to St. Petersburg. Some books cite St. Petersburg—a place from which Jews were generally excluded—as the birthplace of Rose's parents. Frances Godowsky explained the discrepancy this way: "My mother would have said St. Petersburg because that would make her grander." When Morris Gershovitz applied for American citizenship, he gave the date of arrival here as August 14, 1890. Several Gershwin biographies state that he and Rose married in July 1895, but no record of the marriage seems to exist. Kate Wolpin says she cannot recall the ceremony, and this upsets her because she was told she had been a flower girl. The absence of any record of George's parents' marriage is not an isolated phenomenon in the documentation of Gershwin's history (and of many other immigrant families at that time).

There are, for example, no records for him at P.S. 25, the only school he attended that still exists. It is possible that the papers simply fell apart over the years. It is also possible that, because of what Gershwin became, the people in his family who handled his affairs decided to sanitize the entire picture. In 1990 the producers of the album of *Girl Crazy* selected a photograph of the brothers on the terrace of their penthouse apartments. What they liked best was the informality of the shot with Ira unshaven. But Leonore would not release the photograph unless she was guaranteed that Ira's stubble would be airbrushed away. The Gershwin family has devoted time, money, and energy to removing the warts and stubble from all portraits of the Gershwin brothers.

George's school record was not admirable. He was a dirty, neglected child. His grades were bad. He seems never to have read. He fought, stole, and played hooky. The late Jack Miller, a childhood friend, has reported that George bragged to him that he had had his first girl at nine. In 1973 Miller even brought Alan Gershwin, whose identity he always accepted, to West Seventy-second Street, where he introduced him to a "Mrs. Rose Garfield," then in a wheelchair, who had been the recipient of George's early lust. The Goldberg biography confirms Miller's claim:

> [George] had been a hard kid. At six, it appears, he was almost as blasé and worldly as he is today. He had a girl at nine—the age of Dante's first encounter with Beatrice. He remembers now that he was fond of her because she played and sang. . . . Certainly his parents held no high hope for his future. He was, frankly, a bad child. He was guilty of petty pilfering. He ran the gamut of minor infractions. With a little less luck he might have become a gangster, for the neighborhood in which his father's first restaurant was situated was also the neighborhood that bred Lefty Louis and Gyp the Blood.

Obviously Gershwin, who cooperated closely with Goldberg and later gave the biography to colleagues as gifts, felt no need to delete or distort these facts about his childhood. Nor did he appear embarrassed at the now legendary malapropisms of his father; in fact, he advertised them. Frances expresses astonishment that Morris's gaffes—"Fascinating Rhythm" became "Fashion on the River"—which used to humiliate her, were repeated by George to his high-society friends. She says she admired her brother for being able to do that.

Morris Gershovitz had been a cutter for women's shoes in St. Petersburg. In New York he became an entrepreneur. On December 6, 1896, when his first son was born, the birth certificate gave the child's name as Israel, the father's occupation as "laborer." Ira grew up thinking that because he was called Izzy his name was Isadore and had difficulty much later adapting to Israel. A few months before Ira's birth, the Gershovitzes had lived at 302 East Houston Street. When the first child arrived the address was 60 Eldridge Street. The pattern of repeated moves persisted. In 1938 Ira wrote, "We were always moving. When my father sold a business and started another we would inevitably move to another neighborhood. George and I counted over twenty different flats and apartments we remember having lived in during those days."

Before George began supporting the family, Gershovitz was part owner of several restaurants, a number of Turkish baths, and a billiard parlor. For a month he was bookmaker at the Belmont racetrack. Ira writes that his father's bookmaking job came to an end quickly because "too many favorites won." Rose had no influence over Morris at the track. As far as his other enterprises were concerned, it was she who handled the finances and who hocked her diamonds when times were hard.

Frances remembers her father "mostly as my mother's chauffeur." He did whatever Rose told him to do. Those who knew Ira well report that, as a husband, he modeled himself after his father: he never stood up to Leonore.

By September 26, 1898, when George was born, the family name had been changed to Gershvin, often pronounced "Gershwine." The child's name on the birth certificate read Jacob, his paternal grandfather's name, although there is no evidence he was ever called anything but George. At the time of his birth, the family was living at 242 Snediker Avenue in Brooklyn. When George was one, they were at 425 Third Avenue in Manhattan. In 1901 and 1902 they were living again in Brooklyn. But in 1903, when George was five and about to start school, the Gershwins were in Manhattan to stay.

Morris was not a strong father who put himself between mother and son to give warmth where there was none. His mispronunciation of "Fascinating Rhythm" may have been a continuation of the harsh deprecation of George he had meted out when George was a child, when Morris drummed into him that he would grow up to be a bum. George's recounting, then, in his years of great success, the wide variety of ways Morris showed his social obtuseness may not have been an act of filial love but rather a sophisticated kind of revenge.

In addition to drive, Schoenberg, Stravinsky, Varèse, Bernstein, and Boulez each had someone close to him who believed he was great—perhaps even a genius. Bernstein and Boulez got this adulation from their sisters. George received his from Ira, and that was a remarkable gift for, as the firstborn son in a Jewish family, Ira had been the focus of whatever dreams his parents had.

Ira was an orderly boy, a reader, a good student in public

school. When teachers sent letters home complaining about George, it was Ira, not Rose or Morris, who dealt with the trouble, assuring authorities George would behave. Ira was the only son to be given a bar mitzvah. (Although Frances was only three at the time, one incident stands out for her. She was sharing a bed with George, and during the night that followed the bar mitzvah and the reception, she awakened to see a large suitcase being lowered outside her window. She says she tried to awaken George but he continued to sleep. In the morning the family discovered the theft of all of Ira's bar mitzvah gifts.)

The year after the bar mitzvah, when he was fourteen and George twelve, Rose bought an upright piano because her sister Kate owned one. She intended to have Ira take lessons. But as soon as the instrument was hoisted through the window of their second-floor apartment, George sat down and began to play. He had been visiting Jack Miller, pianist of the Beethoven Society, an amateur orchestra whose members ranged in age from nine to fifty. Miller had a piano in his living room which he had invited George to use. George changed teachers frequently because he outstripped them quickly. Miller brought him to Charles Hambitzer, his own teacher.

On one occasion in 1914, when both Miller and George were at Hambitzer's, they exchanged their addresses on the cover of a Grieg sonata that belonged to Miller. Miller saw to it that the Beethoven Society admitted his young friend. In a 1924 interview, Gershwin said, "Studying the piano made a good boy out of a bad one. It took the piano to tone me down. . . . I was a changed person after I took it up."

Hambitzer, a teacher and composer from Milwaukee, recognized George's gifts right away, confirming what George himself sensed. Hambitzer had a reputation then; the New York Philharmonic Society had performed his works and he had composed *The Love Wager*, a light opera. Hambitzer also played in the Waldorf-Astoria orchestra. At the same time, he revealed a more adventurous musical intelligence by playing Schoenberg's Six Short Piano Pieces.

In a letter to his sister, Hambitzer wrote of George, "The boy is a genius, without a doubt. He wants to go in for this modern stuff, jazz and what not. But I'm not going to let him for a while. I'll see that he gets a firm foundation in the standard music first."

George told Goldberg that Hambitzer gave him a sense of harmony. That was a crucial contribution, for in his treatment of harmony George is far more adventurous than any of his Tin Pan Alley colleagues. Not only are the chords daring, the melody is too. For example, consider the "who" in the second line of "Somebody Loves Me." As soon as you hear it, even if you are untrained in music, you know that it is somehow unconventional and innovative.

At first Hambitzer was outgoing and ebullient, a mature version of the temperament George showed to the world. Gershwin later said he was "the first great musical influence in my life." He certainly made many right decisions for him. He sent him to Edward Kilenyi for lessons in harmony and theory and coached him in performances of Chopin, Liszt, and Debussy. If Hambitzer had seen to it that George studied counterpoint too, Gershwin might have felt less vulnerable later when critics attacked him for an absence of technique.

However grateful George was to Miller for introducing him to the piano, music, and Hambitzer, he did not respect him as he did Ira. Jack was a boy with a pronounced Yiddish accent and no apparent intellect. Ira, however, was not only—from George's point of view—an expert in the English language, he was a voracious reader and an able student.

In the January 1972 issue of *ASCAP Today*, Yip Harburg, like Ira a major lyricist, talked about their boyhood friendship through their school days:

> Ira was the shyest, most diffident boy we had ever known. In a class of lower east side raucus rapscallions, his soft-spoken gentleness and low-keyed personality made him a lovable incongruity. He spoke in murmurs, hiding behind a pair of steel-rimmed spectacles. . . . He never laughed aloud. Whenever the other boys went into paroxysms over a professor's joke, the most it evoked from Ira was a multiple bobbing of the head, a muffled chuckle and a sun-burst blush. . . .

> Ira had a kid brother who was a source of embarrassment to him. He wore high stiff collars, shirts with cuffs and went out with girls. Like George B. Shaw, George Gershwin found school an institution to be avoided at all costs. His brother Ira was "my brother Ira the scholar." This admiration for Ira the scholar was lifelong, profound and of the greatest significance in the growth, development and evolvement of George's creative genius.
>
> Twenty hit shows later, George still looked to Ira for guidance, for critical evaluation, for taste. . . . When Ira failed to nod, George would attack the keyboard with renewed dynamic vigor, until he met Ira's intransigent . . . demands.

Just as Ira kept a literary scrapbook, George kept a music book with photographs and captions of major classical musicians—Liszt, Josef Hofmann, Josef Lhévinne, Ferruccio Busoni, and Alexander Glazunov. There were also photographs of Wagner and Massenet as well as programs of the various concerts he attended at Wanamaker, the New Aeolian, and Carnegie Hall. Ira, who had been taking piano lessons with his aunt Kate, stopped them as soon as it became clear that music was his brother's domain.

Long before the upright piano first entered the Gershwin apartment, George sensed that music had special meaning for him. From the time he was six until he was nine, living on 126th Street, he would roller-skate around the neighborhood for the excitement that could be found there. Once he told Goldberg, that, barefoot and in overalls, he heard Rubinstein's "Melody in F" coming from a nickelodeon on 125th Street. This was in 1904. There were no radios or electric phonographs then. Music was unavailable to him. "The peculiar jumps in the music held me rooted," he told Goldberg.

Four years later Maxie Rosenzweig, a student at P.S. 25, played Dvořák's "Humoresque" in a school assembly. Playing hooky at the time, George heard the performance through an open window. Struck by the beauty of what he heard, he ran through the rain after school to Rosenzweig's apartment to express his excitement. The boys became friends. Rosenzweig went on to a career as a concert violinist under the name Max Rosen and may have been the very first in a line of musical colleagues to attack George on his musicianship. Rosenzweig told his friend to forget his ambition; he didn't have what it took.

Ira, on the other hand, never discouraged George. Much shorter than George, Ira was broad shouldered and stocky, like his father. While George's head appeared long and thin, Ira's seemed to be almost square. Whereas George was hyperactive—in too much of a hurry to remain in high school for more than one year—Ira went to Townsend Harris, a public high school run like a private prep school. While there he wrote "Much Ado," a column for the school paper, with Harburg. Later, at City College, he collaborated with Harburg on a feature called "Gargoyle Gargles."

During these years, Ira was as helpful to George as he had been as a child, when he would extricate him from trouble at school. At City College, he arranged for his brother to play in an annual entertainment sponsored by an organization called the Finley Club. George appeared not only as an accompanist but as piano soloist in a work of his own.

While he was at City College, Ira sent an article to Paul Potter, an English playwright who had dramatized *Trilby*. Potter lived in a hotel above the Turkish bath owned by Morris Gershwin, where Ira worked as a cashier. Potter suggested that Ira send it to *The Smart Set*, a magazine edited by H. L. Mencken. The piece was accepted, and Ira received a one-dollar fee. Ira continued to submit pieces but no more were accepted.

In 1973 Ira told jazz writer John Wilson that "Potter seemed to think that a writer doesn't necessarily have to experience everything he writes about, but by being an attentive listener and observer can gain a good deal by second-hand experience." So for the next twenty years, Ira would generally be seen at parties standing in the corner and watching George's every move. Watching his brother closely seems to have provided him with more than a life; it generated his lyrics. And they proved to be a virtual diary of George's life, which turned out to be useful, because George didn't keep a diary of his own.

Ira, on the other hand, a sober and reflective man, wrote in his lyrics what he believed George should have felt about the situations he found himself in. In her writings about Paulette Goddard, the movie actress and the only woman with whom George said he had been "in love," Anita Loos touched on this curious phenomenon saying that George's feeling for Paulette had found expression in one of the last ballads he ever composed. "They Can't Take That Away from Me." The lyric, Loos noted, was by George's brother Ira, who had been inspired to write about the way Goddard wore her hat, sipped her tea, and sang off key.

The United States at this time had no composers who could be considered in the same league with, for example, Verdi and Brahms, artists who represented the culmination of several centuries of high art. But American music did have a freshness and vitality that came mainly from two sources: Jews arriving in New York from eastern Europe and blacks.

Many of the Jewish immigrants worked in sweat shops. The luckier ones had their own businesses. Because Morris Gershovitz had been a leatherworker in St. Petersburg, he was in the artisan class and lived better than most. The apartment buildings where the Gershwins lived were more than decent. Most of them remain in place today, and the dates of the brickwork show they were new when the family moved in. Rose could afford a maid, and family photographs include a young woman servant.

Aware that George was no student, Rose planned an accountant's life for him; that was why he went to the High School of Commerce. But when, in 1914, he left school for a fifteen-dollar-a-week job at Remick's, a music publishing house on Tin Pan Alley, she put up no argument. There might have been only fifteen dollars a week for her son then, but she knew big money could be made in the popular music scene.

Tin Pan Alley got its name because the sounds coming from pianos in the cubicles of the houses on Twenty-eighth Street from Sixth Avenue to Broadway made one writer think of people banging on tin pans. In place as early as 1885, sheet music was its major product.

At first, most of the music sold was noncopyright European and a high-class variety of American pop. The lower-class music that could be heard in dance halls, beer gardens, or concert saloons was ignored by these publishers in favor of the European pieces. In 1891, however, a reciprocal international copyright agreement ended American access to new foreign music and forced the owners of the new publishing firms to draw on the American vernacular. When they did, they used the advertising, sales techniques, and promotion methods that had recently been developed by American business.

Publishers who dealt in the new popular music included the Witmark brothers, Edward B. Marks and Joseph Stern, Maurice Shapiro, Leo Feist, Harry von Tilzer, Will Rossiter, F. S. Mills, Joe Jordan, and Jerome Remick. The owners taught their salesmen how to publicize a song by constant repetition or "song plugging." In 1914, at fifteen, George became fully employed. According to an article written by Ira soon after George died, "He was probably the youngest piano pounder ever employed in Tin Pan Alley. He played all day, traveled to nearby cities to accompany the song pluggers, was sent to vaudeville houses to report which acts were using Remick songs, wrote a tune now and then and whenever he could attended concerts."

It was George's outgoing nature, talent, and drive that got him the job. Ben Bloom, a friend in the business, introduced him to Mose Gumble, manager at Remick's, which was housed in a three-story building squeezed between Warner Music and Clipper Printing, all drab brownstones on the block. Inside, every cubicle burst with action; half English, half Yiddish was the industry's language.

To hide his youth, George wore a conservative suit and tie to work. He slicked back his dark hair and joined his colleagues cranking out pop tunes—love songs, novelty ditties, barroom ballads, whatever would sell. This was activity Hambitzer could not tolerate, so George stopped his regular piano lessons at sixteen.

Ira wrote of George's composing "a tune now and then," but adds he was not allowed to combine songwriting with his regular duties. "One day," Ira wrote, "George submitted a song of his own to the professional manager. He was told: 'You're here as a pianist, not a writer. We've got plenty of writers under contract.' Shortly afterward, in March 1917, he gave up his job. Even before that, at another house [Harry von Tilzer], a song of his had been accepted. This was in 1916 and the song was called 'When You Want 'Em You Can't Get 'Em, When You've Got 'Em You Don't Want 'Em.' George received an advance of five dollars. Murray Roth, who wrote the lyrics, received fifteen."

George explained the discrepancy between his pay and Roth's to Goldberg. Von Tilzer had offered each an advance of fifteen dollars. Roth took it, while George "waived an advance, wanting my royalties—glamorous word—in a lump sum. After some time I went to von Tilzer and asked him for a little cash on the song. He handed me five dollars. And I never got a cent more from him."

Sophie Tucker, the great red-hot mama of show business, persuaded von Tilzer to publish it. The lyrics reflect the sexist tone of the times. This was four years before women were given the vote and when prostitutes lived and worked in almost every neighborhood in New York.

Verse

A little loving now and then
Is relished by the best of men.
That's a proverb old and true,
Still somehow it's always new.
A fellow wants a girlie, bad,
But there's none to be had.
No matter how you try,
You cannot reason why
Things always turn out like this:

Chorus

When you want 'em,
You can't get 'em,
When you've got 'em

You don't want 'em.
All the wise men try to dope it out,
But it seems they're always left in doubt.
When you get 'em,
Then you pet 'em,
When you lose 'em
You forget 'em;
At certain times you have too many,
And lots of other times you haven't any,
When you've got 'em you don't want 'em,
You're never satisfied at all.

At eighteen, George took this very ordinary idea and applied ingenuity to it. The melody is fairly standard for the day, but he played a joke with the pace of the song. The first four lines of the chorus take up a conventional four bars. When the same words return near the end of the song, Gershwin squeezes them into half the original length of time.

A profit of five dollars a song was not what George had in mind when he forsook Hambitzer's lessons and the possibility of a concert pianist's career for a life in Tin Pan Alley. He could not live on this kind of royalty, nor could he help to contribute to the family purse if he depended on it. Even before he left Remick, George began to supplement his income by making piano rolls.

Gershwin in late 1915 was a seventeen-year-old boy going to work every day on West Twenty-eighth Street, making a trip to Perfection Studios in East Orange, New Jersey, to cut piano rolls, continuing his visits to the New York concert halls, and putting entries into his music scrapbook. Gershwin's heart was still partly in the world of serious music, but he dared not commit himself to it. First, he needed money badly. Second, he did not believe he had the right to be in that world.

Until then the only Jews who had achieved impressive careers as composers were the Germans and Austrians—Mendelssohn, Mahler, and Schoenberg—highly educated, assimilated men who had formally converted to other religions in order to make their way in this world. George could not possibly identify with them, so he set out to write popular music. Cornered and frustrated, he worked hard, never taking time off, pushing himself so that one day he would reach the point where he would find himself free from his imprisonment.

Almost immediately his family's standard of living rose. In the movie *Rhapsody in Blue*, neighbors visiting the Gershwins after the start of George's success comment on the family's new furniture. They say it must have been bought with George's income. "And what is the matter with that?" Morris asks.

When George started cutting piano rolls, Perfection was making about twenty rolls a week. There was no notion of a serious artistic effort here, just a production line. The company's purpose was to sell piano rolls.

Those in charge picked pianists who were good sight readers. The pieces were generally divided this way: intro, verse, chorus, and a few concluding notes. The performers repeated the chorus at least twice, rarely embellishing or varying what they had done the first time around. In that way they would fill the roll, which lasted from two to three minutes. Gershwin followed this pattern. The material he was given was generally dull; and before 1920 it was hardly ever his own.

Mike Montgomery, a piano-roll historian who has been collecting rolls for decades, believes that nobody sensed then that the piano roll could last. The period under discussion here—the second decade of the century—did not know of the radio or the electric phonograph. The idea of music historians ever studying these rolls—which is happening now—would have been inconceivable.

George used to go to Perfection Studios on Saturday afternoons, sit down and acquaint himself with the songs. Then he would make them as interesting as he could and walk out, leaving his work behind him. Often he would overdub his own work, creating a heavy texture, in vogue at that time. This was not the same as doing a phonograph recording. The rolls were not as telling as even the earliest phonograph records were. Gershwin had no more control at Perfection than he had at Remick. The piano-roll business was like the sheet-music business; its purpose was to make money, and George's purpose in being there was the same.

It is not surprising then that Gershwin's early rolls are less interesting than rolls by other pianists. He went in and out of the studio fast, the way one biographer claims he had sex with whores—no foreplay, no embellishments. He was there to do a job; over a period of eleven years, between 1915 and 1926, Gershwin made about 130 rolls. The later ones are the best.

At the start, a roll cost fifty or seventy-five cents, enough to buy a steak dinner or a night in a hotel. George got thirty-five dollars for six rolls, more than two weeks' salary at Remick's, far more than the income from his first published song. To convey the impression it had many pianists on its staff, Perfection had George use pseudonyms: James Baker, Fred Murtha, and Bert Wynne. Robert Kimball, a historian of American popular music, claims that Gershwin used the name Wynne because he admired the comedian Ed Wynn. Kimball says that it was for the same reason that, in 1915, George changed the last syllable of his name from *vin* to *win*.

As unimpressive as his early rolls were, the instrument clearly influenced his aesthetic. The Pianola style affected his playing when George sat down at the conventional piano. Gershwin gave peppy, staccato performances, even of his own works. His playing, to cite one example, of "Someone to Watch Over Me" on the conventional piano sounds bored, even mechanical, as though Gershwin had no notion of the loveliness of his own melody.

This was not the way Josef Hofmann or Paderewski played. Gershwin did not achieve what has generally been considered an idiosyncratic piano style from the Europeans playing in concerts or salons in high-class neighborhoods of New York. He got his piano style not only from the player piano but also from the black musicians he watched and heard in Harlem.

Though he drew heavily on the ideas and direction of black music, Gershwin did not adequately credit blacks for their enormous influence on his work. In *The Gershwins*, a book published in 1973 celebrating the seventy-fifth anniversary of Gershwin's birth, Kimball writes, "George Gershwin was certainly one of the earliest [white songwriters] to seek out black music purely from personal interest. He soaked himself in it."

It is impossible to write about Gershwin without acknowledging the profound influence black music had on him from his adolescence. One way he immersed himself in it was through frequent visits to Barron Wilkins's nightclub on Seventh Avenue and 135th Street when, in his mid-teens, he was living on West 111th Street. He went to listen to the black musicians playing there under James Reese Europe. Europe, who studied classical violin as a boy, founded the Clef Club in 1910; it was an organization of a hundred men that provided a kind of booking agency for black musicians. Leading the orchestra that accompanied the dance team of Vernon and Irene Castle, Europe played a crucial role in popularizing the fox-trot.

Europe also conducted his black musicians in music that became known as ragtime. Then he tried to move back into the classical realm. In 1912, he rented Carnegie Hall for three consecutive annual concerts. He engaged as his concertmaster Will Marion Cook, another classically trained black musician, who exerted considerable influence on black music around the turn of the century.

Born in 1869, Cook learned to play the violin and went abroad to train. In Germany he worked with Joseph Joachim, the renowned virtuoso and a close friend of Brahms's. In describing Cook, pianist and composer Eubie Blake said he was "the man who taught me to conduct. I believe he was the reincarnation of Richard Wagner—looked like him, too. Very proud! He studied in Leipzig. Cook never wore a hat because he was proud of his bushy hair. That was what gave him away so you could know he was a Negro. Most eccentric man I ever met."

In 1895, after his return from abroad, Cook gave a recital in Carnegie Hall, and although the debut was a success, the critics enraged him by calling him "the best colored violinist" they ever heard. Cook swore that because of the rampant racism here, he would never appear on an American concert stage again.

Cook's demand to be treated on a par with the most distinguished of white artists revealed itself not only in the choice of Joachim as his violin teacher but in his selection of Antonin Dvořák for composition. When Cook returned to the United States he did so with Dvořák, who loved the music of the Negro and wrote his ninth symphony in a tribute to the music of the "new world." In 1898 Cook attracted considerable attention with a work he called an operetta, in collaboration with Paul Laurence Dunbar, an eminent black poet. Called *Clorindy, Or The Origin of the Cakewalk*, it dealt with the genesis of the cakewalk, a black dance that made fun of white plantation owners. Mounted in the roof garden of the Casino Theater, a legitimate house on 69th Street and Broadway, it provoked so much applause and cheering that Cook wrote, "He simply stood there transfixed."

Both blacks and whites contributed to the development of indigenous music, and each listened to what the other was doing. As early as 1846, Louis Moreau Gottschalk, born in New Orleans and educated in Europe, incorporated elements of the black music he heard around his hometown in his concert works. Forty years later George Whitefield Chadwick, also educated in Europe and one of a group known as the "Boston Classicists," introduced echoes of the cakewalk into his Symphony no. 2. Cook celebrated the cakewalk, a black entertainment that parodied plantation owners, as did many blacks of the time.

In 1912, when James Reese Europe decided to give his concerts with his black musicians at Carnegie Hall, Cook agreed to serve as his concertmaster.

When the black musicians appeared at Carnegie Hall in the first of the three concerts, a great deal of what they did was ragtime. Some musicians used conventional instruments, but others played banjos, mandolins, guitars, drums, and grand pianos. The concerts sold out. In 1913 Victor, already a major record company, started to record the group. But even here the blacks were abused. While white musicians of the time received a two-cent royalty per record, James Europe got only one cent. What was important about the Carnegie Hall concert in 1912 was that it was the first significant public event at which black musicians played their non-European, rhythmically fresh music for a largely white audience.

The name of this music derived from ragged time, or syncopation. It was characterized by irregular accents of the melody against an unvarying, relentless articulation of the beat. Ben Harney, a singer, introduced it to New York in February 1896, and it quickly became a staple of vaudeville. Ragtime historians trace its antecedents to the self-deprecating coon songs of the Negro minstrels that surfaced after the Emancipation.

By the time George was born, ragtime had captivated the country, and when one thinks of today's means of distribution for music that were not available then—radio, records, movies, television—that was a remarkable phenomenon. Ragtime rode in on the back of the cakewalk and spread as no music ever had before. This happened not only through vaudeville but through the guitars and banjos of shoeshine boys on the streets, wax recording cylinders, and piano rolls.

Another reason for the wide dissemination of ragtime was that it was written down; 1897 was the year the first rag appeared in print. Among those who made the first great rags were Tom Turpin and James Scott. But the greatest exponent was Scott Joplin, whose "Maple Leaf Rag" quickly became a national hit. Like Cook, Europe, and dozens more, Joplin used his talent to try to cross over into the world of high culture. His *Treemonisha* is, after all, an opera in ragtime.

In 1899 Joplin met John Stark, a white music publisher. Stark published "Maple Leaf Rag" and many other Joplin pieces. Theirs was a courteous, mutually nourishing connection, an exceptional relationship between black and white. Despite such friendships as this one, prejudice permeated the era.

Look at one example, the story behind "Alexander's Ragtime Band," Irving Berlin's first major hit. It reveals how this songwriter took from the blacks while insulting them in his lyrics and then accepted recognition as the originator of the idiom.

Because Gershwin always said Berlin was his first model in music, it is useful to reconstruct how this song became a success. It was published in the musically remarkable year of 1911, the year Schoenberg wrote his atonal *Pierrot lunaire* and Stravinsky completed the score for his ballet *Petrouchka*, which ended with the innovative combination of a C-major and an F-sharp major chord sounded simultaneously. It was also the year that a hungry and ambitious George Gershwin turned thirteen.

There is, first, the choice of the name Alexander. It was a dignified name that took on comic overtones when it was applied to a black. There were many "Alexander" songs in vogue then.

Second, the only ragtime in use here is one brief phrase of syncopation. Berlin's piece is a march, one that echoes Stephen Foster's "Swanee River." Berlin used the word "ragtime" not because that was his musical source but because the title could be counted on to sell his tune. Laurence Bergreen, Berlin's biographer, quotes Berlin late in life on this subject: "I never did find out what ragtime was."

The song got off to a very slow start. As an instrumental—without lyrics—it failed to attract an audience. At first it appeared in a cabaret show but the producer dropped it quickly, and Berlin called it his "dead failure."

In 1911 he had a little success with a few songs he wrote for Ziegfeld's *Follies*. Perhaps he was encouraged by being singled out there, for he returned to his "dead failure" and gave the song words. The words were what made it possible for Al Jolson to choose to belt it out in one of Lew Dockstader's minstrel shows. Two years later, two million copies of the sheet music had been sold.

Scott Joplin, an American black, helped develop and crystallize ragtime; Antonin Dvořák, a Czech composer, transformed the rags of the American blacks into themes for his concert works. Yet it was not either of these two musicians, but Irving Berlin, an eastern European Jewish songwriter, who, because he used the word "ragtime" in a lyric, became known as the Ragtime King. He also cultivated an image as the most prominent exponent of the vernacular in American music. In 1915 he told critic Julian Johnson: "The reason our American composers have done nothing highly significant is because they won't write American music. They are as ashamed of it as if it were a country relative. So they write imitation European music which doesn't mean anything. Ignorant as I am, from their standpoint, I'm doing something they all refuse to do: I'm writing American music."

Berlin was correct. This was the freshest language to appear in the twentieth century. And the Europeans knew it. Even seven years before Berlin's remark, Debussy had written *The Golliwog's Cakewalk*, and a few years later, Stravinsky was composing ragtime pieces.

At the time of this first big success, Berlin was ten years older than George, an idol to a boy of thirteen. George must have longed to *be* Berlin, a great songwriter who came from the Lower East Side, just where he himself had lived, and whose talents, skill, and energies made him a titan on Tin Pan Alley and a rich man. The first step was to meet Berlin. George managed to get an audition. The purpose was to land a job as Berlin's musical secretary, writing down the tunes he could not notate himself. This meeting took place in 1915 just before he went to work at Remick's and Perfection.

Reports of the meeting are varied and fuzzy. It serves many purposes to suggest Berlin recognized George's great gifts and turned him down so Gershwin could get ahead on his own. But there were no tape recorders then and such a generous reaction is out of character for Berlin. Goldberg reports that Berlin denied remembering the encounter. This much is certain: if George went there to get a job, he came out without one.

George's reception appears to have been warmer among blacks. To enhance his piano technique, he went to Luckey Roberts. According to Harlem historian Delilah Jackson, Roberts told her that George came to his apartment and watched him play. Mike Montgomery identifies Roberts as "the pianistic giant of the New York area prior to World War I." Actress and singer Ethel Waters agrees: "Men like James P. Johnson, Willie the Lion Smith, and Charley Johnson could make you sing until your tonsils fell out. They stirred you into joy and wild ecstasy. They could make you cry. And you'd do anything and work until you dropped for such musicians. The master of them all, though, was Luckey Roberts."

Roberts's mastery of the piano opened doors for him even in the South. He played in such a striking way that wherever he went he was treated like royalty. Garvin Bushell, a black musician who played with Roberts, told historian Mark Tucker that even in the South "they let us use the front door. Luckey was just like a little king. He was polite, but he was also powerful on the piano and a great exhibitionist. People would crowd around him, just listening to him play."

Roberts's trademark was a left hand of dazzling speed and an idiosyncratic way of playing tremolo with the right. In a very crowded field, Roberts triumphed over his rivals and generated excitement wherever he played. Performers consciously took "tricks" from one another. James P. Johnson talked about it: "I was playing a lot of piano then, traveling around and listening to every player I could. I'd steal their breaks and style and practice them until I had them perfect."

Eubie Blake claimed Roberts visited him, sat next to him and copied what he did. Roberts told Delilah Jackson that Gershwin did something like that with him. Gershwin's piano style may have been shaped in part by the Pianola, for his approach was busy and full with an active left hand and frequent octaves in the right. But added to this was a drive and syncopation then unknown to white players.

Gershwin appropriated this from the blacks, ingested it until it was his own, and transformed it into his songs. Blake told jazz writer John Wilson that he remembered hearing about Gershwin as early as 1916, when he first moved from Baltimore to New York: "James P. Johnson and Luckey Roberts told me of this very talented ofay [black code word for white] piano player" at Remick's, Blake said. "They said he was good enough to learn some of those terribly difficult tricks that only a few of us could master."

Gershwin's playing served him in the same way Roberts's performances had served him: it gave him entry into a more elevated stratum of society than he could have entered without it. More than contributing to his performance, ragtime itself became the material for a few early songs. When he was only fourteen, George wrote "Ragging the Traumerie," a piece that was never published. But the title alone suggests that the idea of injecting the vitality of a pop idiom into the stuffiness of European art was then on his mind. It could not have made Hambitzer happy, for he was trying to keep his youthful student concentrating on the old masters.

In 1917, George wrote "Rialto Ripples" with Will Donaldson, another songwriter at Remick's. The next year Gershwin wrote a rag on his own, with his brother Ira contributing the lyrics. The title: "The Real American Folk Song Is a Rag." Ira used the pseudonym Arthur Francis, which he created by putting together the first names of his twelve-year-old brother Arthur and his sister, Frances. He used the pseudonym until 1924, when he began using his own name. Later he explained that he did this because he did not wish to trade on his brother's success.

In 1917 Scott Joplin died. That year the all-white Original Dixieland Jazz Band came to New York and opened at Reisenweber's three-story nightclub in Columbus Circle. The group had originated in New Orleans and spent a year in Chicago. Almost as soon as they started playing in New York, Victor signed them and continued to record them for years. This music was different from the ragtime that preceded it in that it opened up and orchestrated an idiom that had been grounded in an unrelenting beat and the timbre of a piano.

When Eubie Blake spoke to John Wilson about a talented "ofay" piano player, he was using the pig Latin word for *foe*. Every white person was seen as an enemy. In 1987 Judith Anne Still, the daughter of William Grant Still, a black classically trained composer whose works were conducted by Stokowski, Reiner, Ormandy, Szell, and Monteux among others, wrote (in a letter to Paul Hoeffler, a Canadian photographer) that Gershwin stole from her father:

> I think that, to a certain extent, inspiration is "in the air" waiting to be plucked out by refined and spiritual individuals. Sorry, but Gershwin doesn't qualify as such a rare and special creature: my father said that Gershwin came to the Negro shows in Harlem to get his inspiration, stealing melodies wholesale from starving minority composers and then passing them off as his own. "I Got Rhythm" was my father's creation, according to Eubie Blake.

Reconstructing the precise chronology opens up all manner of interpretation. Gershwin's "I Got Rhythm" was written for *Girl Crazy*, which had its first public hearing on September 29, 1930, in Philadelphia's Schubert Theater. One month later, on October 30, William Grant Still, according to *In One Lifetime* by Verna Arvey, his widow, began composing the *Afro-American* Symphony, a work that contains a Scherzo movement with a "brief accompanying figure" similar to the motif of "I Got Rhythm." However, in an article published in November 1969 in *Music*, Arvey writes that her husband was playing oboe in the pit orchestra in *Shuffle Along*, the breakthrough black musical of 1921, composed by Eubie Blake and Noble Sissle. Arvey writes that the players, "tired of playing the same thing over and over," improvised from time to time, and her husband's improvisation, she maintains, took the form of the particular melodic fragment that appears in Gershwin's "I Got Rhythm" and Still's *Afro-American* Symphony. The Gershwins, she believes, were undoubtedly there because the show drew celebrities from Broadway.

This narrative has Still creating the fragment nine years before either he or Gershwin used it. But the fragment itself can hardly be said to have been "composed." It jumps right out of the fingers of the right hand of anyone playing the black notes on a piano. C-sharp, D-sharp, F-sharp, G-sharp—that is the theme of "I Got Rhythm" where pitch alone is concerned. It is also the notes that make up Still's subsidiary motif in his Scherzo movement and in hundreds of other works beside these. There are, after all, only twelve notes in the Western scale and a cluster of any four of them in a particular sequence will inevitably reappear. It is only when several measures present a series of pitches, harmonies, and durations that mirror the same combination of elements in a different work that a case for plagiarism can be made.

The reason for devoting this much attention to Arvey's book and article and Still's letter is to convey the very real sense of rage many blacks continue to feel because they believe a language that was once theirs was expropriated from them and exploited by whites. In a way there is truth in this; consider the "Alexander's Ragtime Band" story. It is a Rashomon-like situation: Those who were there first see the phenomenon as stealing, while historians would characterize it as culture passing-on. One thing is unambiguous: shows created by blacks between Cook's *Clorindy* and Sissle and Blake's *Shuffle Along* provided crucial ingredients for the genre that came to be known as the Broadway musical.

It has been estimated that two thousand whites from downtown went up to Harlem each night during the 1920s and 1930s when Gershwin was going there with Anita Loos, Marilyn Miller, Constance Talmadge, and other glamorous women. This period was the Harlem Renaissance, and George was viewed in the clubs as a star, a glowing presence in an all-white audience watching exotic blacks entertain.

But it was during the decade before that the influence of the blacks on Gershwin became seminal. That was when he hung around Barron Wilkins's Club and sat next to Luckey Roberts, ingesting every pianistic move Roberts made.

Gershwin not only responded to the music the blacks made;

he felt as though he were one of them. That was inevitable. WASP society treated Jews the way white society treated blacks: in a cold and dismissive way.

In 1918 Hambitzer died. The obituary cited tuberculosis, but there were rumors of alcoholism and suicide. Hambitzer's wife had died a few years before, leaving him with a young daughter to raise. Added to that were grave disappointments with George. In the movie *Rhapsody in Blue*, the teacher, here a European, admonishes his student: "Are you just for making a fortune? Look at Schubert. He wore the same necktie for years. He died young, but his voice will never be silenced. Beethoven never asked, 'Is this a hit?' He wrote how he felt."

Hambitzer's tragedy was in having to watch his discovery, this unkempt boy he recognized as a genius, defect from his teachings and move into what he saw as a crass, commercial world. And that was the world—nightclubs, black musicals, stride pianists—the improvisational jazz style that evolved from ragtime—into which Gershwin moved while Hambitzer was living. It had nothing to do with African strains, backcountry blues, or the New Orleans music of the 1880s and 1890s, which some would say were fundamental to jazz. But neither did it have to do with anything remotely connected to the classical heritage.

After Gershwin left Remick's in the spring of 1917, he didn't know where to go. Among those he asked for help was Will Vodery, a black friend and an exceptionally skilled arranger and orchestrator. Through Vodery, Gershwin got a job as pianist at Fox's City Theater to accompany the acts from the pit at a salary of twenty-five dollars a week. He was there to play during the dinner hour when members of the orchestra were eating. Gershwin reported the experience to Goldberg:

> Happy to be working, I attended the Monday morning rehearsal and sat beside the pianist, watching the acts go through their routine. I also sat through the first show watching the music and the acts to make sure I'd make good.

The supper show began. I got along fine with three of four acts. I was especially good with a turn that used Remick's songs.

Then came what I consider the most humiliating moment of my life. A typical vaudeville revue consisting of six chorus girls, a leading lady, the leading man and to be sure, a comedian. . . . This act had special music composed for it, and the music was naturally in manuscript form. You know the cryptic condition of those theatrical scores. I started to play the opening chorus and seemed to be getting along fine, when suddenly I found myself playing one thing and the chorus girls singing another. Evidently I had missed a couple of cues. After all it was my first day at the job, and aside from nervousness I was as yet unfamiliar with all the musical terms you find in such music. . . . I immediately sensed the situation and began to get red in the face. It came to my mind that the City Theater was in my neighborhood and there might be some people out in the audience who knew me—not to mention proud members of my family and a few relations.

The comedian in this act was a typical ham if ever I have seen one. Seeing my predicament, he thought he'd have a little fun with me. He shouted across the footlights: "Who told you you were a piano player? You ought to be banging the drums." He followed this with a nasty laugh. I could have lifted the piano and hurled it at him. I had to stop playing, but the comedian continued having a good time at my expense. The act went on to the bitter end without any music, with the chorus girls giggling, the comedian still joking, and the audience howling with laughter. Certainly my beginning looked like an end.

When the show was over, I went to the box office and said to the cashier, "I was the piano player and I'm quitting." She tried to calm me by telling me it wasn't important. And she said I'd be all right at the next performance. But I couldn't see how I could face that comedian again. . . . How I wish I could remember his name. His looks are forever engrossed [sic] on my memory. I believe that I could pick him out of a crowd this very day.

The whole experience left a scar in my memory. How could

> I have foreseen that one day, hardly more than a dozen years later, I'd be signing up a hundred thousand dollar contract with Mr. Fox, music to be written by the frightened pianist who made such a fiasco of it during that nightmare of a supper show.

There are several reasons for quoting Gershwin as fully as Goldberg did. First, it is rare to hear his voice, and, second, the details he uses for this incident suggest the impact it had on him. Third, it contradicts the notion that many family and friends still entertain—one restated in many books—that Gershwin was invulnerable, that even the critics could not wound him, that he always knew just how good he was and that nothing could threaten his overwhelming self-esteem. Fourth, he may not have been able to throw the upright at the comedian, but he inhibited his wish to hurt him. In fact he did nothing at all. He even suppressed the man's name. Gershwin was invariably polite. When people insulted him—and surprisingly many report that they did—Gershwin never responded with a counterattack. Rather he courteously said, "Of course, you are probably right."

Such internalization of hostility and aggression is not good for one's health. Many physicians today acknowledge that fact. In Woody Allen's *Manhattan*, the star's young girlfriend asks him after he has been insulted why he did not fight back. Allen answers "I would never do that. I get a brain tumor instead."

In 1989, Irving Caesar, the famous lyricist, reminisced about his early friendship with Gershwin:

> I was working at the Ford Motor Company. One day I heard about Remick's and at lunch I went over there. George was plugging when I arrived. I love the piano and began to love George. Nobody has ever played like George. The chords he played were what was special. He was a sweet and sensitive boy but I also knew just how good he was, and I sensed his drive.

I would go to Remick's just to hear George play. And George would come over to Ford to catch onto what was going on there. As far as I was concerned what George was doing on the piano was far more interesting than anything that was happening at Ford.

I wrote my first lyric at five. One day George and I got together. We wrote "You-oo Just You." By this time he had left Remick's, but we went to Fred Belcher of Remick's who listened as I sang and George played. Each of us hoped to make $25. When we stopped Belcher asked, "Well, boys, how about $250?" We were speechless. We both thought he was telling us we would have to pay him that to see the song in print. Belcher took our silence to mean we were not satisfied. He said, "OK, I'll give you $500."

We were so excited that we ran all the way uptown to where George lived. We told his parents the great news. Many years have passed since that day but I've never forgotten what Rose said: "Morris," she told her husband. "Send a lawyer to help them. These boys will be eaten up alive."

To keep from being eaten alive, George continued to look for work wherever he could find it. In October 1918, George traveled with *Ladies First* as Nora Bayes's pianist. The show, a vehicle for Bayes, one of the great stars of vaudeville, played with the women's suffrage movement. In it the heroine runs for mayor against her sweetheart and is pleased when she loses because it is he who wins. Most of the score was by A. Baldwin Sloane, a composer of musical comedies who had had nothing on Broadway for five years.

In musical comedies of those days, plots were usually as simple as this and the songs did little more than change the pace. They did not enrich the characters or move the story. The master of the early twentieth-century musical, the shows that George and Ira saw growing up, was George M. Cohan. Though "Yankee Doodle Dandy" and "Give My Regards to Broadway" were among his memorable songs, his librettos were forgettable.

Sloane was no Cohan but *Ladies First* was a hit. On tour with the show in Baltimore, Gershwin wrote this letter to Irving (Iz) Caesar dated: "Tuesday evening, 7:45 by the clock."

Dear Iz—from the plantation,

Give ah run down to de plantation un tell Seamble Ginsberg that—I sen my love un *kisses un also* tell 'im that I'm in the city of Baltimo', M. D. (Making Dough)

Tell me Iz, how's Jake, Max, Bennie, Seammy, Rosie, Beckie, Lizzie, Daveh, Morris, Oiving, Louie, Elbert—in fect how's all my fren's. Hah? Tell me right away in a letter. Garuss [*greet* in Yiddish] everybody for me.

Are you still increasing Ford's annual income? In Jersey? Les hear. When does 55th St. factory open? When it does open will you have a reserved room and bath? Or what?

In this letter I can only write you about the present & future. It is a funny thing, but in travelling from one town to another, the minute I imprint my O'Sullivans in the soil of the town in which I arrive,—the town that I left completely leaves my memory. Therefore you will have to satisfy your hunger for some news, with what's happening here at present.

First of all—I have 3 songs in the show namely, "Some Wonderful Sort of Someone," "Something About Love," and "The Folk Song." "Wonderful Someone" unfortunately is misplaced, being the first song Miss Bayes does, & coming in a spot where a comedy song is expected. I will be glad if she removed it. It's not worth a nickel the way it's done now. Unless she puts it way back in the show, & has it done with the girls I'd rather have it out altogether.

Many people say it's the prettiest song in the show. I'll let you know later what happens to it.

"Something About Love" is done with a piano. Irving Fields & myself.

"The Folk Song" is ruined in it's present condition. No fault of the songs but the singer. I expect someone else to do it shortly. Hal Forde is now ruining it. So you see it's not merely having good songs that make hits.

Baldwin Sloane who wrote the music to the show gets 3 percent royalty. There are 9 interpolated songs and 8 songs by

Sloane. He told me he got $400 for Pittsburgh week—including one day in Trenton. Pretty soft for him.

My name is on the programme following each of my songs.

S. Greene who is in Washington came on here yesterday.

I. Fisher is sorry there is no place for Mammy . . . in the show.

I may want you to buy back our numbers from Remick before I return. I'll let you know about it. Miss Bayes wanted to sing my march melody (Love is to Live) until I told her Remick's had it. *Don't say a word about this to anyone* or we may not be able to get them back. As soon as I get them back, I may try to place the Kiss song.

I met Belcher in Cleveland. You'll have to excuse me now as I have to run over to the theatre. As I've said before, regards to everybody from me including your family and yourself. Let's get a long letter from you. How about it?

Izzie [Ira] tells me you're writing with Tierney. 'Zat so? Tell me all about it. I'm certainly interested.

Well, S'long. See you soon.

With that Gershwin signed an oversized George, with "Auditorium Theater, Baltimore, Maryland, U.S." underneath.

He writes in a kind of Broadway Yiddish dialect with traces of black usage. Apparently three songs of his were interpolated into the show—"Some Wonderful Sort of Someone" with lyrics by Schuyler Greene, "The Real American Folk Song" with lyrics by Ira, and "Something About Love" with lyrics by Lou Paley, a high school teacher then engaged to marry Emily Strunsky, one of George's good friends.

Harry Tierney was another Tin Pan Alley composer with songs interpolated into *The Canary*, running at the same time as *Ladies First*. The Kiss Song—"There's More to the Kiss Than the XXX"—was written with Caesar. The Xs of course stood for kiss sounds. Four months later, it was interpolated into *Good Morning, Judge*, an English musical at the Schubert Theatre.

In addition to writing songs, getting them interpolated into shows, and traveling when his career demanded it, Gershwin also worked as a pianist for show rehearsals and for some

Sunday-evening concerts. At one of these, in November 1918, Vivienne Segal sang two Gershwin-Caesar collaborations: "You-oo Just You" and "There's More to the Kiss Than the XXX." The manager of the show in which Segal was appearing heard George's songs and recommended him to Max Dreyfus, head of T. B. Harms Company, a major music publisher.

Dreyfus acted immediately. He offered George thirty-five dollars a week to do nothing but write songs; at Remick's, all he had been allowed to do was plug other people's songs.

Remick's had been right for Gershwin when he had Berlin as his model. But by 1917, the year that Gerald Bordman, Jerome Kern's biographer, calls his subject's "annus mirabilis, the year in which the extent of his profligacy and the brilliance of his creativity were to establish him as Broadway's leading composer," Kern was clearly the man to emulate. Not much, of course, can be inherently better than a Berlin song. Yet this is what Gershwin told Goldberg about his newfound feelings: "Kern was the first composer who made me conscious that most popular music was of inferior quality and that musical comedy was made of better material. . . . I paid him the tribute of frank imitation and many things I wrote at this period sounded as though Kern had written them himself."

What Gershwin was responding to was not the quality of melodic writing in this arena; Berlin and Kern were equally remarkable. What he was responding to was definitely a matter of class. Unlike Berlin, a Russian Jew who grew up on the Lower East Side and started his career as a singing waiter in a Chinese restaurant, Kern was born, according to Bordman, to a family that "belonged to the Jewish-American aristocracy that arose shortly after the Civil War." He chose to go to Germany to study music for a while. More important perhaps than even this matter of pedigree was the fact that the musical material that had served as his background came from those very shows playing in the good Broadway houses that charged five dollars a seat, not from black musicals running in inferior houses. At first these were entertainments from London, but in 1907, when Franz Lehár's *Merry Widow* began its run, the Viennese-style operetta and its florid middle-European waltz ambience took over. Kern began his career with these, composing interpolations when needed. Kern even married up: in 1910, in a high church ceremony in St. Mary's Parish Church in London, he married an Englishwoman.

Gershwin has said that he first heard Kern at his aunt Kate's wedding, where the orchestra played some songs from his 1914 *The Girl from Utah.* One of them was the beautiful "They'll Never Believe Me." In 1991 Kate Wolpin, then 101 years old, said that, although she could not be certain, she thought she married on June 21, 1916. This suggests George lost less than one year in moving out of Remick's and beginning his separation from the idea of churning out individual songs to the connection with the theater. So a few months after Kate Wolpin's wedding, he not only went to Harms, the firm that had discovered Kern in 1903, but also got himself employed as rehearsal pianist for *Miss 1917*, a show produced by Florenz Ziegfeld and Charles Dillingham, and composed by Kern with Victor Herbert, an even earlier master of the lyric theater here. In the 1950s, Will Vodery said it had been he who got Gershwin the job with the Kern-Herbert musical.

Berlin, back from serving in World War I, decided to withdraw from Waterson, Berlin, and Snyder, the firm that had represented him until then. He intended to set up a publishing house of his own. But at that moment he had a new song, "The Revolutionary Rag," that he said was inspired by the Russian Revolution, and he called on Dreyfus for help. He needed someone to write the song down. Dreyfus called in Gershwin and asked him to do for Berlin what George had offered to do a few years before, take down his music.

Like a good secretary Gershwin complied and notated the piece. Then he tore into his own stunning improvisation in his best Luckey Roberts–Gershwin manner. Berlin is reported to have said it was so good "I hardly recognized it." The remark has been interpreted as a generous compliment from the older man. But because giving such a compliment was out of character for Berlin and because anyone who has ever known a composer will agree that what he wants above all else is for his work to remain intact, this was surely a cutting down of the younger man.

Still under twenty, George was cheeky to do what he did. What his behavior said was "I am better than you." It is what his behavior said every time he quoted his father's malapropisms for sophisticated people to hear. Such an attitude appears to be inevitable for young men obsessed with getting to the top.

The work in which Gershwin seems to have ingested Berlin and used his example to make himself famous was "Swanee," which did for him what "Alexander's Ragtime Band" accomplished for Berlin: it made him rich and renowned.

From the first days of their friendship, Gershwin and Caesar wrote songs together. Caesar estimates there are about fifty such pieces. One of them, he says, was "I Was So Young, You Were So Beautiful," which he characterizes as "off the beaten track for the time." But then one evening, at Dinty Moore's restaurant, they began a conversation that led both of them, in Caesar's words, "to strike gold. We were talking about a particular hit, 'Hindustan, where I came to rest my tired caravan.' Because it was such a success, I thought we should come up with something like it."

"Hindustan" had been a manifestation of the fashion of the time for the pseudo-oriental effect that had begun a few years before with songs like "Chinatown, My Chinatown." Caesar recalls that he suggested George keep the one-step but that they put their own song in an American context. George agreed and mentioned "Swanee River." He surely could have had in mind the way Stephen Foster's song was used by Berlin eight years earlier in "Alexander's Ragtime Band."

They began to write in the restaurant. They continued to work on it on the Riverside Drive bus. By the time they arrived at the Gershwin apartment it was almost completed. Morris was in the middle of a poker game but he invited the two young men to join them. Caesar and Gershwin continued to work, however, and when they finished, Morris put tissue over a comb and gave the song its first performance. George did something unusual for the time; he changed the key between verse and chorus.

According to Caesar, the line between composer and lyricist was not tightly drawn. He says it was he who hummed some of the music and tells the following story about a lyric. He had come up with "I've been away from you a long time. The birds are singing . . ." and then he paused and nothing came right away. It was George, Caesar said, who contributed the next line: "It is song time," not a bad lyric line for a composer to improvise.

It is one thing to create a song. It is another to see it become a hit. At the time the men came up with "Swanee," Gershwin was working as rehearsal pianist for the Ziegfeld Follies, with music by his old model Berlin. During a quiet moment he played not more Berlin but his own "Swanee," and the girls clustering around him went wild. "Girls always clustered around George when he played," Caesar says. "Pianists used to be called piano pimps because women always clustered around them and no pianist had more women clustering around than George." Ned Wayburn, the show's director, heard "Swanee" and saw the reaction and said he would use it in a show that was going to open the Capitol Theater, then the largest theater in the world.

Many months passed before the opening, but when it happened the Capitol had sixty girls dancing to "Swanee" with electric lights in their dancing shoes. Seventy musicians played "Swanee" from the pit and everyone on stage sang "Swanee." Caesar says the applause was fine but that the sale of sheet music in the lobby was dreadful. He admits he and George hung around buying copies in a futile effort to stimulate sales.

It is impossible to know if George, at thirteen, had been aware that Jolson brought the turnaround for "Alexander's Ragtime Band." The denouement of the "Swanee" story suggests that he did. He worked it out so that he was invited to a party that Jolson was hosting at Bessie Bloodgood's whorehouse in Harlem. By this time Gershwin had become a friend of Buddy DeSylva, a first-rate lyricist as driven and ambitious as he. DeSylva had dropped out of the University of California after Jolson had heard one of his songs and bought half interest in it. When Jolson went back to New York, DeSylva was with him. At the time of the party, Jolson was interpolating DeSylva's song into *Sinbad*, a show with music mostly by Sigmund Romberg, at the Winter Garden Theater. The party began at midnight, after the theaters had closed. DeSylva invited George to play and among the songs he chose was "Swanee." Jolson responded immediately and interpolated "Swanee" into *Sinbad* the following week.

Within a month, Dreyfus bought the entire front page of *Variety* to advertise "Al Jolson's greatest song." On the back page he described it as the "Hit of Hits." "Swanee" became the biggest hit Gershwin ever had; his share of the royalty income is reported to have reached $10,000 the first year. He never again earned this much from any song he composed for Broadway.

"Swanee" traveled fast. In *Passport to Paris*, songwriter Vernon Duke writes that when he was still the composer Vladimir Dukelsky, he heard it in Constantinople in 1920 and that "the bold sweep of the tune, its rhythmic freshness, and especially its syncopated gait . . . sent me into ecstasies."

In the years between 1917 and 1919 Gershwin moved from having songs interpolated into shows, to writing part of a show, to being the show's sole composer. After *Ladies First*, Dreyfus recommended Gershwin for *Half-Past Eight*, which starred comedian Joe Cook and used a twenty-five-piece black orchestra. The show opened and closed out of town in a few days. Gershwin had some pleasure seeing his name on a marquee but he told friends he couldn't bear the idea that he had wasted time on a flop. While it was playing that short time in Syracuse, "You-oo Just You," which Vivienne Segal had introduced the year before, was being interpolated into *Kitchy Koo of 1918*.

Then something happened that Gershwin later told a radio audience was "the lucky break" every career needs. He had had, of course, a number of lucky breaks by that time. But the one he was speaking about happened in 1919 when Arthur Jackson, a lyric writer, introduced him to Alex Aarons, the twenty-nine-year-old son of Alexander Aarons, a major figure on Broadway. The younger Aarons wanted to start his own Broadway career with a show called *La La Lucille.* His father suggested he hire Victor Herbert but he wanted a younger, fresher, steelier sound and had heard some Gershwin and loved it. For the lyrics he chose DeSylva and Jackson.

Gershwin pulled out two old songs, wrote some new ones, and this show was not a flop. It opened in Boston, and in the *Evening Transcript*, Brooks Atkinson, then using the byline J. B. Atkinson, gave the music a good notice. He wrote that it was "vivacious and surprising of detail, and harmoniously pleasing." Gershwin, who had long before stopped keeping his scrapbook, filed the clipping away. Dreyfus published seven of the songs.

Gershwin's treatment of Kern repeated his treatment of Berlin. In 1917, when Gershwin had served as rehearsal pianist for *Miss 1917*, he was in awe of the older man—Ira has noted this in his diaries—and hardly a word was exchanged. But in 1918, when he was rehearsal pianist for Kern's *Rock-a-Bye Baby*, a warm relationship developed. Kern told George that if he were ever offered a show, he should consult with him before committing himself to it. In his biography of Kern, Bordman writes that when Kern learned Gershwin "had signed to write a musical without first consulting him, Jerry's feelings were hurt. For several years thereafter, he was noticeably cool to George."

It is possible that, like Berlin, Kern had belittled him in some way. But it is also possible that now that Gershwin had access to Broadway, his sights were set even higher, on the classical music world. As early as 1919 Gershwin composed *Lullaby*, a string quartet. It showed no evidence of contrapuntal technique or sophisticated writing for strings. *Lullaby* was all substance and idea, a hauntingly beautiful, melancholy little piece.

It was around the time that he composed this quartet that Gershwin's social life began to include people in the classical music world. One of them, Abram Chasins, had attended the privately funded Ethical Culture School, Juilliard, and the Curtis Institute. In *Speaking of Pianists*, he writes about George bringing him into "the fresh and forbidden fruits of a jazz world that my parents and teachers had carefully taught me to resist and reject." Chasins's widow, Constance Keene, the concert pianist, goes even further. She reports that her husband's parents forbade him to go to the Gershwin house, where cards were always being played for money and a vulgar atmosphere prevailed. Chasins writes about a fight he had with George:

> My nose was stuck to the musical grindstone. George was having a love affair with music: no regular piano practice, no slaving away at theory, harmony, counterpoint, orchestration or form. One day, in 1919, on the corner of Lenox Avenue and 113th Street, he confided more of his big ideas. "George," I said, "don't you think it would be a good idea to take some lessons with [Rubin] Goldmark? Nobody can do what you want without basic training."
>
> He stood still and glared at me. "You're just the kind of person who is keeping me from doing my greatest work," he shouted, and stamped off, leaving me standing there. Meanwhile the musical comedy career . . . was already launched with *La La Lucille*, and "Swanee" was blaring from every phonograph and player piano.

George got angry with Chasins because while part of him believed he should study music in a disciplined way, he was incapable of doing that. At the start of his life he played hooky from school. But he did make the effort from time to time with one composer or another. Hambitzer had recommended Edward Kilenyi for harmony and, in 1919, when he composed *Lullaby*, he was taking lessons with the Hungarian teacher. Four years later he even went to Goldmark for three lessons. Afterward he enjoyed repeating his experience with Goldmark to prove teachers were charlatans. At the last of his three lessons, he would tell whoever would listen, he presented Goldmark with *Lullaby*, composed four years before, as though he had written it for him. Goldmark complimented the piece and said it showed just how much Gershwin had learned during the brief period of study with him.

The evidence suggests that when Gershwin began to succeed, he became grandiose. But, because it grew out of the rapid success that came after years of self-contempt, that confidence rested on a fragile base. Still people did suffer from his rough treatment. Ira, who at this time had achieved little success on his own, later said the use of a pseudonym was his own choice. But Irene Gallagher, Max Dreyfus's employee for forty years, told it differently in a conversation in 1972. "George would not permit Ira," she said, "to use his own name during the early years of his success. George was a pretty odd fellow," she added. "We were dating. Suddenly one day he called and said, 'I can't go out with you anymore, because you're just a telephone operator and I'm a composer.' "

Gallagher, who started as a messenger for Dreyfus when she was twelve, worked her way up to a position of authority in the firm. She listened to the songs when the writers brought them in and offered advice, coffee, and food. Trusted not only by Dreyfus but by all those songwriters who revered him, her words about Gershwin can be trusted.

How to explain his behavior to her? As a child, George felt that he was a social outcast, an embarrassment to his brother, a source of aggravation to his parents. According to Caesar, George frequented whorehouses in Harlem, which may be interpreted as a sign of his low self-esteem. His sudden success, at twenty, shifted the ground. Because he had received harsh judgments from others, his new achievements led to an arrogance that was at the least insensitive and at the most, cruel. Isamu Noguchi, the sculptor, once said that Gershwin possessed "an exterior of self-assurance verging on conceit." He was as hard on Irene when he dropped her as a girlfriend as he was on his brother when he forbade him to use a name that, after all, was his own.

Still, long after Gershwin stopped going out with Gallagher, he bought clothes for her at Saks Fifth Avenue because, friends say, he thought "she dressed too plain."

. . .

In 1912, in good measure because of profits garnered from its pedal-operated player piano called the Pianola, the Aeolian Company built its own office building on Forty-second Street between Fifth and Sixth avenues. Stretching through from Forty-second to Forty-third streets, across the street from Bryant Park and the brand-new New York Public Library, the seventeen-story limestone and buff building housed offices, showrooms for its instruments including the Pianola, and a 1,500-seat concert hall.

In 1917 Gershwin stopped making rolls for Perfection and started making them for Aeolian. Caesar says that Felix Arndt, the composer of "Nola," brought Gershwin to Aeolian. From then until 1926, apart from seven rolls he made for Welte, which were distributed in Europe, Gershwin worked exclusively for Aeolian. In 1925 he cut two rolls of *Rhapsody in Blue*. "Sweet and Low Down" and "That Certain Feeling" of 1926 were the last piano rolls he made.

Before 1920, Gershwin's rolls—more than a hundred by then—were generally arrangements of other people's songs. Gershwin never did his best when interpreting the works of others. Take, as one example, "Grieving for You" by Sam Coslow, a song he put on a roll in 1921. Zez Confrey, three years older than Gershwin and educated at a Chicago conservatory, also made a roll of the song. Confrey's rendition sounds clever when compared to the barren, pedestrian Gershwin performance. Confrey's even suggests Debussy or Ravel subjected to syncopation.

An interview published in *Jazz Review* in 1959 has James P. Johnson saying that Gershwin's interests lay elsewhere: "It was at Aeolian Hall . . . in 1920 that I met George Gershwin who was cutting 'oriental' numbers there when I was making blues rolls which were popular then. He had written 'Swanee' and was interested in rhythm and blues. Like myself, he wanted to write them on a higher level. We had lots of talks about our ambitions to do great music on American themes."

Nothing illustrates more dramatically the difference between the piano and Pianola for Gershwin than comparing his pre-1920 performances on each. Gershwin live was mesmerizing, a slender, 5-foot 9½-inch white Luckey Roberts, who could dazzle with any number of tricks and would often sing to his own accompaniment. On the player piano he was dull. Whether this was because he was rarely performing his own material, or because the machine was an inherently defective medium is hard to say.

The point is that the piano roll produced soulless music. The tempo of the instrument adjusted like a metronome. The instructions might read: "Play it 80 for singing, 100 for dancing." In addition a lot of editing was done if the producer wanted a thicker, richer, more orchestral sound. The player rarely had control over what the purchaser would hear.

Artis Wodehouse, who, with the help of computers, is converting Gershwin's player-piano performances into notated scores, has made an intensive study of his rolls. (For the most part his name appears on the rolls simply as George Gershwin. But on some rolls he made for Welte, he is characterized as George Gershwin, composer of *La La Lucille.*) She finds the rolls he made after 1920 contain intimations of what was to come in the compositions of his more mature years: "In making piano rolls, Gershwin, like Mozart, based his music in a pre-existing commercially viable musical idiom. During the course of producing this salable music, Gershwin assimilated the stylistic conventions of the piano roll song arrangement so thoroughly that when his unique voice as a composer began to emerge around 1920, he was prepared to use these conventions as a frame for a more refined artistic statement."

The year Wodehouse dates the emergence of Gershwin's "unique voice," 1920, was also when Gershwin went to the Victor studios for an audition that until now has escaped historians' attention. Gershwin's aborted effort to enter the recording world came on Wednesday, July 20. The "Recording Log Books" at the Victor Archives states that he appeared there for an audition, but there are no data on the log sheet that suggest that a successful trial recording was made. This is how the personnel were listed:

THE GERSHWIN TRIO
SAXOPHONE—Mr. Ralton
BANJO—Mr. King
PIANO—Mr. Gershwin

TITLES: *Kismet*—Arabian Fox Trot
Chica Mexican Dance by George Gershwin

Mr. Ralton was Bert Ralton, who had come from San Francisco to New York with Art Hickman and his orchestra in 1919. Mr. King was George King, part of the Vernon trio, which signed a recording contract the following year with Emerson. Apart from showing Gershwin's interest in making records, the incident reveals his involvement with the saxophone, an instrument that had been invented sixty years earlier but was not used much until then. During the period when Gershwin expected to be drafted into the army, he had taken up the saxophone, hoping he could play in an army band. He was never called up, but his interest in the saxophone did not disappear with the armistice.

In 1919 the saxophone began to show up in a new context in New York. During the war, dance orchestras, apart from those that performed at the Clef Club, were mostly small string ensembles. They played at such hotels as the Plaza and the Waldorf-Astoria—Hambitzer played piano in the Waldorf group—where couples danced the one-step and the waltz. But on the West Coast, Art Hickman created the first modern dance orchestra by hiring Ralton and Clyde Doerr, creating the first saxophone "section" in history. Although some performing groups of the day had trumpets and trombones, the saxophone started something new, and violin players began to turn to that instrument.

When Hickman brought his group to New York, they played at the Biltmore Hotel. Until then musicians there played on a little balcony, in the old European way. But Hickman refused to do this, insisting his men be on the floor so they could "feel" the dancing. Ziegfeld invited Hickman to play in his *Midnight Frolic*, the show that played upstairs in his theater, the New

Amsterdam, on Forty-second Street, while his *Follies* was downstairs. They performed there for two weeks. The next year he brought them back, only this time they went directly into the *Follies*. A dance band had become an organic part of the theater.

Gershwin's sister says that whenever he returned from a performance he would show her the dances he saw. Fred Astaire not only credited George with choreographing an exit step for him but summed him up saying, "He wrote for feet." What Hickman was doing obviously interested Gershwin, who went wherever there was anything that interested him. Ralton and King apparently went to Victor with him to see what they could do.

But the Gershwin Trio disappeared from view. Nor did Gershwin ever make the records of his own work that one would have expected from him, not even one of the Concerto in F, which he himself had performed at its premiere.

Considering his intense reaction to the humiliating experience with the comedian at the Fox Theater and his fleeing without even asking for his day's pay, it is possible that whatever happened at Victor prompted him to avoid risking a similar experience.

It was probably fortunate that Gershwin did not try to work for Ziegfeld during the early years of his career. Ziegfeld was genuinely abusive to people, and Gershwin's temperament might not have been capable of withstanding the abuse. Ziegfeld not only infuriated and alienated most of the composers who worked for him but he abused animals as well. When at twenty-two he produced *The Dancing Ducks of Denmark*, the Society for the Prevention of Cruelty to Animals closed the show when it was discovered that Ziegfeld got the ducks to "dance" by applying heat to the bottoms of their feet.

The *Ziegfeld Follies of 1915* was the most lavish *Follies* until then. The show had sets by Josef Urban, a Viennese architect who had designed a palace for Count Esterházy. Opening with simulated underwater effects with rippling blue lights and "The

Gates of Elysium" surrounded by huge, reared-up elephants spouting multicolored water, this *Follies* starred Ed Wynn, Leon Erroll, and W. C. Fields in his first speaking role. Bert Williams appeared as a put-upon houseboy, and Ina Claire and Ann Pennington headed the glamorous Ziegfeld girls. All of it diverted attention away from an undistinguished score with the best songs by Louis Hirsch. George White got his start as a dancer in the show.

In 1919 White started his own *Scandals* to rival the *Follies*. Richard Whiting was his composer, but the show ran only four months. For his next show he was looking for someone else. White had danced in *Miss 1917* when Gershwin was the rehearsal pianist and by this time Gershwin had done "Swanee" and *La La Lucille*. Gershwin was twenty-two when he approached White. Actually he took a train to Detroit, where White was auditioning for his next revue. White was looking over chorus girls when George introduced himself. White congratulated him on "Swanee" and *La La Lucille* and George made some self-deprecating remarks about *Half-Past Eight*. He also said he had heard that White was unhappy with Whiting and was looking for a new composer.

On February 27, 1920, White sent Gershwin a handwritten letter from the Statler Hotel in Detroit noting he had secured his services from Harms for $75 a week. For the next *Scandals* in 1921, White raised the fee to $125. Gershwin worked on the *Scandals* for the next five years with increasing renown.

Although there were many run-of-the-mill songs in the shows, others illustrated a fearlessness in breaking away from all conventions. Thirty-four songs from the *Scandals* were published, including "Drifting Along with the Tide" (1921), "I'll Build a Stairway to Paradise" (1922), and "Somebody Loves Me" (1924).

Unimpeded by the conventions impressed upon Chasins and hundreds of other composition students, Gershwin was free to invent as he went. Even his 1919 "Swanee" contains idiosyncratic touches. Listen to the shift from minor to major on the "Somehow" that precedes "I feel." And think of the idea behind accompanying "Swanee" with two long held notes and following them with the hard accent on the "How" after that.

Stanley Adams, former president of ASCAP, who knew George, recently described him as a "composer with balls." The aggression and drive Gershwin often conveyed by his use of small melodic fragments and his love for the repeated note contribute to the sense of virility to which Adams referred.

Between 1920 and 1924, in addition to composing for the *Scandals*, he settled on collaborators who proved indispensable to him. Aarons, producer of *La La Lucille*, did more than give George the opportunity to produce his first score for Broadway. He virtually led him to both these men. One was Ira. As late as 1919, Ira had had no real success. He often joked about belonging to "the ranks of Brothers of the Great." One day George learned that *The Sweetheart Shop*, a show in previews in Chicago, needed a song for its leading ingenue. That evening he and Ira came up with "Waiting for the Sun to Come Out." It had to have been a joke for them because of its almost comical banality. The sun says "Howdy" as it chases the clouds away.

The next day George brought it to Edgar J. MacGregor, the producer, who offered $250 for the right to interpolate "The Sun" into the show. The score had George as composer and Arthur Francis as lyricist. When MacGregor asked George who Francis was, George replied "a smart college boy with talent," which was probably George's candid assessment of his brother.

In May 1920, *Variety*'s Chicago correspondent called *The Sweetheart Shop* "the biggest musical comedy money maker in America," which is probably what prompted the Gershwins to do the song. But the show folded after five weeks on Broadway. When George asked MacGregor for their money, the producer said that because the show failed in New York, he would be hard pressed to come up with it. According to Ira's account of the story in *Lyrics on Several Occasions*, George said that was all right with him "but the college boy really needs the money." Ira continues: "Whereupon a most welcome check for $125 was made out to Arthur Francis. 'Waiting for the Sun' was my first published song. The $125 plus, within the year, earnings of $723.40 from sheet music and $445.02 from phonograph records, kept the 'college boy' going for some time."

Despite the debacle, MacGregor commissioned the brothers to come up with a score for his next show, *A Dangerous Maid.* They wrote ten songs. Eight were used, five published. The show closed in Pittsburgh.

In the spring of 1921, Aarons was making plans for his second Broadway show. George brought Vincent Youmans and Ira to Aarons. The result was that Aarons's *Two Little Girls in Blue* had a score by Youmans and composer Paul Lannin and lyrics by Arthur Francis. It opened May 3 and was a hit. Three songs—"Who's Who with You," "Dolly," and "Oh Me! Oh My!"—sold widely. *Two Little Girls in Blue* did better than *La La Lucille.*

Ira's intelligence and careful planning were not lost on Aarons. He brought the brothers together for his *Lady, Be Good!* This led to a collaboration that, for thirteen years, made it seem as though words and music were coming from the same source.

This is how Ira, in his only book, treats those years between his first Broadway show and when he teamed up with George and began using his real name. All the activity of that period is contained in one paragraph which appears between parentheses:

> (As Arthur Francis I did the lyrics for *Two Little Girls in Blue*, with composers Youmans and Lannin: *A Dangerous Maid*, with my brother; and a dozen or so songs interpolated in various revues, with composers Lewis Gensler, Raymond Hubbell, Milton Schwarzwald, and one or two others. In 1924 I dropped Arthur Francis. He was beginning to be confused with lyricist Arthur Jackson; also I'd been made aware that there was an English lyricist named Arthur Francis. Besides, all who knew me knew me as a Gershwin anyway.)

Ira's terseness in describing his professional activities just before he began his collaboration with George may be due in part to his natural reticence. It may also come from the fact that he knew well—but chose not to point out—that his own interest in the musical theater preceded his brother's by about eight years. In 1911, the week that W. S. Gilbert died, Ira read *Trial by Jury*. From that point, he went on to collect poems by Gilbert as well as the Gilbert and Sullivan songbooks. George took over the piano that Rose had bought for Ira, just as he went on to capture fame and fortune through his work in a genre discovered by his brother. Ira, throughout it all, remained in the shadows. However little Ira wanted to practice piano, however little he desired celebrity, some significant part of him inevitably resented the way things turned.

Aarons not only led George to view Ira with new eyes, he also led him to William Daly, the other person who proved central to Gershwin's career. *For Goodness Sake*, Aarons's third Broadway show, had a score by Lannin and Daly and lyrics by Arthur Jackson.

Born in Cincinnati, the son of a successful song-and-dance man, Daly attended high school in Chelsea, Massachusetts, and received his A.B. from Harvard in 1908. For some years he worked as an editor for *Everybody's Magazine*, a post that would surely have appealed to Ira. In 1915 he married, settled down in a Fifth Avenue apartment, and fathered a girl, his only child. But just about the time he married he shifted into show business. Here was an intelligent, cultivated man who was also an educated musician. Aarons chose Daly as one of the composers for *For Goodness Sake*. Fred and Adele Astaire with sixth billing danced to two Daly songs—"The Whichness of the Whatness" and "Oh Gee, Oh Gosh"—which, according to the *Evening Telegram*, elicited "storm after storm of applause." The same could not be said of audience or critical reaction to the Astaires' presentation of "All by Myself," a Gershwin song interpolated into the show.

Therefore, at this particular moment, early spring 1922, Daly and Ira had book shows, not revues, that were hits on Broadway. George made an effort to combine forces with Daly; on December 4, 1922, *Our Nell*, with a score by both Gershwin and Daly, opened at the Nora Bayes Theater in New York and ran only forty performances.

EARLY in 1922, Buddy DeSylva, by then established with "April Showers" and "Avalon," visited George at his office and suggested they write a hit. George began to improvise a slow, sensuous melody. DeSylva, enthusiastic, said, "Do it again." Delighted with the double entendre, they kept the lyric line. The song remains a jewel in Gershwin's exceptionally rich output.

As always he played his newest creation at a party as soon as he finished it. Actress Irene Bordoni was there and insisted it be hers. She introduced it to the public in a farce, *The French Doll.*

"I'll Build a Stairway to Paradise," composed for Gershwin's third *Scandals* in 1922, signals his mature style and the start of his career as a musical theater composer. By this time he had been collaborating with Ira and DeSylva for several years. In this instance he collaborated with them both. DeSylva suggested expanding on a line in a song by George and Ira. The brothers had written a good deal together, much of it unpublished, but one line in one song attracted DeSylva's attention. He told Ira he saw the germ of an idea in the song's ending: "I'll build a staircase to Paradise, with a new step every day." So one evening, in DeSylva's apartment in Greenwich Village, the three got together and wrote a new song for George White. They kept only that line from the original and even a syllable in that was changed: stair*case* became stair*way*.

When White heard the song, he built a production number around it, using it for his first act finale. Called "The Patent Leather Forest," it featured a gleaming white stairway as wide as the theater's proscenium and performers dressed in shiny black strutting up and down the steps. Paul Whiteman's orchestra played on stage, pounding out that brassy, thumping beat.

Songwriter Alec Wilder, who was also an analyst of popular American music, writes that this song is "one of the earliest associated with the broad definition of jazz given in those years by non-jazz writers and critics." Wilder believed there was this perception because Gershwin emphasized the so-called blue notes—the flatted third (E-flat in the key of C) and the flatted seventh (B-flat in the key of C). This song, Wilder writes, "probably thrilled listeners familiar with the more polite melodies of Friml and Romberg. . . . Gershwin's bald insistence here on notes which have been virtually the early jazz players' and blues singers' private property must have been delightfully shocking to the average theater-goer."

Writer Carl Van Vechten was thrilled too. He wrote that the song "represented the most perfect piece of jazz written." Here Gershwin combined those lessons he learned from emulating Kern with the sounds he had ingested for years when he was hanging out uptown with black musicians.

Ira, delighted to be used for a *Scandals* production, wrote that he was pleased with the results. Seemingly obsessed with money, he noted his royalties came to "$3500, enough to support me for a year."

The growing collaboration between George and Ira worked well. In the mid-1920s, Ira became a full-time lyricist for George. Ira was able to support himself well the rest of his life. Ira's self-effacing temperament, his pragmatic nature and attention to detail, his ability to extricate George from trouble as he had when they had been children, all this seemed to be what his younger brother needed.

Before Gershwin and DeSylva finally parted professionally,

they worked on, among others, a twenty-minute piece that appeared in the same *Scandals* as "I'll Build a Stairway to Paradise." Even though the running time of *Blue Monday Blues* was a fraction of that of a Broadway show, the work was important for Gershwin because it was what might be called his first opera, contained one beautiful melody, inventive rhythms and—more to the point—dramatic passages that clearly led to *Porgy and Bess*.

Gershwin dated the stomach troubles—constipation and physical pain—he suffered from that time on to the anxiety he associated with this particular work. He later referred to these problems as his "composer's stomach," not his songwriter's stomach. The plot of the short opera is intriguing not because of its strengths (DeSylva's libretto was ridiculed by the press) but because it was the story behind Gershwin's first serious music-theater work. It is about a young man who died because he loved his mother too much. By the time Gershwin talked about *Blue Monday Blues* to his biographer Goldberg, he was dismissive of it. He had even lost the score. But he gave Goldberg enough information for him to produce the following account:

> Buddy DeSylva, one of the cleverest lyricists that ever forced a rhyme in Tin Pan Alley, in the early 1920s was discussing with Gershwin the possibilities of an opera written especially with a colored audience in mind. It was the hey-day of the new jazz, and Gotham was in the midst of a concurrent Negrophilia. Together they brought this black idea to the producer, George White. At once he saw its possibilities and suggested that it be done as a one-act specialty for the *Scandals of 1922*.
>
> On second thought, White suggested that DeSylva and Gershwin hold back a while. He expected to have white performers blackened up for the opera, and this would involve many changes because of the make-up. Nevertheless, three weeks before the show opened he came to the collaborators and announced that he would like to have a try at the experiment, anyway. DeSylva took out his pencil, and Gershwin dug into the cornucopia of his portfolio, fishing out a couple of viable tunes. For five days and nights they toiled on this pi-

oneer one-act vaudeville opera and on the sixth day they arose and found it good.

At the rehearsals everybody was enthusiastic about it; Paul Whiteman and his orchestra, it will be recalled, were in the show. Whiteman, himself a doughty pioneer of the higher jazz (much as he has always shied away from that but halfnaturalized noun), fell at once into the spirit of the thing.

George was keyed to high pitch. Here was something that was feeding his insatiable appetite for novelty and advancement. The opening night in New Haven was a tremendous tax upon his nerves. From this occasion, indeed, he dates his famous nervous indigestion.

The opera—in New Haven—went over magnificently. "This opera," wrote one critic the next morning, "will be imitated in a hundred years."

The story is simplicity itself; a step further and it might have eventuated in a setting of *Frankie and Johnny*. The scene is laid in "a basement cafe near 135th Street and Lenox Avenue." Joe, a gambler, is the favored lover of Vi. Tom, an entertainer in the cafe, is his rival. Joe receives a letter from his mother in Georgia and makes up his mind to visit his mammy. Amid this hard-boiled atmosphere, however, he is ashamed of the softness that distinguishes this mother-love, and pretends to Vi that he has been called out of town for a few days. Tom sees his opportunity and, behind Joe's back, convinces Vi that this out-of-town business is nothing but another woman. Vi, blinded by jealousy, shoots her Joe, only to discover the truth, too late.

Gershwin used recitative here, as he would later in *Porgy and Bess*. But while he wrote the orchestration for his bona fide full-length opera, he had Will Vodery, his black friend and colleague, orchestrate *Blue Monday Blues*. There was nothing in this that would have surprised anyone. Vodery had been orchestrating for Ziegfeld for many years by then. With this short work he applied principles that were virtually eighteenth century; sections of the piece sounded Haydnesque. The critical reaction was mixed but mainly negative. But there was this from a critic identified by Goldberg only as W. S.:

> Although Mr. White or any of his confreres may not be aware of it, they will have done a thing which will, or ought to, go down in history; they have given us the first real American opera in the one-act musical piece called *Blue Monday Blues*. Here at last is a genuinely human plot of American life, set to music in the popular vein, using jazz only at the right moments, the sentimental song, the blues, and, above all, a new and free ragtime recitative. True, there were crudities but in it we see the first gleam of a new American musical art."

Here is a review by Charles Darnton published in the *World* that characterized the critical response:

> *Blue Monday Blues* was the most dismal, stupid and incredible blackface sketch that has probably ever been perpetrated. In it a dusky soprano finally killed her gambling man. She should have shot all her associates and then turned the pistol on herself.

White canceled future performances, saying the opera was too depressing for the particular audience he needed to please. Al Jolson, a financial backer of the *Scandals*, ordered it killed.

Orson Welles once spoke of the "confidence of ignorance" that permitted him to take big risks when he was young. "If you're walking on the edge of a cliff and you don't know it, there is no basis for fear." Like Welles, Gershwin had no sense of the existence of a cliff when he was at Remick's, making up a song on the Fifth Avenue bus with Caesar, serving as rehearsal pianist for Ziegfeld, or writing the score for *La La Lucille;* with *Blue Monday Blues*, he caught sight of that cliff and lost his footing for a while.

The following spring he left the country for the first time when he went to Britain to write the score for *The Rainbow*, a revue that opened at the Empire Theatre in April 1923. Later he said that he considered it his weakest effort. Goldberg agreed and wrote, "The music is among the most insignificant that George has ever written. Much of it is strangely insipid. Was he deliberately toning himself down for the English? . . . George's English debut was a fiasco."

Still, *The Rainbow* had been a lucrative deal. The London producers gave him $1,500-plus passage. And the show brought him together with James P. Johnson, the black musician he had met when they both were making piano rolls for Aeolian three years before. "Plantation Days," a number from one of Johnson's shows, was included in *The Rainbow*. The New York *Times* wrote, "A scene in which Negro performers appear . . . provoked much agitation because . . . there are quite a few white American artists in the cast."

In 1933 Gershwin wrote that "not many composers have ideas. Far more of them know how to use strange instruments which do not require ideas. Whoever has inspired ideas will write the great music of our period. We are plowing the ground for that genius who may be alive or may be born today or tomorrow. If he is alive, he is recognized to a certain degree, although it is impossible for the public at large to assimilate real greatness quickly."

His *Rhapsody in Blue* suggests that he was talking about himself. It sent a message around the world that a Tin Pan Alley songwriter had successfully used popular music idioms in a concert work. It sent that message from a historic concert at Aeolian Hall on February 12, 1924, normally the home of Walter Damrosch and the New York Symphony.

But before that date, Gershwin had committed himself to composing his fifth edition of the *Scandals*. It opened in late June 1924. Daly conducted, DeSylva wrote the lyrics. The remarkable "Somebody Loves Me" came from that show. But there was another song in this revue, "I Need a Garden," that was as undistinguished as its title. Writing of this song, Alec Wilder says: "I have to believe Gershwin wrote it under duress; it was part of his contract. It shouts of resplendent production—even a stage filled with young ladies dressed as daffodils and hollyhocks, and frozen in graceful floral postures. The song might have been dashed off at a party as an imitation of a Kern ballad but given scarcely more attention in its published form. I believe that both Buddy DeSylva and Gershwin perpetrated a jape for a florid production number which must have bored them both to extinction."

Wilder was right. But it is worth mentioning because it signaled that Gershwin no longer held Kern in awe. The fun was being poked not at White but, more likely, at Kern and his tepid, operettalike numbers. Gershwin had taken what he needed from blacks, from Berlin—his improvisation on "The Revolutionary Rag" showed he no longer looked up to him—and finally from Kern. Now, in 1924, he was his own man.

Here is how the historic composition and performance of *Rhapsody in Blue* came about: Late on the evening of January 3, Gershwin and DeSylva were shooting pool at the Ambassador Billiards Parlor on Fifty-second Street and Broadway. Ira, as usual, was watching and reading the morning paper when he came upon an article publicizing an upcoming Paul Whiteman Aeolian Hall concert. He read aloud that George Gershwin was "at work on a jazz concerto" that would be played by Whiteman and his orchestra at Aeolian Hall on February 12. The announcement also noted that a panel of distinguished musicians —Rachmaninoff, Heifetz, Zimbalist, and Alma Gluck—would determine what constituted American music. Apart from Gershwin's contribution, the item claimed that Victor Herbert would compose something new and that Irving Berlin would create a "syncopated tone poem" for Whiteman.

Herbert did give Whiteman four serenades, which turned out to be the last pieces he wrote; he died in May 1924, just months after the *Rhapsody*'s premiere. But Berlin never gave Whiteman anything. He could not notate music, so a tone poem in the manner, say, of Liszt, was clearly out of the question. Whiteman had to have known that, but he probably wanted to dangle the Berlin name while he was selling tickets. To deliver on his promise of a work by Berlin he had Ferde Grofé, a sophisticated musician then working with Whiteman a few years, orchestrate some Berlin songs—"Alexander's Ragtime Band," "Orange Blossoms in California," and "A Pretty Girl Is Like a Melody."

When Gershwin asked Whiteman why he had given a release to the press before letting him know of these plans, Whiteman said that Vincent Lopez, a rival bandleader, had stolen the idea for the concert from him and had already booked a similar venture. Whiteman set out to win the contest. First, he spent $7,000 to rent Aeolian Hall. Second, he got a commitment from Victor Herbert, one of America's most prestigious musicians who was a founder of the American Society of Composers, Authors and Publishers (ASCAP) and its first president. So ASCAP supported Whiteman. Herbert and Whiteman had become friends when Whiteman played under Herbert at the 1915 San Francisco Fair.

Herbert's participation in the Whiteman event gave it respectability. In addition to the panel of experts on music, there was a list of patrons that included Fannie Hurst, Amelita Galli-Curci, Leopold Godowsky, Fritz Kreisler, Frank Crowninshield, Otto Kahn, Max Reinhardt, Heywood Broun, Carl Van Vechten, Gilbert Seldes, Deems Taylor, and Pitts Sanborn.

Hugh C. Ernst, Whiteman's manager, wrote the following explanation of what Whiteman had in mind for the nineteen-page brochure that would be given out at the concert: "The experiment is purely educational. Mr. Whiteman intends to point out, with the assistance of the orchestra and associates, the tremendous strides which have been made in popular music from the day of the discordant jazz, which sprang into existence about ten years ago from nowhere in particular, to the really melodious music of today which—for no good reason—is still being called jazz." Thus, with a stroke of the pen, for an event which was designed to celebrate the union of jazz and art, Whiteman ignored the role that blacks had played in the origins and development of what may well be America's most vital gift to world culture.

. . .

Gershwin created *Rhapsody in Blue* for that concert in less than six weeks. Gershwin's strength lay in musical ideas, not aesthetic ones. As an adolescent he sensed he wanted to combine pop and concert music and he wrote "Ragging the Traumerie." Still it took Buddy DeSylva to suggest a black opera with a jazz idiom at its base in order for him to compose *Blue Monday Blues*. Two years later Whiteman suggested Gershwin compose an orchestral work with the same jazzlike idiom as its roots.

Whiteman played a singular role in making *Rhapsody in Blue* the landmark piece it has come to be. A son of the superintendent of music in the Denver, Colorado, public school system, Whiteman was subjected to a rigorous music education. First he worked on violin, then viola. At seventeen he landed a job as violist with the Denver Symphony. Continuing to live at home, he upset his father by drinking and womanizing. When his father made it clear he would have to go out on his own, Paul went to San Francisco and got a job with its symphony orchestra. He went to work on December 17, 1915, with a guarantee of sixteen weeks at twenty-five dollars a week. He was twenty-five.

Thomas de Long, Whiteman's biographer, quotes from a published interview: "Jazz was beginning to be popular, and I made the surprising discovery that while I was able to earn only $40 a week in the symphony, I could get $90 playing what was called jazz fiddle. The music was often sketchy, the arrangements inexpert, and a great deal was left for the player to improvise."

What Whiteman never did tell his biographer was how it came to be that his first band was such an outstanding ensemble. In August 1991, jazz historian James T. Maher wrote:

> Red Norvo, the highly respected pioneer jazz xylophonist and vibraphonist, has recalled that when he joined the Paul Whiteman orchestra in 1930 it was common knowledge in the band that Whiteman had got his start as a band leader in San Francisco by "fronting" a band led by the banjoist Mike Pingitore. "No one tried to cover up the fact; it was just taken for granted," Norvo has recalled. "I learned about it from the

> older fellows who had been with Whiteman from the beginning." . . . Pingitore was already well known in San Francisco dance music circles in 1919. Whiteman himself told me that "the young, carriage trade dancers at the Palais Royal made Mike their favorite after we opened there in 1920. When they danced by they'd call out Hello, Mike and greet one or two of the other players." Norvo recalled Pingitore with great affection: "He was a wonderful person, very nice to work with. A sweet sort of guy. Apparently the way it started was that he had this band in San Francisco—right after the end of World War I—and he hired Whiteman. Now you know that Mike was short; hunchbacked with one leg shorter than the other. The way old-timers in the band told it, Mike decided that Whiteman would look good up in front of the band. Tall and impressive. You have to remember that Whiteman was a lot thinner then. So Mike made Paul the leader."

Even before World War I, San Francisco's Barbary Coast, the waterfront district, was the jazz center of the West Coast. Sometime after he began fronting the Pingitore band, Whiteman ran into Ferde Grofé, who worked as a freelance pianist and an arranger for dance orchestras. Other excellent arrangers included Arthur Lange, who worked for New York publishers. But what drew Whiteman to Grofé was not only his talent and education but his use of the saxophone. He gave it a jazzy, lush, vocal quality altogether unlike the violinlike character it had in the hands of a classical composer such as Bizet. Whiteman engaged Grofé, whose name he always mispronounced as GROW-fee, with the accent on the first syllable. With Grofé he instituted fixed arrangements with virtually no improvisation by his musicians.

Whiteman met Gershwin in 1922 when they were both working for White's *Scandals*. He conducted "Stairway to Paradise" and *Blue Monday Blues*. Gershwin liked what Whiteman did with his pop song, and Whiteman admired Gershwin's black opera. Later he said that soon after this he began to suggest to Gershwin that he write an orchestral work in a similar mode, that is, using a jazz-derived language. And that's why a number of first-rate musicians and one excellent orchestrator were all in place to give their best to whatever Gershwin would create.

At the same time Whiteman was looking up to the concert world, the high-culture scene in Europe was being captivated by jazz. In 1917 Carl Van Vechten, who spent two years in Paris as a correspondent for the New York *Times*, wrote an article, "The Great American Composer," published in *Vanity Fair*. Van Vechten predicted that American art music would grow from American popular music. In fact even French art music was beginning to grow from American popular music. In October 1923, Darius Milhaud's ballet *La création du monde*, which drew on some of the same jazz conventions that Gershwin would use only months later, received its world premiere in Paris.

The idea of combining pop with art was very much in the air abroad. According to his own account, Van Vechten persuaded Eva Gauthier, a French singer, to include a group of American songs in her November 1923 recital at Aeolian Hall. Van Vechten also claimed that he persuaded her to ask Gershwin to accompany her.

On November 1, 1923, less than four months before the Whiteman concert, in the same hall, Gauthier had sung Berlin, Kern, and Walter Donaldson along with "Stairway to Paradise," "Innocent Ingenue Baby," "Swanee," and "Do It Again," all with Gershwin at the piano. Gauthier placed the American songs after a group by Hindemith and Bartók and before Schoenberg's *Gurrelieder*. In the *Literary Digest*, Deems Taylor wrote of Gershwin's participation: "A pause. The singer reappeared, followed by a tall, black-haired young man who was far from possessing the icy aplomb of those to whom playing on the platform of Aeolian Hall is an old story. He bore under his arm a small bundle of sheet music with lurid black and yellow covers. The audience began to show signs of relaxation; this promised to be amusing. . . . Young Mr. Gershwin began to do mysterious and fascinating rhythmic and contrapuntal stunts with the accompaniment." Whiteman was working nightly at the Palais Royal and attended the Aeolian Hall event. The Gauthier concert surely mobilized his efforts to move quickly with something even more innovative.

What put Gershwin at the center of all this? Neither parent possessed musical talent nor any degree of cultivation. Yet as Luckey Roberts entranced him when he was in his teens, so European concert music held him in awe from an even younger age. The Library of Congress has Gershwin's music scrapbook, begun in 1909, when he was eleven years old. Most of the items were taken from *Étude*, a music magazine. George cut and meticulously lettered his own index tabs. He gave prominent space to "Great Pianists of the Keyboard," pasting underneath this heading photographs of Liszt, Josef Hofmann, Harold Bauer, William Mason, and Busoni. Sometimes he included descriptive passages that had appeared in print. There was a clipping, to cite one example, that Josef Lhévinne "amazed the critics and music lovers by the virility of his technique and by his finely trained artistic judgment."

George's scrapbook gave space to composers, too, particularly the Russians. There were photographs of Mussorgsky, Balakirev, and Glazunov as well as of some who were less well known: S. M. Liapunov, A. A. Ilyinsky, and W. Sappnikov. Another entry was the program of a Cooper Union concert performed by a twelve-year-old American Jew named Max Rosenzweig, who played a thoroughly European program of short works by Grieg, Corelli, Mozart, Vieuxtemps, Wagner, Puccini, Wieniawski, Beethoven, and Tchaikovsky with the assistance of Gina Ciaparelli-Viafora and the Sinsheimer String Orchestra.

By 1913 George attended concerts regularly. On April 3 he went to Leo Ornstein's recital at Wanamaker Auditorium. On June 13 he heard Lhévinne play Liszt transcriptions of Bach and Mendelssohn and works by Beethoven, Brahms, Chopin, Glazunov, and Balakirev. That same spring the Beethoven Society celebrated Wagner's centenary, and George was in the audience. Efrem Zimbalist was violin soloist with the Russian Symphony Orchestra. A playbill for Aeolian Hall with Damrosch's picture on the cover is another of Gershwin's mementos. He also heard Hofmann at Carnegie Hall.

Then Gershwin's own name begins to appear among the memorabilia. He has cut and pasted "Played by George Gershwin" with titles of piano rolls he made and pasted underneath: "Bantam Step," "Harry Jentes," "When You're Dancing the Old-Fashioned Waltz," "You Can't Get Along with 'Em or without 'Em," and "O Promise Me That You'll Come Back to Alabama." George must have sensed the discrepancy between this material and works by the great European composers.

Gershwin's serious concertgoing continued even after he began to write Broadway shows. In 1920, after *La La Lucille*, he attended a concert where Damrosch conducted the Musical Arts Society in works by Palestrina, Brahms, Johann Michael Bach, and some recondite Renaissance composers. Even more surprising is his attendance at an International Composers' Guild concert for a performance of Schoenberg's *Pierrot lunaire*, a trailblazing, atonal work.

By the time Gershwin set out to write a concert piece for Whiteman's Aeolian Hall concert, he had heard a good deal of the music that stretched from the fifteenth century to his own lifetime. Five or six years later, in a long letter to Goldberg, Gershwin detailed how the *Rhapsody* evolved in his mind:

> . . . no set plan was in my mind—no structure to which my mind would conform. The rhapsody, as you see, began as a purpose, not a plan.
>
> At this stage of the piece I was summoned to Boston for the premiere of *Sweet Little Devil* [December 23, 1923]. I had already done some work on the rhapsody. It was on that train, with its steely rhythms, its rattlety-bang that is so often stimulating to a composer—I frequently hear music in the heart of noise—I suddenly heard—and even saw on paper—the complete construction of the rhapsody from beginning to end. No new themes came to me, but I worked on the thematic material already in my mind, and tried to conceive the composition as

> a whole. I heard it as a musical kaleidoscope of America, of our vast melting pot, of our national pep, of our blues, our metropolitan madness. By the time I reached Boston, I had a definite *plot* of the piece, as distinguished from its actual substance.

Gershwin went on to write that the middle theme came to him at the home of a friend, "just after I got back to Gotham. . . . All at once I heard myself playing a theme that must have been haunting me inside, seeking outlet. No sooner had it oozed out of my fingers than I knew I had it."

In 1985 filmmaker Paul Schrader wrote a screenplay about the life of Gershwin that never made it to film. But Ira Gershwin recalled for Schrader's researcher how George had spoken to him about the work. It does not contradict but rather supplements what Gershwin had written to Goldberg. Here is the Schrader screenplay with George speaking to Ira (Iz):

> You start with an ice-breaker, an ascending clarinet to get attention, to start the engine. Just after the first theme, four bars in, I stress an unaccented beat. First bump in the road.
>
> (gesture)
>
> Same thing two bars later but fool with the harmony too. The second bump is also the first turn! With the second theme five bars later you're on your way with the scenery all blue and jazzy—but where are you headed? Keep changing keys, turn, detour seven times before hitting straightaway A Major, like the cycle of fifths rag players use.
>
> (George dashes to the keyboard, demonstrates)
>
> Meantime I'm pitting four notes against three so you feel like you're accelerating all the time. Add a few classical conventions and you think you're listening to Tchaikovsky or Liszt. It's a rhythm for our time, Iz. Not just pep. Our pulse.
>
> (a beat)
>
> And Grofé will orchestrate.

Gershwin told Goldberg that when he wrote the *Rhapsody*, what he knew about harmony could be put on a three-cent stamp. Still, the harmonic trajectory of the piece is bold. It begins in B-flat major. The conventional path would be to move to F major or G minor, keys closely related to the tonic home base. But instead of going either way, Gershwin takes the music to a far distant place and the A major he refers to here moves us to the E-major blues theme, as far removed from the tonic key as possible. Then the composer skillfully brings the listener back to B-flat major, where he began.

It has been claimed repeatedly that it was Ira who changed George's *An American Rhapsody* title to *Rhapsody in Blue*, calling attention to the E-major (blues) theme. This may be true. But the final title echoed *Blue Monday Blues*, George's most extended work until then. For a man known as unflappable, Gershwin's emphasis on blues in his titles and blues in his art supports his biographer's description of a "puzzled solemnity" in the man.

Kurt Dieterle, one of Whiteman's eight violinists at the time of the concert, recalled in a 1991 conversation that during rehearsals Gershwin tried to delete the E-major theme. He probably felt that after the initial brilliance, that sensual melody would slow the piece down. Dieterle recalled that Grofé persuaded the composer to keep it in. Gershwin had originally scored the clarinet opening as a seventeen-note scale passage, with each pitch clearly delineated by the player. But, says Dieterle, Ross Gorman, a brilliant reed player, either out of boredom or whimsy, impulsively "smeared" the clarinet to the top, something that few other clarinetists could do with the same precision. Gershwin liked the effect and wrote it into the score. And so *Rhapsody in Blue* acquired a brilliant opening, one of the most quickly identifiable aspects of the work and a gesture that set the tone for the piece.

The incident not only reveals Gorman's inventiveness; it also illuminates Gershwin's willingness to accept good ideas from others. Gershwin composed the *Rhapsody* in the 110th Street apartment he shared with his parents, brothers, and sister. A back room was reserved for his work. Grofé went there every day, taking the pages as they were completed and orchestrating them right away. Although there is no date on the last page of the score, Gershwin probably finished it by January 25, when he went to Boston for final rehearsals of *Sweet Little Devil.* The score looks like one by Mozart; there are virtually no erasures.

Whiteman had more riding on the concert than Gershwin, who, after all, was not yet a household name. Yet Milton Rettenberg, one of Whiteman's pianists, has said that when the orchestra rehearsed the *Rhapsody* at the Palais Royale, Gershwin kept offering apologies, saying that he had not had enough time to do the job he wanted to do, while Whiteman was so moved by it that he wept.

February 12 was a cold, snowy day. Cabs and limousines crowded the streets around Aeolian Hall. Posters on the building advertised "An Experiment in Modern Music" by Paul Whiteman and his Palais Royal Orchestra. Fred and Adele Astaire came. So did Kilenyi, Gershwin's harmony teacher, whom he consulted for this score. So did Vodery, who also probably gave advice. And there was the cream of the musical world: Heifetz, Kreisler, Rachmaninoff, Sousa, Stokowski, Godowsky, and Stravinsky. The Gershwin brothers watched them enter from a darkened alcove.

The concert began at 2:45 P.M. Gershwin's work was the twenty-second in a program of twenty-three pieces. The concert was to start with a tongue-in-cheek Dixieland Jazz Band number and move on to Irving Berlin to Zez Confrey to Victor Herbert and Edward Elgar with a lot of material in between. At 5:05 the *Rhapsody* still had not been played. People were restless. The ventilating system had broken down, and even though the concert was being held in February, musicians and listeners were bathed in sweat. Some of the audience began to leave when Herbert's *Oriental Serenade* ended to polite applause. Then Gershwin's *Rhapsody* was announced. There was a rustle of anticipation and Gershwin walked briskly onto the stage and sat down at the piano. When the clarinet gave forth with that never-before-heard startling whooooop, those who had started to leave went back to their seats.

Rhapsody in Blue was a historic event in world music. With Schoenberg's *Pierrot lunaire* and Stravinsky's *Sacre du printemps,* two of the major European composers of the twentieth century took music based on tonality as far as they thought it could go. Both spent the rest of their lives dealing with ideas that would give structure to compositions without using tonality as the base which automatically confers structure on a work. In 1923 Schoenberg presented his Five Piano Pieces, op. 23, which revealed his twelve-tone method designed to give music the structure that tonality had provided.

That same year Stravinsky composed his Octet, a work that demonstrated a revised concept of tonality that his colleagues labeled neoclassic. The following year Gershwin composed *Rhapsody in Blue*, which, while building as it did on the popular musical idioms of the day, was rooted in tonality. Yet the inventive rhythms, the swinging touch that came directly from jazz, brought a quality to the classical-music world that was perceived as genuine freshness.

The audience loved *Rhapsody in Blue*, and many critics wrote favorable reviews. Olin Downes said that despite some "technical immaturity," Gershwin had "expressed himself in a significant, and . . . highly original manner." In the *Sun*, Gilbert W. Gabriel wrote that the *Rhapsody* was "the day's most pressing contribution. Mr. Gershwin has an irrepressible pack of talents and there is this element of inevitability about his piece." In the *Herald*, William J. Henderson said the *Rhapsody* was "highly ingenious" and Deems Taylor, in the *World*, wrote the piece "hinted at something new, something that had not hitherto been said in music." Some major critics attacked the work. In the *Tribune*, Lawrence Gilman, its chief music critic, wrote a scathing piece: "Recall the most ambitious piece on yesterday's program and weep over the lifelessness of its melody and harmony, so derivative, so stale, so inexpressive." For Gilman the *Rhapsody* and other works on the program contained "trite and feeble conventional . . . tunes" and "sentimental and vapid harmonic treatment."

But even those attacking the work mentioned Gershwin's remarkable pianism. He had written out the cadenza, but the score contained an empty page allowing him to improvise as he chose, and the house went wild when he performed with his unique pyrotechnics. The concert was such a success with the public that Whiteman scheduled a second on March 7 at Aeolian Hall and a third on April 21 at Carnegie.

After the Carnegie performance, Whiteman took the orchestra on a two-week tour to Canada and followed that with an extensive itinerary through the United States. Gershwin was the soloist but he had to leave in June to return to work on his last *Scandals*. When he left, Whiteman used Milton Rettenberg to play in his place.

Immediately after this thirty-concert stint, Gershwin, with Whiteman, recorded the *Rhapsody* for Victor. Though more sophisticated equipment was already being developed, this first recording was done with giant acoustic horns. Still it remains the most aesthetically satisfying version to date. Three years later the same personnel came together and rerecorded it, using an electrical recording system. Despite its technical improvement, this new recording does not compare with the first version. Little of the original substance remains.

Nine months after the Aeolian concert Van Vechten approached Gershwin with the idea of their creating an opera together. Bruce Kellner, Van Vechten's biographer, writes that "there was talk, late in 1924, that Gershwin and Van Vechten would collaborate on a jazz opera with a Negro subject." In a diary entry on October 16, 1924, Van Vechten wrote: "George Gershwin came at ten and stayed until after twelve. I told him the scheme for the opera." That meeting must have held promise because one week later, on October 18, Van Vechten wrote to Hugh Walpole: "I am going West next week. . . . When I return I *may* write an opera, for the music of George Gershwin. He has an excellent idea, and I am tempted—a serious jazz opera, without spoken dialogue, all for Negroes! He has unlimited funds to produce this. By the way, I had Ernest Newman here the other evening to listen to Gershwin, an historic occasion."

Less than a week later the project appears to have dissolved. In a letter dated October 23, written to his wife, Van Vechten says that he and Gershwin had come to an impasse: "I've been thinking more about opera and I have more ideas, but I'm sure Gershwin wants something different and nothing will come of it."

That Van Vechten sought out Gershwin for a collaboration, that the British critic Ernest Newman spent hours listening to Gershwin play, that someone—probably the investment banker Otto Kahn, who headed the Metropolitan Opera—had offered him "unlimited funds" reveals the heights to which Gershwin had risen since the evening of January 3 when he and DeSylva played pool on Fifty-second and Broadway.

Dreyfus published the *Rhapsody*, making it Harms's first concert piece. It was a two-piano version in which the second piano part was a reduction of Grofé's score for jazz band. It sold rapidly, surprising Gershwin, for both parts were exceptionally difficult to play at that time. When one computes the money the work brought in for Gershwin during the next ten years—not only from sales and rentals of the score but for permissions to use the work in other ways—the sum is $250,000. (Financial considerations did not always preclude personal ones. In 1927, Gershwin gave George White the use of the *Rhapsody* for a ballet that closed the first act of the season's *Scandals*.)

Although DeSylva continued to write lyrics to some of Gershwin's music for a time, Ira's role grew. He and his wife jealously guarded his position not only in their day-to-day dealings during George's lifetime but also in the manipulation of history after his death. The books written under their supervision hardly mention other lyricists. Irving Caesar says no biographer of Gershwin has ever given his work with Gershwin the attention it deserves for he and George collaborated on dozens of Gershwin's early songs.

Donald Kahn, son of Gus Kahn, who wrote the lyrics with Ira for "Liza," one of Gershwin's most enduring songs, confirms Caesar's remarks. In 1990 he reported that the Gershwin lawyers never permitted "Liza" to be used in a retrospective of Gershwin's career, because Ira would then have had to share both credit and money with the Gus Kahn estate.

Rose Gershwin exulted in her newfound wealth. Milton Rettenberg, who knew the family before Gershwin's success, told conductor Maurice Peress that one day Rose, seated in an open limousine with a chauffeur at the wheel, shouted to him on the street, simply to get him to look at her. Leopold Godowsky, her grandson, said in 1990, "There was always the feeling that if only Rose had more money, she would be happy. She was geared to a life of material things."

Along with the dramatic rise in Gershwin's career, a similar jump in his social life took place. His first circle of friends as a young adult was the closely knit group that spent Saturday nights at the home of Lou and Emily Paley at 18 West Eighth Street. Lyricist Howard Dietz and his wife lived on the floor below the Paleys in a house in Greenwich Village. Two years older than George and a Columbia College alumnus, Dietz was on a higher level—from a social and cultural standpoint—than George. According to Dietz's own account, some time in 1920, on Saturday evenings, the chandelier in his living room would start to shake. The disturbance seemed to come from the floor above. One Saturday, before he and his wife were to leave for the theater, he decided to go upstairs and complain about the problem:

> I knocked at the door of the Lou Paleys. Someone opened the door carefully and put his finger to his lips, cautioning me not to disturb the music. About forty people were sitting on the floor around the grand piano at which a dark-haired chap was playing and singing in a rich guttural. He was vastly entertaining. I took a seat on the floor. My wife below got impatient waiting and came upstairs to find out what had happened to me. I went to the door, put my finger to my lips and motioned her to come in and sit beside me. We never got to the theater and we stopped bothering about our chandelier. We became regulars at the Saturday nights at the Lou Paleys to hear George Gershwin.

Gershwin's friendship with the Paleys predated their Eighth Street apartment. Herman Paley, Lou's brother, twenty years older than George, had worked at Remick's when George was there. Immensely impressed with Gershwin's gifts, he brought him home when the Paleys lived on 112th Street and the Gershwins on 110th. Like Dietz, Herman Paley was an educated man. He had graduated from City College, studied composition with Edward MacDowell, theory and harmony with Kilenyi, and piano under Hambitzer. Mabel Pleschette, a niece, also had been a Hambitzer student. In 1989 she described Hambitzer as a "marvelous man. He always sat at the other side of the room, not next to you at the piano. And he never demonstrated how to play a piece by playing it himself. He gave you that important sense of freedom."

Mabel and George were good friends. On Saturday nights the Paleys and their friends listened to George play and sing. He had written some of the songs with Lou, a published lyricist. The participants also talked about books, which was useful to George, for he did not read. Through him these people, throughout their lives, enjoyed the pleasure of seeing one of their own get public recognition.

Howard Dietz did not remain so friendly. In his autobiography, *Dancing in the Dark* (the title of the song he had written with Arthur Schwartz), he wrote of how he filled in for Ira some years later when Ira had an appendectomy and George needed fast help with a score. He complained he was given credit for an undistinguished song written by Ira and no credit for "Someone to Watch Over Me," to which he claims he contributed a great deal. "George needed a substitute and selected me. He wanted Ira to retain as much credit as possible. He chose me because I would be least demanding on both credit and money and I showed promise. . . . Realizing that any sum paid me would have to come out of Ira's royalties, George paid me next to nothing. It was decided I was to get one cent for every copy of sheet music that was sold. When Ira sent me my first paycheck it was for 96 cents."

In 1921 George met Jules Glaenzer, an executive at Cartier's, the jewelers. Glaenzer was a famous New York host, and Gershwin was invited regularly to parties at his East Side town house. Glaenzer helped George rise to his new status. He taught him not to talk with a cigar in his mouth. Glaenzer also took George to a tailor to have his suits made. Gershwin continued to entertain at the piano as he had done on Eighth Street. But now the guests included Douglas Fairbanks, Jack Dempsey, Charlie Chaplin, Lord and Lady Mountbatten, Noel Coward, Jascha Heifetz, Fanny Brice, Maurice Chevalier, Gertrude Lawrence, and Fred and Adele Astaire. Fred Astaire and George had met years before at Remick's and even then discussed the possibility of working together on Broadway.

But most of Glaenzer's guests were new to Gershwin. Noel Coward became a friend. On October 29, 1924, he wrote George, "The Rhapsody record is marvellous and it's given me more pleasure than you can imagine—I sit down to listen to it a normal healthy Englishman and by the time the second half is over, I could fling myself into the wildest excesses of emotional degeneracy. Please be careful what you write in future or I won't be answerable for the consequences."

Glaenzer had a house in Paris, at 5 rue Malakoff, and, in 1923, when George went to London to do his first revue outside the United States, Glaenzer invited him and DeSylva to join him on the Continent. In a 1973 biography of Gershwin, Charles Schwartz says that one evening, after making the rounds of restaurants and clubs, the three men went to a Paris whorehouse. Glaenzer had made arrangements in advance for DeSylva and him to look through a peephole while George was fornicating in a private room. "Though they had not necessarily expected a virtuoso performance . . . they were amazed when Gershwin showed almost no sophistication in the art of love. He seemed neither to enjoy nor desire the experience and dispensed entirely with foreplay. Instead, he completed the sexual act quickly, in an almost mechanical way. . . . When Glaenzer and DeSylva met with him afterward, their stupefaction was heightened by Gershwin's boastful claim regarding his vitality with the courtesan as well as his prowess as a lover."

The incident certainly suggests Gershwin wanted always to project the image of a great lover. Perhaps his potency, so pleasurable to him at the age of nine, had started to decline about the same time he began to suffer his stomach pains. In a conversation in 1990, Al Hirschfeld, the Broadway newspaper caricaturist, who frequently saw George at parties in the late 1920s and 1930s, said, "I know stories of his womanizing were prevalent but I never saw him go steady in any sense of that word. George was so in love with work that he seemed asexual to me. Like Crowninshield and Woollcott. Neither was homosexual or interested in women; their passions were all tied up in their work."

Gershwin left Van Vechten's at noon on October 16, 1924. He returned later that day for dinner escorting Pauline Heifetz, the younger sister of the renowned violinist Jascha Heifetz. She entered this event in her appointment book. Pauline and George probably met at one of Jules Glaenzer's parties.

By October 16 she had made five entries for occasions she had shared with George. On October 9, she had already indicated interest in him with this entry: "4:30. George Gershwin comes to tea. We go for a walk. I like him."

Pauline Heifetz was the second child of a Jewish family that had come from Russia. Jascha started playing in public at five. While he was touring the United States, the Russian Revolution broke out. His family, touring with him, decided to remain in America. Isidor Achron, Heifetz's accompanist in Russia, had not come with him, so Heifetz had to choose another pianist. He selected Samuel Chotzinoff. The pianist was then sharing a studio over Carnegie Hall with another bachelor, playwright S. N. Behrman.

According to Chotzinoff's memoir, Pauline and her younger sister, Elsa, used to pop out from behind a screen and make faces at him as he was working with Heifetz. Pauline became a voracious reader and a brilliant pianist.

Reuven Heifetz, their father, had played in a pit orchestra in Russia and was ambitious not only for his son but for his daughters. The family eventually bought a town house on West Eighty-fifth Street in Manhattan and a summer house on Narragansett Pier in Rhode Island. Reuven and Anna Heifetz hosted many parties. Anna Koch, a cousin, remembers a New Year's Eve when she heard Anna Heifetz say she had asked the orchestra to come early to prevent George from sitting down at the piano and monopolizing the music for the entire evening.

When George first appears in Pauline's appointment books, almost as a footnote, it is clear her concentration was on the British film director Rex Ingram. Indeed, a clipping about him found in her appointment book includes quotes from other renowned directors including Erich von Stroheim, who calls him "the greatest director in the world." September 30, Pauline dines with Ingram. October 1, she notes, Ingram sails for France on the *Paris*. But that is the last time his name appears. The night he leaves, she dines at "Chotzie's." On the bottom of the entry she notes that Gershwin was there.

A couple of months before this, her sister, Elsa, married without warning. Anna Koch remembered the event: "Elsa and Harold Stone arrived in a shiny black Packard. 'We are married,' they said. Everybody bustled around fixing up a bed for them." Pauline was in a state of shock. Her younger sister had married before she did. On that day, in her diary, Pauline entered the following: "Elsa marries Harold" and drew a skull and crossbones below her words. She wrote frequently about how "adorable" Rex Ingram was. But in October he was gone from her life and Gershwin was in it.

Pauline Heifetz was cultivated and moved in sophisticated circles. In a letter to Jascha, she writes of a party he had asked her to arrange and wonders if she left anyone out. The list includes Helen Hayes, Charles MacArthur, Frank Crowninshield, Gene Tunney, Alfred Knopf, Lynn Fontanne, Gloria Swanson, Marc Connelly, Irving Berlin, and George Gershwin.

On October 9, 1924, Gershwin came to tea and a week later

he invited her to Van Vechten's. After that they spent at least one out of every three evenings together going to movies, to the theater, to friends' houses, to Narragansett. Apart from times when George was working out of town, this went on for more than a year.

Gershwin gave Pauline a first edition of *Rhapsody in Blue* bound in wine-colored suede with "For Pauline" and the title embossed in gold. Inside was the inscription: "With admiration and deep affection." Theirs was not a sexual liaison but a conventional courtship of the time. Anna Koch insists that she would have known if it were more than that.

Finally, on December 9, 1925, fourteen months after they had started to spend time together, Pauline wired George in Wilmington that Chotzinoff had proposed to her and what was she to do. Gershwin replied that she should say yes.

There are reports that Gershwin remarked that he was so busy at the time that he didn't even notice what had happened. But Kate Wolpin, his aunt, says that on his return to New York he was very depressed. She says that "everybody in New York knew Pauline married Chotzie to spite George," and that may have been true. But she adds something that suggests the marriage could not have worked: "Rose [her sister and George's mother] told me that Pauline had snubbed her. That really ended it with George. On Passover my sister entertained the whole family and George and I took a walk. I asked him why he didn't marry Pauline. He said, 'I don't think we could be happy together. I like to get up in the middle of the night to work and she likes to keep going out.' "

Also, of course, he did not love her.

The end of the relationship pleased Rose Gershwin and displeased Reuven Heifetz. According to Anne Grossman, the daughter of Samuel and Pauline Chotzinoff: "On December 9 my grandfather gave my father the family diamond ring. He said, 'I had hoped for something better but . . .' " One can't know from this whether he would have thought Gershwin better than Chotzinoff or only that, in his eyes, Chotzinoff did not rate very high.

. . .

Back in October 1924, when Gershwin had begun to see Pauline with some regularity, he was having his most successful year. He had watched *Sweet Little Devil*, with lyrics by DeSylva, open at the Astor Theater. It was still running when *Rhapsody in Blue* was born. He had also put together his last score for White's *Scandals*. Gershwin's fortunes had turned even in England, where the success of *Primrose* wiped out the memory of the *Rainbow* revue. It opened September 11 at the Winter Garden in London and ran 255 performances. In the face of all this activity, Gershwin still managed to complete his score for *Lady, Be Good!* in time for a December 1 opening.

By this time the revue, as a Broadway format, was in a decline. Shows such as these simply staged a group of unrelated sketches and musical numbers, not necessarily all by the same composer. During the 1924–25 season, hardly any revue, including the *Ziegfeld Follies*, did well. Berlin had been composing scores for his own Music Box Theater since 1921, and Jerome Kern had had a string of successes at the Princess Theater. But by 1924, their shows were losing money. Berlin's fourth edition of the *Music Box Revue*, which evoked a courteous and genteel past, closed after 186 performances, and Kern's *Dear Sir* lasted only two weeks.

The terrain was wide open for *Lady, Be Good!*, which had a libretto and songs and dances that fitted into the story for the most part. A brother and sister dance team, down on their luck, manipulate their fortunes through disguises that bring a happy ending.

Vinton Freedley, who had performed in musical comedies, joined Aarons as a producer. Guy Bolton, who had contributed to the *Primrose* book, wrote the libretto with Fred Thompson. Fred and Adele Astaire headed the cast. The pit orchestra, conducted by Paul Lannin, was augmented and dominated by the two-piano team of Phil Ohman and Victor Arden, whose quirky, angular style brought a new dimension to Broadway. Norman Bel Geddes designed the sets.

The Gershwins created twenty-five songs for the show—including some never used and others added to a London production. "Oh, Lady, Be Good!," "The Half of It, Dearie, Blues," "Little Jazz Bird," and, most particularly, "Fascinating Rhythm" pointed the way to a jazzy, brassy, hard-edged future for the Broadway musical.

Another song that Gershwin started in the spring of 1924 did not make it into this or any future production, though it was often tried. Like the E-major theme in *Rhapsody in Blue*, "The Man I Love" slowed down the action. But in 1925, when Lady Mountbatten brought the unpublished score to London, her favorite dance band played it, and it eventually became a hit not only in England but in France and finally in the United States.

Twenty years after Gershwin composed it, Australian composer Percy Grainger wrote a foreword to a new edition. He traced its melody as well as a theme from *Rhapsody in Blue* to the music of Edvard Grieg. The yellow front cover of the Schirmer score of Grieg's piano sonata op. 7 had served as a kind of notepad for Gershwin and Jack Miller when they were studying with Hambitzer.

Along with the American sounds of James P. Johnson, Luckey Roberts, Irving Berlin, and Jerome Kern, Gershwin was obviously influenced by the European music he had studied in his early years. Unlike the intellectual and well-educated Jerome Kern, Gershwin had no sense of history, nor did he care about the antecedents of the particular kind of music he was making at any given time. In a 1989 conversation, Mabel Schirmer, the Mabel Pleschette of Gershwin's youth who married a member of the Schirmer music publishing family, said George never talked about ideas or, for that matter, about people. His reluctance to be introspective or to assess what he was eager to do revealed itself in his response to a request from *Vanity Fair*. In 1925 Frank Crowninshield, the magazine's editor, asked him along with several other celebrities, to write his own epitaph. Here was what George submitted:

Here lies the body of GEORGE GERSHWIN

American composer

. . .

Composer?

American?

Virgil Thomson, critic and composer, once said, "It is very easy to write American music. All you have to be is American, and then write any kind of music you wish." It is not as simple as that. The critical question is how much of Europe the American has absorbed and how he has dealt with that part of him.

In the nineteenth century, Edward MacDowell and Horatio Parker, two of the best-known American composers, got their training in Europe. Unlike Schoenberg and Stravinsky, the first an Austrian, the second a Russian, neither MacDowell nor Parker felt the need to cause a revolution about anything.

But revolution was in the air in Europe, and a man born in the town of Villars in the French province of Burgundy was the most radical of all. Edgard Varèse left Europe for the United States in 1915, much earlier than those artists who fled because of the rise of Hitler. What he wished to do was assault the physical principles on which music was based. He did not accept the fact of twelve equal semitones, regarding it as an arbitrary division of the octave. From the start of his life in Greenwich Village, Varèse strove toward a pitchless sound, deemphasizing melody and harmony. Eventually he was perceived as the father of electronic music.

In 1919 he became the conductor of the New Symphony Orchestra, a cooperative in which participating musicians shared in the profits. His goal of performing well-rehearsed contemporary works was what also prompted Arnold Schoenberg to found the International Society of Contemporary Music (ISCM) in Vienna only months before Varèse began the New Symphony Orchestra. ISCM had sponsored the Gauthier concert where Gershwin made his performing debut. Schoenberg always had in mind a limited attendance by an enlightened elite whereas Varèse was then reaching for a large public.

Varèse failed quickly. The orchestra died before its second event. In the press Varèse attacked contemporary musical organizations as "Bourbons who learn nothing and forget nothing. They are mausoleums, mortuaries for musical reminiscences."

Because his departure from the New Symphony Orchestra left him without an outlet for his work, he and his friend harpist Carlos Salzedo started the International Composers' Guild (ICG). This was less costly to run because the repertoire was limited to works written for small ensembles. In July 1921, the ICG published a manifesto in which Varèse praised composers and attacked performers. It was a very different approach from the one pursued a few years later for the Aeolian Hall concert by Paul Whiteman, who invited the most distinguished musicians in the concert world to participate in his experiment in modern music.

Gershwin probably felt no affinity for Varèse's musical activity. Melody and harmony were too central to his work. Then, too, in 1922, when the ICG began, Gershwin could hardly have conceived of himself as an artist who could associate with these figures. The chances are that he was more than grateful when Whiteman took an interest in him.

But from his childhood, when he pasted photographs of the masters in his scrapbook, Gershwin had longed to be a part of this world. By early in 1925 he was. On January 1, he escorted Pauline Heifetz to a Koussevitzky concert, then to a party at the home of newspaper publisher Herbert Bayard Swope. On January 7, Gershwin met Stravinsky at a reception following Stravinsky's first American concert at Carnegie Hall, where he conducted a program of his own works. By this time Stravinsky had shown his enthusiasm for American pop with *Ragtime for Eleven Instruments* (1918) and *Piano Rag Music* (1919). Ernest Ansermet, a Swiss conductor, had stimulated his interest with sheet music he brought back to the Continent from the United States.

On January 8, Stravinsky and Gershwin met again at a party. This time some misguided guest forced the two to sit at the piano. Stravinsky and Gershwin both appeared to shrink at the prospect. Fortunately John Jay Hammond of the organ-manufacturing family knew this piano well; he pulled a switch that rendered it silent. His action not only saved the evening but also the relationship between the two men, for Pauline Heifetz wrote that on the morning of January 9, she, Jascha, George, and Ira visited Stravinsky in his hotel suite. Later Stravinsky told the press that he found Gershwin "nervously energetic."

During these meetings with Stravinsky, George met Stravinsky's friend Samuel Dushkin, the Russian violinist, who had made his American debut in 1924. Dushkin asked Gershwin if he had anything Dushkin could play at a recital on February 8. George offered him his notebooks and Dushkin selected two pieces that together would make a suitable violin and piano composition. At this premiere at the University Club, Gershwin called the piece "Short Story," which again suggests the idea of a plot underlying the music thinking that he used to describe *Rhapsody in Blue* to Goldberg.

For the opening, Dushkin chose a piece dated August 30, 1923. It had "Andantino con fantasia" on its first page. For the closing he chose one composed in 1919 in ragtime. Under its original title, "Novelette in Fourths," Gershwin had recorded it on a piano roll. For Dushkin, he changed that title to "Allegretto scherzando."

Gershwin's markings in a foreign language testify to his notion that "American" was not the language of art. He fancied up his concert scores with foreign directions. One could hardly fault him for that. Music in New York in the 1920s was still very much a European property. Varèse had not been able to find an American work he deemed worthy of performance for his first New Symphony Orchestra concert. Virtually anyone who wanted to pursue serious music went abroad to study.

Walter Damrosch, an American conductor who attended the Aeolian Hall concert and conducted the New York Symphony in regular concerts, had helped found a music school for Americans in the Paris suburb of Fontainebleau. The school's head was François Casadesus, the uncle of pianist Robert.

Most important was the fact that Nadia Boulanger taught there. Boulanger had embarked on an almost spiritual voyage to help young composers find their musical personalities. It began after the death at twenty-four of her sister and composition student, Lili, who was the first woman to win the Prix de Rome.

Boulanger had an apartment on the fourth floor of an old building on rue Ballu, where she gave private lessons. Those Americans who studied with her—and there were many—were not immersed, like Gershwin, in showgirls and big Broadway money but in the genteel poverty associated with art and a world of ideas that grew from the works of T. S. Eliot, Ezra Pound, Marcel Proust, André Gide, André Breton, Gertrude Stein, Ernest Hemingway, and James Joyce. The Guggenheim Foundation had a hand in promoting this exodus by giving fellowships to those Americans who went to Paris, beginning with Copland. All this European training not only intimidated American autodidacts like Gershwin but helped bring about the descent in the United States of the reputations of those eminently national composers Charles Griffes, Edward MacDowell, Daniel Gregory Muson, and Henry Hadley.

Aaron Copland went to Paris in 1923 with his cousin Harold Clurman (who a decade later helped create the Group Theater in New York) and began to work with Boulanger. They remained in France for three years, returning in June 1924, four months after the premiere of *Rhapsody in Blue*. By the time Copland had returned to New York, some of the composers associated with the ICG had left to found the League of Composers, an organization over which Copland reigned.

There was not as much distance between Copland and Gershwin as between Varèse and Gershwin. While Varèse was fifteen years older than Gershwin, Copland was about the same age. Copland and Gershwin were both born in Brooklyn, and both were Jews. Neither Copland nor Gershwin had gone to college. Despite their similarities, they had little connection. In 1990 Nicolas Slonimsky, the music lexicographer, said, "Gershwin was among the theater people. Copland was not. I introduced them. Not much was said." But because of their similarities,

Copland must have felt threatened by Gershwin's presence on the concert scene. To him this man was strictly Tin Pan Alley, a Broadway boor with a cigar, and he did not want to be tainted by that image because of his own commitment to the idea of European art.

There seems to be no evidence that Copland ever discussed Gershwin while Gershwin was alive. Nor is there any sign Gershwin talked about Copland, although it is safe to say that despite his active social and musical life, he coveted the increasing respect Copland garnered in those circles that mattered dearly to him. After Gershwin died, composer George Antheil wrote, "He has been recognized by everybody except those whose . . . understanding he most craved—the American composer."

That attitude survived Gershwin's death. Despite the countless performances his concert works receive throughout the world, despite the fact that Copland's music has never entered the public consciousness in a comparable way, music critics and composers in the United States have joined in anointing Copland as the dean or the father of American music.

In the mid-1970s, Daniel Brewbaker, a student of composition at the Juilliard School, asked Copland what he thought of Gershwin. "He was a good Broadway composer," Copland said.

Here is Copland's own description of his student days from a memoir published in 1984:

> Perhaps my three student years in France are so vivid in my memory because they had such an enormous influence on my future career. Man has not yet devised a method for measuring influences on an artist—influences can be direct or indirect, positive or negative, sharp or subtle. All this notwithstanding, it was in France in the early twenties that I reached my majority, that my ideas came of age, and it was there I came to know those who were to be the major and continuing influences in my life. I speak of Nadia Boulanger, my teacher, and Serge Koussevitzky, the great Russian conductor. I cannot imagine what my career would have been without them.

Boulanger, a devout Catholic, was as adoring in her devotion to Stravinsky. People would often see her walking several paces behind him carrying his bags. In his memoir Copland tells of the excitement he felt on seeing a Stravinsky score on Boulanger's piano before its premiere and on seeing Stravinsky himself. He tells of meeting the composer at "one of Mademoiselle's Wednesday afternoon classes and I was one of the dozen or more students who stood about in awe of the Master's presence." A far cry from Gershwin's attitude toward Berlin or Kern, it remained constant in Copland's feeling for Stravinsky throughout his long life.

Copland's attitude toward Koussevitzky was just as deferential. From 1920 to 1924, Concerts Koussevitsky were held in Paris. The music was of the twentieth century. Copland writes that it was there he heard premieres of works by Honegger and Prokofiev as well as an all-Stravinsky program with the composer as soloist in the first performance of his piano concerto. Copland and other Boulanger students—known collectively as the Boulangerie—followed Stravinsky in adopting the neoclassic mode, composing with tonality as their base, but without the form that tonality had earlier generated.

During the years abroad, Copland heard jazz in Vienna bars. "Hearing it in a fresh context," he wrote in the 1980s, "heightened my interest in its potential. I began to consider that jazz rhythms might be the way to make an American sounding music." It is true that by the time he heard jazz in Vienna he probably also had heard Stravinsky's ragtime pieces and the dozen or more European pieces—even Debussy's *Golliwog's Cakewalk* of 1908—but he writes as though Gershwin had never lived.

In the spring of 1924, the press reported that Koussevitzky would leave Paris to take over as conductor of the Boston Symphony Orchestra. As Copland reconstructs it, Boulanger made an appointment with the conductor and brought along Copland, her prize pupil. He played one of his works for Koussevitzky, who promised to program it during his first American season. Knowing Boulanger planned to make a trip to the United States about that time at the invitation of Damrosch, Koussevitzky invited her to appear with the BSO as organ soloist in a work he commissioned from Copland. "Boulanger must have written to Damrosch," Copland says in his memoir, "for the next thing I knew, a big unwritten composition for organ and orchestra was scheduled for performance in the 1924–25 season by both Walter Damrosch with the New York Symphony and Serge Koussevitzky with the Boston Symphony Orchestra. Two major performances were at stake. It was very tempting but very *scary*."

Perhaps scary for Copland, surely unsettling for Gershwin, for in the spring of 1925, there was this onslaught by Copland as the first accredited serious American composer, complete with an education abroad. Gershwin had to feel gratified when, in the spring of 1925, Damrosch commissioned him to compose a piano concerto. Damrosch did not have Koussevitzky's stature; Copland makes that clear in his memoirs. Still it meant Gershwin had a chance to enter the world he admired.

If Copland became scared at the thought of writing for the organ, consider Gershwin's reaction to the notion of writing for a full orchestra. Those who had attacked his *Rhapsody* had ammunition in the fact he had not orchestrated that himself, something forgivable in show business but never tolerated in serious music. So he bought Cecil Forsythe's book on orchestration, a comprehensive manual published in 1914, and decided he would do it himself. He may have had some help from his friends Will Vodery, who had orchestrated *Blue Monday Blues*, and Bill Daly, who helped him in many ways.

Through all the vicissitudes brought about by this ambitious commission, Gershwin kept working for Broadway. *Tell Me More*, produced by Aarons with lyrics by DeSylva and Ira, opened on April 13, and although it contained such gems as "That Certain Feeling" and "Kicking the Clouds Away," it ran only 100 performances.

On May 26 it opened in London at the Winter Garden. Gershwin rented an apartment with Sammy Lee, the dance director of *Tell Me More*, who had started his career as a member of Gus Edwards's kid revues. While in London Gershwin wrote to Pauline Heifetz, telling her he would accompany Eva Gauthier there and in Paris as he had done in New York.

49, Pall Mall,
S.W.1.

Dear Pauline—

Outside of lonesome spells that I get now and then, I am enjoying this trip very much.

The new production of "Tell Me More" looks good and the management is very satisfied.

Sammy Lee and I have engaged a flat at the above address and find it very comfortable. We've bought a couple of cases of wine and sit around the fire-place drinking as much as we like. I've developed a taste and capacity for wine that would surprise you. Yes—you wouldn't recognize me as the man who nearly fell under your brother-in-law's table after one scotch and soda. I'm sorry you are not here to join me in drinking the marvellous wines that are obtainable here.

What are you doing these days? Stepping out? Or spending quiet evenings at home? Perhaps you have gone to Narragansett. I do wish you'd write a fellow and let him know all about yourself.

Eva Gauthier is giving a recital here on May 22nd and in Paris on June 11. In both these concerts I will accompany her in the Jazz group.

Expect to be back home in about 6 or 7 weeks. Is that Narragansett invitation still open? I hope so.

Please give my best to Elsa and Harold and to your family and write without fail.

Love,
George

During his stay in England Gershwin began to sketch the work Damrosch had commissioned, which Gershwin was then calling the *New York Concerto*. On his return home he found more chaos than usual. He had bought a five-story house at 103d Street off Riverside Drive, and the family was getting ready to move. So, when Ernest Hutcheson, who taught a summer music program at Chautauqua, New York, offered him quarters there, he accepted the invitation. The last page of the first movement of the two-piano sketch for the piece is dated July 25.

In August, from Chautauqua, Gershwin sent another letter to Pauline indicating he had not completely finished the first movement by July 25. The letter is remarkable, considering its author had not gone beyond one year of high school.

Dear Pauline—

Your letter was most charming. It seemed as sincere as your handwriting seemed bad. It made me feel, after a restless Wednesday night (it arrived Thursday AM) happy and warm.

I've been in this place 9 days and I must say I made a happy choice in coming here. The atmosphere is quite different from any other I've been in. There are, for example, 40,000 people here, pious people with one foot in the grave, whose greatest pleasure is to go to lectures and sermons on Christ and His Return or Evolution versus the Bible. You know the type. The kind Ruth Draper portrays so well. However they are very quiet, homely Americans who, aside from their narrowness, are very nice people.

The New York Symphony has a six weeks season here with Albert Stoessel as conductor, which makes the place attractive musically. He tries occasionally to awaken the populace by playing Stravinsky or Honegger, but the church-loving Americans haven't yet emerged from the magic spell of "The Rosary" or "Oh Promise Me." And they tell him in letters they wish he would be forced to conduct "Pacific 231," for example, 231 times in succession before foisting it on them once more.

Mr. E. Hutcheson has very kindly given me the use of one of his studios every afternoon and evening, so every day between 2 & 6 and evenings between 8 & 10 you will find me diligently writing notes, playing piano or praying (you've got to pray in Chautauqua) to the God of Melody to please be kind to me and send me some hair-raising "blues" for my second movement. The first movement is practically finished, needing only a few changes and about 8 bars.

I am so sorry not to be with you this weekend. I'm sure you

> and I would have won the treasure hunt—especially if you knew all the clues beforehand.
>
> I met Chotzie's sister here. She is the wife of one of the Symphony players. She is a charming girl full of good Yiddish stories.
>
> Next Wednesday night I leave for the village of Manhattan. Write and let me know of your plans. My best wishes to your family and the gang staying there. I miss your yodle.

Next to his signature, Gershwin drew a two-bar staff in which he notated a melodic motif which, with its use of the dissonant interval of a second, points to the taxi horn notes in *An American in Paris*, which received its first performance two-and-a-half years later.

On July 20, Gershwin found his face on the cover of *Time* magazine. He was the first American and the youngest person to have achieved this distinction in the two-year-old publication. But the magazine then was not what it is now, and the story on Gershwin was genuinely perverse. He is, it read, "a young Jew . . . a Jazzbo," who, as a child "nourished himself smearily with bananas." It was replete with mistakes: "For some time the neighbors suffered; then they advised him to study in Europe. His first teacher died when he was still torturing Chopin's preludes. . . . When he was 15, he tried to write a song. It began decently in F, but ran off into G, where it hid behind the black keys, twiddling its fingers at Gershwin. Discouraged, he went to work as a songplugger for a music publisher."

But Gershwin was still young and strong. He continued his writing and dated the completion of the second movement August–September 1925, the third movement September 1925. On November 29, an article he wrote about the work appeared in the New York *Herald-Tribune*. It shows his continued love of dance music. True to form, Gershwin does not credit the black man who originated the Charleston rhythm, which created the dance craze. It was James P. Johnson, and he introduced it in his show *Runnin' Wild*, which opened on August 25, 1923. The rhythm—a dotted quarter and an eighth note in a four-four bar—did not appear in Gershwin's music during the first year of its life; he did not include it in his score for *Lady, Be Good!* But when that show was produced in London in April 1926, the added song, "I'd Rather Charleston," became a big hit. As for the Concerto in F, the final title of the commissioned work, composed the previous summer, he emphasized the importance of the Charleston rhythm in his program notes and then went on to assure the reader that orchestration was very much on his mind during the composition of the work:

> The first movement employs the Charleston rhythm. It is quick and pulsating, representing the young, enthusiastic spirit of American life. It begins with a rhythmic motif given out by the kettledrums, supported by other percussion instruments, and with a Charleston motif introduced by bassoon, horns, clarinets and violas. The principal theme is announced by the bassoon. Later, a second theme is introduced by the piano.
>
> The second movement has a poetic nocturnal atmosphere which has come to be referred to as the American blues, but in a purer form than that which they are usually treated.
>
> The final movement reverts to the style of the first. It is an orgy of rhythms, starting violently and keeping to the same pace throughout.

Bill Daly conducted the Concerto in F at a run-through at the Globe Theater a few days before the premiere. Gershwin was at the piano. The audience consisted of Damrosch and Gershwin's friends. Revisions and some cuts were made.

During this rehearsal, Allan Lincoln Langley, a member of the orchestra, accused Damrosch of commissioning the concerto because Gershwin was good "box office," not for any inherent artistic reasons. Langley also revived the rumor that Gershwin could not orchestrate and that Daly did it for him.

Morton Gould, the composer and conductor, and an orchestrator of great distinction, served as a young man as rehearsal pianist for the original *Porgy and Bess.* Throughout his career, he has conducted Gershwin frequently. He considers the Concerto in F "a unique and highly original piece that bypassed all the fashions and trends. It is one of the few concertos of the twentieth century—and there have been many—that is firmly established in the repertory." But Gould concedes that, as inspired as it is, "Gershwin's orchestration needs thinning out in spots." If Daly, a consummate craftsman, had orchestrated it completely, it is unlikely that the work would have needed such "thinning out."

The period from November 12 to December 10, 1925, can best be captured by quoting excerpts from Pauline Heifetz's appointment book, which was divided into Morning, Dinner, and Evening segments. Here are a few of the more interesting entries:

> *Thursday, November 12th*
> Morning: Play the concerto with George at his house
> Dinner: Dance the tango at Ciro's with Manuello Valentino
> Evening: Ciro's with George, Edgar Selwyn and Jules Glaenzer
>
> *Friday, November 13th*
> Morning: Rehearse with George at his house
>
> *Saturday, November 14th*
> Evening: Hofmann's concert
>
> *Monday, November 16th*
> Morning: orchestra reading of George's concerto. Go with Chotzie to the Globe Theater
>
> *Tuesday, November 17th*
> Evening: Philadelphia Orchestra with mother
>
> *Monday, December 7th*
> Morning: George leaves for Washington [Performances of the concerto were scheduled for Washington, Baltimore and Philadelphia.]
> Dinner: At Elsa's with Chotzie, Art and Morton
>
> *Tuesday, December 8th*
> Morning: very unhappy. All over.
> Evening: Go with Morton to the opening of "The Coconuts." After, Swope's party

Wednesday, December 9th

[Under the Morning category, Pauline has drawn a skull and crossbones, her sign of sadness. She used it before when Rex Ingram had disappointed her.]

C. here in afternoon. [C. stands for Chotzie.]

Dinner: Talk it over. All settled.

Evening: Theater with Peter Visher "The Butter and Egg Man." Go to Reubens with Peter and C.

[On December 9 Pauline wired Gershwin that Chotzinoff had proposed to her; he replied that she should marry him.]

Thursday, December 10th

[Here two tiny hearts lightly drawn in pencil are joined and marked "P. to C."]

Peter Visher with us. Marry Chotzie.

Evening: *Faust* with Chotzie, afterwards the Swopes.

In the New York *World*, music critic Samuel Chotzinoff gave the concerto a rave review, one quoted frequently in the intervening years: "Of all those writing the music of today . . . he alone actually expresses us."

Gershwin was probably grateful for that review, because Pitts Sanborn of the New York *Globe* and Olin Downes of the New York *Times* thought the concerto less successful than the *Rhapsody*, and Lawrence Gilman of the *Tribune* said that it was "conventional, trite . . . a little dull."

It may seem that Gershwin was acting childish when he had the protagonist of his first opera come from Georgia because his own name was George. But artists often show such traces of irrationality and superstition. No less an artist than Arnold Schoenberg said "it is not superstition; it is belief." To Schoenberg the number 13 represented the height of malevolent magic. Born on September 13, he considered this to be an evil portent and was so convinced of the inherent destructive power of 13 that he claimed that if he interrupted a composition and left it for a week or so, he invariably found he had stopped on a measure that was a multiple of the number 13. This prompted him in his later years to use 12A instead of 13 when he numbered his measures.

This belief overpowered Schoenberg: he feared he would die during a year that was a multiple of 13. He so dreaded his sixty-fifth birthday—5 times 13—that a friend asked an astrologer to prepare Schoenberg's horoscope. It revealed that although the year was dangerous, it was not necessarily fatal. Schoenberg survived. But in 1951, on his seventy-sixth birthday, another astrologer informed him that the coming year would be critical, because 7 plus 6 equaled 13. Until then, he had only been wary of multiples of 13 and had never added the digits of his age. Now he became obsessed with this new idea, and several of his friends report that he frequently said, "If I can pull through this year, I shall be safe."

On Friday the thirteenth of his seventy-sixth year, Schoenberg stayed in bed, sick, anxious, altogether upset. Shortly before midnight, Gertrude, his wife, leaned over and whispered to him: "You see, the day is almost over. All that worry for nothing."

He looked at her and died.

Coincidences involving letters and numbers can be seen not only as omens but as signals from God. Leonard Bernstein made a great deal of the fact that he met Aaron Copland, who became his mentor, on Copland's birthday, November 14, and that, a few years later, on this very same date he was called to conduct the New York Philharmonic because Bruno Walter fell ill. That event catapulted him to stardom.

Gershwin made his own secret equations. Seven years before "Georgia" from *Blue Monday Blues*, he chose Gershwin as his last name. He did it in 1915 when he was beginning his career. Gershwin was a more euphonious name. And, as historian Robert Kimball suggests, Wynn was the name of the popular comedian. But probably more important than either of these factors was that the last syllable of his new name was *win*, exactly what he had set out to do in every aspect of his life. To give a part of one's own name such symbolic content is no more farfetched than Schoenberg's precipitating his own death on a Friday the thirteenth of his seventy-sixth year.

Virtually all of Gershwin's shows include women whose fictional names were the same as women in his own life. A 1920 show called *Dere Mabel* (for Mabel Pleschette) with lyrics by Caesar closed out of town. In *Funny Face*, the female has the name of Frankie, his sister's name.

Gershwin's infatuation with the dance craze known as the Charleston may well have played a role in his initial attraction to Mollie Charleston, a beautiful woman, three years older than he. That may in turn have led him to invest the Charleston with more significance than he otherwise might have. He met the stunning brunette just before he determined to use the Charleston beat as the underlying motif in the Concerto in F.

Anna Koch recalled that during the summer of 1925, Gershwin visited the Heifetz family in Narragansett. She said that he and Pauline would sit on the glider on the porch while the family remained indoors. When the couple returned to the living room, Pauline, out of George's line of vision, would shake her head to let her cousins know that he had made no proposal. At that time, Gershwin had much going on in his life. For one thing, he was having an affair with Mollie Charleston.

The 1910 U.S. Census lists the Charleston family this way:

		Age	*Immigrated*	*Occupation*
CHARLESTON	Joseph	40	1892	tailor, ladies' clothing
	Ida	40	1892	none
	Fanny	18		operator, ladies' waists
	Abraham	16		apprentice, millinery
	Mollie	14		none, school
	George	11		none, school

Records indicate that Joseph and Ida had then been married twenty years. Joseph's name had been changed from Charlkovitz. Mollie's younger brother was not only named George but was George Gershwin's age. For a man who took messages from such striking parallels, that and the name Charleston might have made this connection more compelling than the one he was experiencing with Heifetz.

When she and George met, Margaret, formerly Mollie, was married to a man named Eriksen, perhaps thirty years older than she. Murray Charleston, a cousin now living in Florida, recalled in 1990 visiting the family when he was a child. The event was a children's birthday party; Mollie had a young son then. The year was 1919 and Murray was six years old:

"Mollie Charleston was generally known as May. She and her husband lived on Rockaway Avenue in Brooklyn. There were toilets in the hallway. It was a ghetto neighborhood. When I went to the party that day Mollie was dressed to the nines. Her husband was short and stocky and I remember him wearing a homburg. But the place was slovenly and Mollie's face was painted in a way I had never seen."

Evelyn Morris, Murray's sister, says: "Mollie was tall and had dark hair. She lived in Brownsville when I knew her and we lived nearby in East New York. Her mother, Ida, was called by her Yiddish name. There was always hush hush when the talk came around to Mollie. The grown-ups didn't want the children to hear what was being said."

Larry Charleston said that even twenty-five years later, whenever Mollie's name came up, the reaction of family members suggested a scandal involving the name Gershwin, and that while George seemed to be at the center, it was Ira who appeared to handle whatever money changed hands.

The basis of the scandal was the fact that George impregnated Mollie in August 1925. That was the summer he was composing the Concerto in F in Chautauqua and visiting Pauline Heifetz in Narragansett. The pregnancy brought about major changes in Mollie's life. She and Eriksen got a divorce. But Gershwin's career was at stake: the question was how would this affect the reputation of the man who was recently honored on the cover of *Time*?

In these days of casual public sexual relationships among celebrities, it is easy to forget that in the 1920s a wide gulf existed between public and private morality. People remembered the way a monstrous scandal and a public trial ruined the career of Fatty Arbuckle. There was almost certainly great concern about Gershwin's career. Reinforcing this apprehension was an episode that occurred seven months later. Paul Whiteman himself got into trouble in March 1926, two months before Mollie and George's son was born. A woman married briefly to him eighteen years before sued him for desertion and the hospital bills for their sick child, who had died at six months of age. Whiteman's lawyer advised him to settle out of court and Whiteman did, but by that time, the publicity of the case had caused some damage to his reputation.

Repeating the pattern of childhood, Ira, who used to go to the teacher after George had misbehaved and rectify what he had done, took charge of the situation. Ira handled all the arrangements for the birth of the child, who was born at the Brooklyn Hebrew Maternity Hospital on May 18, 1926. The registered number of the birth certificate is 20735. His mother is listed as Fanny Schneider, Mollie Charleston's older sister, who had married Ben Schneider, a junk man. Two older boys were living in the Schneider house. A third, Murray, born four years after Gershwin's son, said in 1990 that he remembers overwhelming poverty as a child as well as his own envy when a car would come to take Gershwin's son to visits with his famous father.

Although the child's name on the birth certificate was Albert Schneider, he was called Alan and knew from an early age that he was George Gershwin's child. The Schneiders, who raised him in Brooklyn, never let him forget that. Through this connection, they kept hoping they would get money. Alan says he remembers an envelope with five hundred dollars in cash being hand-delivered every two weeks by two men in an automobile, but this is hard to reconcile with Murray Schneider's portrait of a disadvantaged home. It could have been a fantasy Alan created to help him feel that his father cared for him. There is also the possibility that the Schneiders merely served as a conduit for money to be paid to Mollie, who lived for many years after Alan was born.

Mollie Charleston's name on her Actors Equity union card read "Margaret Manners, see file for Marguerite Eriksen." She joined the union on April 27, 1926, and continued to pay dues through November 4, 1929. George White and Buddy DeSylva, among Gershwin's closest friends, employed her regularly in their shows. She started in the chorus of the *Scandals* in June 1926, one month after Alan was born. When the show closed on July 1, 1927, after 432 performances, she went into rehearsal in August for a September 26 opening of *Manhattan Mary*, an Ed Wynn vehicle with a score by DeSylva, Brown, and Henderson. *Manhattan Mary* closed on May 12, 1928. In June Manners worked again in the *Scandals*. On February 5, 1929, she appeared in a show called *Fioretta* that ran 111 performances, closing on April 20, 1929. Four months later, in August, Manners once again joined the *Scandals* for its tenth year. That run ended February 8, 1930.

In October 1929, the stock market crashed and devastated Broadway along with the rest of the nation. Manners stopped working four months after that. The Schneiders told Alan his mother had been in show business but died of leukemia when he was a small child. He believed that for most of his life. Yet Manners remained geographically close to Gershwin, continuing a relationship with him until the mid-1930s, when she married Morris J. Fox, a man Evelyn Morris remembers as "tall and financially comfortable." Alan appears to have had a sad childhood, not understanding who or what he was. He says that on one visit to his father, Gershwin and he wrote a sixteen-bar song which his father entitled "Just Something That I Can't Explain."

While George may have been a neglectful father, seeing the child only occasionally and, at those times, introducing him as "the son of a friend," Gershwin comes through as more concerned about Alan than was his mother, who seems to have cut her child out of her life.

Marge Sevo, a former Ziegfeld girl now living in Los Angeles, said in 1990 that she remembered Manners well, particularly because their first names were the same. "She was in with all of the top who's who of show business," Sevo said. "She was a close friend of Ira Gershwin's. I saw them together a great deal. She traveled to Europe a lot and always seemed to be going on a cruise. I remember her putting money into a revue."

Stravinsky's description of Gershwin as "nervously energetic" surely must characterize his life during this particular period. In addition to balancing Pauline Heifetz and Margaret Manners during the summer of 1925, he began work on *Tip-Toes* with Ira as lyricist and *Song of the Flame* with Herbert Stothart as co-composer. Having someone write the music with him may have been an acknowledgment that he might have had too much to do by himself.

At this same time, Gershwin was buying a house between Riverside Drive and West End Avenue on 103d Street. The closing took place on September 22, 1925. George had a half interest; Ira and Rose each had quarter interests. There were two mortgages totaling $20,500. The purchase price was not recorded. While the renovation and the move were going on, George rented rooms at the Whitehall Hotel on Broadway.

The entire family moved into the house. The kitchen and a billiard room were on the ground floor; a dining room and living room with twin Steinways occupied the parlor floor; Rose and Morris had a bedroom and sitting room on the second floor; the third-floor bedrooms were for the younger children, Arthur and Frances; the fourth floor was reserved for Ira, who was then courting Leonore Strunsky, sister of Emily Strunsky Paley. The fifth floor belonged to George. The house even had an elevator.

When Gershwin first moved in, the works-in-progress on his piano included the Concerto in F, *Tip-Toes*, and *Song of the Flame*, which opened in Wilmington on December 9, 1925. That was the afternoon that Pauline Heifetz had sent George the telegram informing him that Chotzinoff had proposed.

Meanwhile Paul Whiteman had had Ferde Grofé reorchestrate *Blue Monday Blues* for a Carnegie Hall performance to give it a more jazzlike sound than the version done by Will Vodery in 1922. The new title: *135th Street*.

Pauline Heifetz's appointment book contains unexpected entries during the last three weeks of 1925. After marrying Chotzinoff, Pauline continued to invite Gershwin to their dinner parties, and Gershwin invited Pauline and her husband to his shows and concerts. Perhaps more startling is the entry for the evening of Thursday, December 17. Heifetz writes: "Go with Chotzie to George's rehearsal of the 'Nigger Opera.' " On December 29, the night of the actual performance, she uses those words again and adds that afterward they all went to Reubens, the delicatessen for which the sandwich was named: "Go with mother to George's 'Nigger Opera'—Whiteman—George & C. to Reubens."

The fact that she put "Nigger Opera" in quotes strongly suggests that this is what Gershwin was then calling the work he had composed a little more than three years before. Black associates of Gershwin report—sixty years later—that he frequently used the word "nigger," with some explaining that this was common usage at the time. Whether or not it was, "nigger" has almost always had pejorative connotations, and Gershwin's use reveals a sensibility not finely tuned to race relations. Still, on a personal basis, he seems to have behaved decently. To W. C. Handy he gave a first edition copy of *Rhapsody in Blue* inscribed "to Mr. Handy, whose early 'blue' songs are the forefathers of this work. With admiration and best wishes."

The year 1926 brought the front-page news that Irving Berlin was marrying Ellin Mackay, the daughter of Clarence Mackay, at the time one of the richest men in the United States. In a memoir, S. N. Behrman, the playwright who married Elsa Heifetz after her divorce from Harold Stone, writes: "George had a knack for making enigmatic remarks. One of them I puzzled over for years without hitting on an explanation. I was walking up

Broadway on a hot August night with George. The papers were full of the sensation of the moment: the announced engagement of Irving Berlin to Ellin Mackay. George and I were deep in it. He stopped suddenly, gave me an earnest look, and said: 'You know, I think it's a bad thing for all songwriters.' " Perhaps what he meant can be read from what he said to his aunt Kate to explain why he did not marry Pauline: she would interfere with his work.

Behrman continues:

> George was becoming one of the most eligible bachelors in America; there was curiosity among his friends from the beginning as to who the girl would be. I began hearing about the "Dream Girl." The Dream Girl was a Chicago physical culture teacher whom I never met. She gave George elaborate workouts, which he thought were good for him. Physical well-being led to infatuation. Perhaps some of us thought it was a bit naive of George to enhalo his sweetheart in this way, but on the whole we didn't mind. We liked the concept; we believed in Dream Girls. It was a more guileless time.
>
> We waited for a wedding announcement. It didn't come; it kept on being delayed. Years passed. One day Ira called me to tell me some devastating news: "Dream Girl" (we never referred to her in any other way; I never knew her name) was married! He hadn't the heart to tell George. He begged me to relieve him of this disagreeable chore. I took on the job. I went up to Riverside Drive where the Gershwins were then living. I went up to George's room; he was working on the Concerto in F. He played me a passage; he completed a variation on it. "George," I said, "I have some bad news for you. Dream Girl is married."
>
> His brown eyes showed a flicker of pain. He kept looking at me. Finally he spoke.
>
> "Do you know," he said, "if I weren't so busy I'd feel terrible."

This was as unfeeling a response as the one he made on receiving Pauline's wire about her marriage. It appears that both women married after being rejected by George at about the same time. This means he was courting Heifetz, Dream Girl, and possibly others while Margaret Manners/Mollie Charleston was pregnant with his child.

In 1926, Emily Strunsky Paley sent Gershwin a copy of *Porgy*, a novel by Dubose Heyward set in Charleston, South Carolina. Though he was not generally a reader, Gershwin not only read the book but decided immediately to transform it into the most ambitious work of his life.

Emily Strunsky was three years older than her sister Leonore. Married to Lou Paley, a high school teacher and lyricist, she first met Gershwin when Paley was writing lyrics for him. In a memorial brochure prepared after Emily died in 1990, Kate Mostel, Zero's widow, made the point that she was so good that she bored everybody to death. Still, Leonore was jealous of Emily, Frankie Godowsky has said, because Emily was so beloved and Leonore generated the opposite feeling.

Yet Leonore was a gracious and vivacious hostess and helped people seeking to gain footholds in Hollywood. She and Ira met in 1926 and, according to her own account to relatives and friends, she pursued him until he married her. Throughout their lives, no situation appears where Ira ever said no to her. Most of the choices she made dealt with the accumulation of wealth. In 1989, Kate Wolpin, George's aunt, said that Leonore was worth $25 million. Nancy Gershwin, whose father was a first cousin to George, Ira, Arthur, and Frankie, paints a picture of an exquisite life Leonore lived in southern California even into her eighties: "The house and grounds are incredibly beautiful. Time has stood still. When you're there as a guest a servant calls up: 'What would you like for breakfast?' Lee gets her own breakfast on a silver tray served in bed. There is a swimming pool and tennis courts magnificently landscaped. She has numerous servants. One of them can identify all the birds."

Frankie Godowsky says Ira had affairs before he married Leonore on September 14, 1926. Those who knew Ira and Leonore note they always had separate bedrooms, and, for the last fifty years of their marriage, these bedrooms were separated by a large living room. However this may have affected Ira, he did not reveal himself any more than did his gregarious but enigmatic brother.

The marriage ceremony took place in the parlor of the 103d Street house. Ira and Lee stood under a chuppah, the traditional marriage canopy, held by four friends wearing yarmulkes. The Gershwin and Strunsky families stood side by side. Leonore's mother had been a feminist, and her father owned considerable real estate in the city, including tenements on the southwest corner of Washington Square where the New York University law school now stands.

George served as best man. He wore a tuxedo and a yarmulke. He probably felt uncomfortable in what may have been the first situation in which he was relegated to a supporting role. At his side was a beautiful woman, not a Jew, who expressed astonishment at all the exotic goings-on. Behind them were Rose and Morris, both fifty-one, Arthur, twenty-six, and Frankie, twenty.

Ira lifted Leonore's veil and kissed her. They sipped the glass of wine handed to them by the rabbi who said:

"We pause to reflect on suffering and a world in which redemption has not yet come. Joy returns after the breaking of the glass." Ira crushed the glass according to tradition. The guests shouted, "Mazel tov." And Leonore Gershwin moved into the fourth floor of the 103d Street house.

The brothers went back to work for another Aarons and Freedley show, *Oh, Kay!*, scheduled to open at the Imperial Theater on November 8.

Six months after Gershwin began courting Pauline, he met Kay Swift Warburg at a party she was giving for Jascha Heifetz. On April 17, 1925, Pauline's entry reads: "Party at Warburg's." Then, in large letters and underlined: "George goes to Europe." This was accompanied by her drawing of a skull and crossbones as well as "Finita Really." This was Pauline's shorthand for "La commedia est finita," which she borrowed from the end of *Pagliacci.*

By November 1926, Kay Swift, a year older than George, had been married to James Paul Warburg for eight years. Warburg, son of a German-Jewish investment banking family, was a graduate of Harvard and a World War I flier. Kay was born in modest circumstances, on Ninety-sixth Street and Broadway. Her English mother was an interior decorator. Her father, Samuel Swift, was a music critic for the *Sun*, the *World*, and the *Evening Mail.*

Kay showed talent even as a toddler. A diary entry by her paternal grandmother, who was a composer, noted that when the child was fourteen months old, "she evidently has an excellent ear, recognizing little songs by the tune without the words and taking her own part by filling out with the right word or gesture at the critical moment." Kay's grandfather may not have had as discriminating an ear as his wife; he drove the Deadwood Gulch stagecoach in the days of Calamity Jane and Wild Bill Hickok.

Heifetz may have drawn the skull and crossbones on April 17, 1925, because Gershwin's attentions to Swift suggested she could not count on him. Reconstructing her meeting with Gershwin, Swift does not mention Heifetz. She does not acknowledge that any other woman was important in Gershwin's life. She readily acknowledges his infidelities with showgirls, but she insists on exclusive treatment when it comes to the matter of "love."

In an earlier biography, Swift is quoted as saying that Gershwin came to the party that first evening with Marie Rosanoff, an old friend and a cellist, with whom she played chamber music for years. After the party, Gershwin left for London and Paris. When he returned in July, he began working not only on the Concerto in F but on *Tip-Toes*, his second Aarons and Freedley show. The success of *Tip-Toes* was undoubtedly generated by Gershwin's being surrounded by people he could depend on. Ira was the only lyricist. Gershwin decided to engage the two-piano team of Arden and Ohman and place them in the pit. Bill Daly conducted, and since the heroine was named Tip-Toes Kaye, it is possible that Kay Swift had already become a significant part of Gershwin's life. The show opened at the Liberty Theater on December 28, 1925.

On March 26, 1926, the Warburgs gave another party; Gershwin stayed at the piano all night. Afterward he left for London again to prepare for the English opening of *Lady, Be Good!* It was then he composed "I'd Rather Charleston," added an opening choral number to the show, and interpolated a 1919 song he had written with Lou Paley. Vladimir Dukelsky, a Russian composer who, at Gershwin's suggestion, later changed his name to Vernon Duke, was in London at the time and has written that Gershwin was "the darling of Mayfair." Sir Harold Acton, a contemporary British writer, confirmed Duke's observation: "The invasion of jazz had begun. . . . Couples clung together forlornly, swaying to some raucous Blues. George Gershwin's *Rhapsody in Blue* accompanied every rough and tumble on the sofa. It seemed to contain all the intoxication of black and chromium cocktail bars . . . high pressure vitality followed by the hangover of yesterday's newspapers blown along gusty streets soon after a sour city dawn. Gershwin himself . . . I heard play it to perfection at the Savoy Hotel."

Apparently Gershwin was showered with invitations from royalty, including the duke of Kent and Lord and Lady Mountbatten. It was also on this trip that Gershwin first met George Antheil, one of the few American composers who expressed admiration for his work. Americans were not the only composers who showed contempt for this Tin Pan Alley upstart. Even the premiere of the Concerto in F had a painful aspect for its composer. The first work on Damrosch's program was a symphony by Alexander Glazunov. After the concert, Glazunov and Gershwin went backstage to see Damrosch. The narrator of the following story was Glazunov's interpreter. He told it almost thirty years later to David Platt, who reported it on January 4, 1956, in *The Daily Worker:*

Then we went backstage and met Gershwin. I have never seen any man's face become so radiant as Gershwin's did when he was introduced to Glazunov.

"Will you please tell Mr. Glazunov that it has been the dream of my life to go to Russia to study orchestration under him."

I translated Gershwin's remarks with great glee. But Glazunov responded coldly with a shrug of his shoulders.

Then he said to me in Russian, "He wants to study orchestration? He hasn't the slightest knowledge of counterpoint."

I kept quiet. I didn't have the heart to translate Glazunov's seemingly cruel words.

The two composers faced each other in a deep silence that lasted for several minutes.

Finally Glazunov broke the ice. Summoning up all the English he knew, the Russian composer slowly but precisely told Gershwin the bitter truth—that he lacked theory, that that defect had to be remedied before he could begin to think of studying orchestration. Needless to say, we left Gershwin in a crestfallen mood.

Gershwin was upset by this exchange because this was a time in his career when he held the Russians in particularly high esteem. Soon after his conversation with Glazunov, he told *The Musical Digest* for its January 4, 1927, issue, that his New Year's resolution was to "write another piece to catch Serge Rachmaninoff's attention."

Incidents like the one with Glazunov and a mother who relentlessly asked him why other composers always got the good reviews must have caused him great anguish. All the more reason that Swift would be a welcome companion for Gershwin. She was a cultivated woman, the daughter of a music critic, herself a knowledgeable musician who had expressed admiration for his concerto.

What made Kay especially valuable was that she had studied counterpoint—the discipline that Gershwin lacked—with theorist Percy Goetschius. She could give George sound advice and notate the music he played, an enormously time-saving service.

Kay Swift did this not only with his songs, but she helped transcribe the three piano preludes, which were first performed in December 1926 and published the following year. Moreover she had no Tin Pan Alley or Broadway roots. Gershwin had to have envied her superior musical training. She had studied piano with Bertha Tapper in New York and Heinrich Gebhard in Boston, both reputable music teachers. She studied composition with Arthur Johnstone and with the composer Charles Martin Loeffler.

In May 1926, while her husband was in Europe, Gershwin began appearing in public with her. The Warburgs already led independent social lives.

The relationship with Gershwin had a sexual component as well, which Swift acknowledged in a 1987 conversation. She was not only older than Gershwin; she had three children by then, and moved in sophisticated circles. During the spring of 1926, Gershwin began work on a show that was being called *Mayfair*. It did not yet have a book. A little later it became known as *Cheerio*. By November, when it opened, and Kay was the most visible woman in his life, the title of the show was *Oh, Kay!*

The play centered on rum-running on Long Island, and its most lovable character was someone who openly flouted the law. The show ranked with *Lady, Be Good!* as a gem of the American musical theater. Aarons and Freedley were again the producers, Arden and Ohman were again in the pit with their two pianos. Bill Daly conducted, and Guy Bolton was one of the collaborators on the book as he had been for *Lady, Be Good!* and *Tip-Toes*.

The genesis of *Oh, Kay!* lies in the *Lady, Be Good!* period. Bolton had just agreed to write the book for that 1924 show, his first with Gershwin. He was not a typical Broadway librettist. Born in England of American parents, he studied architecture in France and helped design the Soldiers and Sailors Monument in New York. Before *Oh, Kay!* he and P. G. Wodehouse had written the books for Kern's Princess Theater shows. Bolton and Wodehouse, his regular collaborator, saw Gertrude Lawrence, the British actress, in *Rats*, a London revue. Bolton wrote her a fan letter saying that if she were to come to New York, he would star her in anything she wished. Lawrence replied with a six-page telegram saying yes. This may have been the first American musical with a British star.

Later Gershwin spoke about a particular song in the show: "In the second act of *Oh, Kay!* the glamorous Gertrude Lawrence had the stage to herself to sing 'Someone to Watch Over Me.' It was all very wistful, and, on the opening night, somewhat to the surprise of the management, Miss Lawrence sang the song to a doll. This doll was a strange-looking object I found in a Philadelphia toy store and gave to Miss Lawrence with the suggestion that she use it in the number. That doll stayed in the show for the entire run."

Alan Gershwin says that family members repeatedly told him that his father had written the song for his mother. In *Lyrics on Several Occasions*, Ira admits that Howard Dietz gave him the title for the song. Although Dietz claimed in his own memoir that he gave Ira more than the title, the lyric still follows Ira's pattern of chronicling George's private life. Here a woman sings to a doll that she's looking for the man "I cannot forget, only man I ever think of with regret," whose initial she would add to her monogram.

In this lyric, Ira, as his brother's cryptobiographer, is suggesting that Margaret Manners wanted to marry George. She never did.

During the summer of 1926 Bolton and Wodehouse stayed at Bolton's house in Great Neck, Long Island. Wodehouse had come over from England in response to a cable from Bolton asking him if he would work on a show starring Lawrence and Oscar Shaw with music by Gershwin. In an April 1960 issue of the New York *Herald-Tribune*, Wodehouse wrote that Oscar Shaw, "the best singing, dancing, light comedy juvenile of that epoch or any since, plus Gertrude Lawrence was a musical comedy writer's idea of heaven."

He did not include Gershwin as part of that heaven, probably because he had been excluded from *Lady, Be Good!* and *Tip-Toes* when Ira became the sole lyricist for both. Not permitted to write the lyrics, Wodehouse did not collaborate on either book with Guy Bolton, his usual partner. Bolton's collaborator on those scripts was Fred Thompson. But Wodehouse relented and agreed to work on the book for *Oh, Kay!*, even if Ira were writing all the lyrics, because he would be working with Lawrence and Oscar Shaw.

During the preparation of the show, Ira had an appendectomy and was unavailable for work for six weeks. Normally Wodehouse, already working on the show, would have been called in as his substitute. But Dietz was selected to fill in for Ira. Dietz was chosen over Wodehouse, Dietz later claimed, because the Gershwins wanted Ira to retain all the credit and money, and they knew that Wodehouse would not be as accommodating.

Ira had always looked up to Wodehouse as a giant in his field second only perhaps to W. S. Gilbert. Under these circumstances his winning out over Wodehouse to do the lyrics for his brother's shows must have been unsettling for him. Clearly money took precedence over everything else, and George owed his brother a great deal. Ira had, after all, quietly and effectively arranged that no public scandal resulted from Margaret Charleston's pregnancy and delivery.

Oh, Kay! ran 246 performances against fierce competition. When the show opened, Kern's *Sunny* was at the Casino, Rodgers and Hart's *The Girl Friend* at the Vanderbilt, and Rudolph Friml's *The Vagabond King*, an operetta, was the longest-running musical on Broadway. When *Oh, Kay!* closed, Sigmund Romberg's *The Desert Song* was at the Casino, Rodgers and Hart's *Peggy-Ann* at the Vanderbilt, Harry Tierney's *Rio Rita* at the Ziegfeld, and Vincent Youmans's *Hit the Deck* at the Belasco. In addition, Mae West was in *Sex* at Daly's, Eva Le Gallienne in repertory at the Fourteenth Street Theater, and *Abie's Irish Rose* was in its fifth season on Broadway.

Despite the competition, the Gershwins' songs sold well. By the end of December 1926, these were the figures for the sales of the sheet music of the songs in *Oh, Kay!*:

Do, Do, Do	20,247
Clap Yo' Hands	13,388
Someone to Watch Over Me	10,107
Maybe	7,099
Oh, Kay!	1,924
Fidgety Feet	1,579
Heaven on Earth	1,498
Show Me the Town	1,388

Gershwin wrote these songs soon after he composed the Concerto in F. Kay Swift was not surprised by this. She says that, where Gershwin was concerned, the concert pieces and music for Broadway were "cut from the same cloth. You take a piece of cloth and make one thing of it and then turn around and make another thing from it. It's still from the same cloth."

In her recollections, she emphasized Gershwin's "ability to latch on completely to anything he did. For instance, he wanted to ride horseback. He had never done it. Now here is a picture of him sitting beautifully on a horse. That was in Connecticut where my husband and I had a house. Then he took up tennis. He did that very well. Not instantaneously, of course, but he had this quality of putting every ounce that was in him into each and every thing. If he found something he did not understand, he would take it and pull it apart. He didn't waste his time on things that were dull. But if he found it interesting and didn't conquer it right away, he worked at it until he did."

In December 1987, Kay Swift spoke about their affair: "I came from a loving family. In 1918 I married. I had a happy career, was fond of my husband, had three children. Everything seemed all right. But I didn't like being in love with somebody else while I was married." She remained in this unhappy position for a long time. Gershwin would not ask her to leave her husband and she stayed in her marriage to Warburg for another eight years.

. . .

Ira admired George without reservation where his art was concerned. On February 28, 1949, writing from his home at 1021 North Roxbury Drive in Beverly Hills, Ira attacked a columnist for suggesting that George owed anything to the Europeans in his incorporation of jazz elements into his music. The letter reveals the anger provoked in him whenever anyone suggested George took anything from anybody:

Dear Mr. Goldberg:

In this morning's column your palpitating readers get the musical scoop of the century. You reveal that the "rhythms and germinal themes" of Milhaud's 1923 ballet [*La création du monde*] later became the "backbone" of Gershwin's *Rhapsody in Blue*, and you invite "immediate comparison."

I lived with my brother at the time he was composing *Rhapsody* and he was about as influenced by *Creation of the World* as by Frescobaldi's *Chaconne and Passacaglia* or Patagonian Bebop.

If *Rhapsody in Blue* owes anything to anything it is to "135th Street" [*Blue Monday Blues*], a one-act blues opera my brother wrote in 1922. This work so impressed Paul Whiteman that two years later he asked my brother to write a piece for what turned out to be the (you'll pardon the expression) historic concert given at Aeolian Hall, Feb. 12th, 1924. As for "rhythms and germinal themes" you will find in Dr. Isaac Goldberg's *George Gershwin* (Simon & Schuster, N.Y., 1931), page 218, that Whiteman liked the themes of "135th Street" better than those in *Rhapsody in Blue*.

And since you are coupling the names of Milhaud and Gershwin, here's another curious coupling, this time by the eminent H.T.P. (H.T. Parker of the old Boston *Transcript* if you're too young to know) on Jan. 30th, 1924: "From him (Gershwin) the Europeans—Casella, Milhaud and others—might draw hints and profits."

Sincerely,
Ira Gershwin

The issue in Ira's letter—the use of the jazz idiom in concert music by Europeans and Americans—is important. By the mid-

1920s many European composers had turned their backs on jazz. It had been an exotic import for them but, by then, they were done with it. In an article, "The Day after Tomorrow," published in the November–December 1925 issue of *Modern Music*, Darius Milhaud addresses this:

> In 1918 jazz arrived in our midst from New York and became the rage. A whole literature of syncopation grew up to convince a hesitant public. Stravinsky wrote his *Rag Time for eleven instruments*, his *Piano-Rag Music*, his *Mavra* [a comic opera]; Wiener wrote his *Sonatine Syncopée*, his *Blues*, and almost created a public scandal by bringing a famous jazz band into a concert hall. During the winter of 1921–1922 in America, the journalists regarded me with scorn when I made out a case for jazz. Three years later jazz band concerts are given in New York, there is talk of a jazz opera at the Metropolitan, banjo classes are organized in the conservatories. Jazz is comfortably installed with official sanction.
>
> Here it is finished. The last works of Stravinsky owe it nothing; they return to a severe classicism and an ascetic sobriety. His *Concerto* and his *Sonate* are sure proofs of this change. The *Concerto* of Germaine Tailleferre leads back to Bach, *Les Biches* by Poulenc carries us into a French park, *Les Matelots* of Georges Auric is unhampered.

Milhaud was a member of a group of French composers one critic labeled Les Six. It included Tailleferre, Poulenc, Auric, Honegger, and Durey. Because he was in the center of musical activity in France, what Milhaud writes must be given credence. But there are some striking omissions. Milhaud claims that jazz in Europe had run its course by 1925. Yet Kurt Weill's *Die Dreigroschenoper* and *Mahagonny*, both with books by Bertolt Brecht, were created after that year. And Ernst Krenek's *Jonny spielt auf*, a jazz opera, premiered in Leipzig in 1927.

Still, the essence of what Milhaud writes is true; the European composers finished rather quickly with jazz. Even Copland, who took his cues from the Europeans, incorporated jazz elements into a major work for the last time before World War II in his piano concerto of 1927. At that, one of the melodies he uses is strikingly similar to the theme Gershwin created for his Piano Prelude no. 2, written just before the Copland work.

But Gershwin could not follow the path of these others. Unlike Milhaud or Stravinsky or Hindemith or Shostakovich or Krenek or even Copland, he was constitutionally incapable of walking away from the American vernacular; that was what was in his brain, his ears, his fingers, and it is what had been there from the beginning of his professional life. If it could not generate works of art in the way that the popular clichés of the eighteenth century had, then Gershwin would find himself in trouble, because he had nowhere else to go.

If Gershwin sensed he was in artistic trouble in1926–27, he gave no sign of it. He and Ira founded the New World Music Company, making it a subsidiary of T. B. Harms. The company published all the Gershwin works, not only the songs for the shows but all the concert works. The profits went two-thirds to George, one-third to Ira.

The Preludes for Piano dedicated to Daly, which Kay Swift had helped to transcribe, appeared under this new imprint. They were played by Gershwin for the first time at a joint recital with the contralto Marguerite d'Alvarez in New York late in 1926 and in Boston a few weeks later. The two had been brought together by Carl Van Vechten, who had also first suggested to the singer Eva Gauthier that she use Gershwin for her recital of art songs in late 1923.

On February 12, 1924, Van Vechten accepted an invitation to sit in d'Alvarez's box for the Whiteman concert. Two days later he wrote to Gershwin:

> The concert, quite as a matter of course, was a riot, and you crowned it with what, after repeated hearings, I am forced to regard as the foremost serious effort by an American composer. Go straight on and you will knock Europe silly. Go a little farther in the next one and invent a new form. . . .

> Marguerite d'Alvarez, by the way, was reduced to a state of hysterical enthusiasm by the concert, especially by your contribution. She wants to sing at the next one! You might tell Whiteman this: she would certainly give the audience a good time.

Whiteman never did use d'Alvarez. Perhaps her "enormous size," in Van Vechten's words, put him off. But that did not deter the contralto. She made her own plans to present a recital at the Roosevelt Hotel on December 4, 1926.

After the Aeolian Hall concert and before he left for England to prepare *Primrose*, Gershwin wrote sixteen musical sketches in his notebook. They were dated March–April 1924. Some of that material found its way into the preludes he performed at the d'Alvarez concert. On October 7, 1924, Van Vechten wrote to Gershwin: "I hear that you have written some jazz preludes. Are these published? . . . I want to talk to you about a number of things. I know that you must be very busy, but if you can spare me an evening next week let me know. . . . The *Rhapsody in Blue* is on the phonograph constantly."

On March 25, 1925, Van Vechten wrote an article for *Vanity Fair* titled "George Gershwin: An American Composer Who Is Writing Notable Music in the Jazz Idiom." He referred to projects of "epic proportions." He included this information at the end of his piece, writing that "it is probable that the production of his twenty-four preludes and his tone poem for symphony orchestra, tentatively entitled *Black Belt*, will award him a still higher rank in the army of contemporary composers."

Black Belt never materialized, nor did the bulk of those twenty-four preludes. One that was dated January 25 became the opening of the last movement of the Concerto in F. Gershwin was prolific at this time, and even he had difficulty keeping track of what he did. Still, virtually everything he valued was put to use somewhere.

The December 4 concert was less than a month after the opening of *Oh, Kay!*. Only six days before d'Alvarez's recital,

Gershwin was not sure what he would play. On November 29 the following notice appeared in the New York *Times:*

> George Gershwin and Marguerite d'Alvarez, afternoon, Hotel Roosevelt. Last of this series, with program including a group of Gershwin's jazz songs, with the composer at the piano. Mr. Gershwin is to play his "Six New Piano Preludes" and, with William Daly, a two-piano arrangement of the *Rhapsody in Blue.* He will accompany a closing group of "jazz" songs for Mme d'Alvarez, who also has groups of French and Spanish airs.

The idea of the recital was too similar to Eva Gauthier's to generate much press attention. Probably the most reliable account of what took place that evening appeared on December 5 in the New York *World.* The critic was Samuel Chotzinoff:

> Mr. Gershwin played five new piano preludes for the first time, two of which are at least as fine as anything he has done in the idiom of American music, which bears no deep or vital relation to jazz, although it is still called by that somewhat doubtful name. The second prelude in particular has a great deal more than mere technical brilliance. . . . It is full of feeling and should find its way to the programs of pianists who are not afraid of something new. The fourth is more directly in the blues tradition, a thoroughly fascinating bit.

What Chotzinoff was saying here was that although Gershwin's preludes may have been making use of minor thirds and minor sevenths and syncopated effects, they transcended any reductionistic category such as "jazz."

In a 1987 conversation, Kay Swift, who also attended the event, gave her own assessment: "The preludes are swell pieces and he played them beautifully, with a lot of spirit and determination." What she was saying more than sixty years after the event was that the pieces were good and that their composer, the man she loved, played them as though he believed in their worth.

. . .

In *The American Popular Song*, Alec Wilder connects the meteoric rise of Gershwin's career to the advent of radio. "The enormous exposure provided by this medium," he writes, "had much to do with the public's enthusiasm for his songs. For the jazz musician liked his songs, and, more important, so did the dance band arranger." Wilder contrasts this situation with the one that characterized the decade before: ". . . during the early years of Berlin's and Kern's careers there were only vaudeville, primitive acoustical recordings and stage productions to promote their songs, and neither of these men wrote as much to the liking of the players and arrangers as Gershwin."

Until the early 1920s, the big money in the business was going to performers and music publishers, not to songwriters, unless, like Berlin, they owned their own publishing businesses. Berlin, the first to do this, had been America's best known songwriter since "Alexander's Ragtime Band." During World War I his sheet music brought in almost $160,000 annually in royalties. That seems extraordinary, but by 1922 record sales were exceeding sheet music sales. Berlin's "Say It with Music" sold 375,000 copies of sheet music in a seventy-five-week period as compared to one million records and 100,000 piano rolls of the same song. Most songwriters had no idea of the sales of their music and received little or no share in sales income or royalties. Nor did the music industry get money from the performance of songs on radio.

Still, from the beginning of commercial broadcasting, radio's potential as a promotional tool was apparent, and publishers in those cities that had radio stations tried to win the friendship of radio performers. In 1922, the number of stations escalated from 28 in January to 570 by the end of the year, and broadcasters were trying to figure out how to fill their time. Major music publishers sent song pluggers to help them. Song pluggers often became well-known radio personalities providing subsidized entertainment for the new medium. Soon more than a hundred hotels across the country had set up broadcasting facilities from which their dance orchestras, often formed with financial backing from music publishers, played the latest songs.

The introduction of network broadcasting in 1926, the year of *Oh, Kay!*, brought escalating audiences. To understand the power of radio, one need only to consider the sales figures of that Gershwin show within a month of its opening. Nothing was more effective than a commercially sponsored radio show when it came to the making of a hit. The industry actually began to complain that this concentrated air play limited the life of a song. On May 4, 1930, in the New York *World*, Gershwin himself articulated this problem:

> Never in all our history of popular music has there been such a plethora of composers—professional, amateur and alleged—as we have today. Responsible, of course, are those two fresh hot-beds—the soniferous cinema and the radio. The merciless ether, by unceasing plugging, has cut down the life of a song to but a few weeks, with the result that anyone who thinks he can carry a tune—even if it's nowhere in particular—nowadays takes a "shot" at music-making.

The cynicism and opportunism of the decade left their mark on every aspect of the music business. On April 10, 1929, *Variety* noted: "It is doubtful whether in any other field there is so much chicanery, double-crossing, double-dealing, duplicity and hooey, a condition that comes about not so much because of economic jealousy but because of the petty business of landing a plug." In the context of what was going on, it was entirely understandable that the Gershwin brothers would set up their own imprint so they could profit from their own work.

Radio served not only as a major conduit for songs; it exploited America's ethnic and racial diversity. On the one hand there was *The Goldbergs*, featuring Molly, the ultimate Yiddish Mama, created by Gertrude Berg in 1929. On the other there was *Amos 'n' Andy*, in which the central characters used "sumpin' " for "something" and "regusted" for "disgusted." It was probably not too difficult for Jews to accept Molly because she had been created by one of their own. But it must have been difficult for blacks to accept Amos and Andy because they were created and performed by two whites—Freeman Gosden and Charles Correll. Both shows played on idiosyncrasies of the groups and were enormously popular, but the scripts did little to enhance the image of either group.

Emily Paley said in December 1987 that "George saw blacks and Jews as being the same in relation to the rest of society." Even the creation in 1922 of a black man from Georgia in *Blue Monday Blues* supports this view. American society confirmed such a perception relentlessly. According to Kate Wolpin, the beaches in Florida in the 1920s displayed signs reading: NO JEWS OR DOGS ALLOWED. (Where did that put blacks?) And when Gershwin went to Lake Placid to visit Pauline Heifetz, he was denied admission to the Lake Placid Club because he was a Jew.

Yet Gershwin could behave in a patronizing way to a black musician. In an interview conducted in March 1974 by Frank Driggs, a jazz historian, Greeley Walton, a black tenor saxophone player, told this story:

> I went with Elmer Snowden [banjo] into the Nest Club on 133d Street and Seventh Avenue in 1927. We had a nine-piece band that included Preacher Jones, Walter Johnson on drums, myself, and Charlie Lewis. "Dizzy" [Lewis] was in the band. He was some pianist. He was a highly trained musician, a graduate of Fisk University.
>
> One night while we were working there, Paul Whiteman and George Gershwin came in. The dance floor was small; very seldom would anybody dance—but it was a money-making place. They had been seated by the maître d'—Jeff Blunt, before he went over to the Lenox Club—and both of them got up and came over to the piano and asked Charlie if he could play *Rhapsody in Blue*. They put two fifty dollars bills on the piano. Charlie was kind of mush-mouthed and said, "You want part of it or all of it?" So Gershwin said, "All of it." Charlie said, "Preacher, put that money in the box" and he stood up, rubbing his hands together and said to the audience, "Ladies and gentlemen, we have a request for *Rhapsody in Blue*,

> and I'll do it from memory." Then he sat down and played *Rhapsody in Blue* better than George Gershwin could ever have played it in his life. The house came down when he was finished. You see, the gag was they were going to make a fool out of Charlie, so when Charlie finished he got up and took a little bow. He said, "Anything else you want—a little Bach, a little Beethoven?" And I mean he could have played anything they wanted. He was some pianist.

Whether or not Whiteman or Gershwin were trying to make a fool of Lewis, the point is that the black musicians who were there saw it that way. However much Gershwin may have recognized his indebtedness to black musicians, he tended to identify with whites even when their behavior was bad. Whiteman, after all, used only white musicians and cheerfully took the title "King of Jazz," which, no matter how you define jazz, certainly was not rightfully his.

As early as 1926, Whiteman began distorting the *Rhapsody* through his use of it as a signature piece. The following year, when he and Gershwin recorded *Rhapsody* a second time using Victor's new electronic equipment, Whiteman set the style and pace and Gershwin responded with a tight performance and probably some angry words as well because, at the moment the recording began, Whiteman walked off the podium. Nathaniel Shilkret, Victor's director of light music, replaced him, but his name was not put on the record label. Whiteman is listed as conductor.

A few months later, in the fall of 1927, Whiteman abused Gershwin again when he recorded the Concerto in F. Despite the composer's heroic effort to orchestrate an extended concert work for the first time, Whiteman had Grofé reorchestrate it for the unusual arrangement of jazz band and orchestra. That Gershwin took umbrage at this is revealed by the fact that Roy Bargy, not he, is the piano soloist on the recording. But again something must have happened at the start of the session because Whiteman walked off and Bill Daly replaced him. Again the substitution was not shown on the record label where Whiteman is listed as conductor. Gershwin never recorded the Concerto in F, probably among the most frequently programmed piano concertos of the twentieth century.

If one searches for a motive for Whiteman's behavior, two possibilities come to mind. The first is that he genuinely believed his interpretation of the *Rhapsody* and reorchestration of the concerto made more musical sense than the composer's. The other is that he felt betrayed by Gershwin when the composer gave the concerto to Damrosch after Whiteman had made clear he wanted Gershwin's next big work.

HOWEVER vulnerable Gershwin may have been to a critic's humiliating review or to Whiteman's replacement of his orchestration or to serious American composers dismissing his concert works or to his mother's diminished view of him, to the world outside, he was a shining image of success. In March 1927, Fritz Reiner, one of the most rigorous and demanding conductors of the time, conducted the Concerto in F with the Cincinnati Symphony. Gershwin played the solo piano part. And as a Broadway composer he was lionized.

In the spring of 1927, Margaret Manners was dancing in a choreographed version of *Rhapsody in Blue* in the White *Scandals.* White used the work first the year before when Manners had joined the *Scandals.* Song-and-dance man Harry Richman introduced the number with his own performance in "The Birth of the Blues." In *A Hell of a Life*, Richman's memoir, he writes of a tryout in Atlantic City. DeSylva, Brown, and Henderson, the show's songwriters, were there. So was Gershwin, no longer professionally connected to White. One might think he was there because of Manners, but Richman tells a funny story.

One night the girls in the show finished rehearsing early. Richman stayed on to rehearse some sketches with comedian Willie Howard. He had taken a suite at the "best" hotel and, along with the suite, an additional room for his girl, who, he says, was one of the prettiest in the show. Richman told her he would be gone for a few hours but he finished quickly, soon after White left the theater.

Richman went to the woman's room and knocked. There was commotion inside. He let himself in and the young woman "jumped out of bed and started putting on her lingerie."

Enraged because he thought George White was somewhere in the room, he "looked under the bed. I looked under the bureau, I said, 'I know he can't be hiding in one of the drawers. . . . He's small, but not that small.' I looked into the bathroom. Over to the clothes closet I rushed.

"It was George, but not White. It was George Gershwin. He hadn't had time to put his shirt on, but he had struggled into his coat. His shirts and pants were still in his hand. He looked at me. One of the most wonderful expressions I have ever seen on a man's face.

" 'Mr. Richman, what can I say to you? *I'm waiting for a streetcar?*'

"The floor came up to meet my ass. He literally knocked me down with that remark, and I sat there laughing so hard I thought I would never recover. When I got my voice back I said, 'Gershwin, to me you're one of the most talented young men in the world. You've been like a god to me. You're a great man. For me to pick a beautiful girl and to be honored by your picking her too—that's a real honor.' "

Once Gershwin reached this level of celebrity, at least one significant relationship grew out of the adoration of a fan and pen pal. Correspondence between Gershwin and Julia Thomas Van Norman (acquired in 1991 by the Library of Congress) and an interview with her husband, Horace Van Norman, in June 1990 reveal the nature of this relationship. Like Pauline Heifetz and Kay Swift, Julia Thomas Van Norman from Minneapolis, Minnesota, was a first-class pianist and musician.

The Van Normans were married in 1920. "I was aware from the start," Horace Van Norman says, that I had an exceptional human being on my hands. She was talented as a writer and very ambitious. She had begun writing poetry in her teens. Both of us believed I was to come into a fortune when I reached twenty-one. She and her father had lived in an apartment house owned by my father. Her father was a wayward kind of person who exerted no discipline.

As it turned out, I inherited nothing. By 1925 the relationship between us had changed perceptibly. We had two children; one was retarded, one mentally ill. I was aware that my wife was profoundly unhappy. I went to a local conservatory to teach and played piano for silent movies. For her birthday in 1927 I gave my wife the Victor Blue Label Paul Whiteman recording of the *Rhapsody in Blue* with Gershwin at the piano.

One day, to my complete astonishment, my wife showed me a blue envelope postmarked Long Island. It began "Dear Mrs. Van Norman:

"Your letter, which I received some time ago, gave me a feeling that is difficult to describe. I receive quite a few letters from various sources, due to the nature of my work, but I must say yours stuck in my mind longer than any other. That a composition of mine should do all the things you claim the *Rhapsody* has done for you is more than I could expect.

"Perhaps it will interest you to know my Concerto in F has just been published by T. B. Harms Co. On the 25th of this month I am playing with the Philharmonic Orchestra of New York at the City College Stadium. Will you by any chance be in New York at this time? Or are you already there?

"Hoping you are entirely finished with your illness and that we may meet some time when you come to New York and thanking you for your letter I am

"Most Sincerely,

"George Gershwin"

Gershwin included his telephone number. Van Norman continues:

The whole thing stunned me. My wife had never shown any interest in anything other than classical music. Since I had already thought of moving to New York, we made plans to move there right away. At that time the children were ages three and one.

Off we went. We found a place in Manhattan and Julia's sister, ten years older than she, and the children came along. No sooner did we arrive than she began trying Gershwin on the telephone. She would always find Arthur instead. I was more than an interested spectator. I wanted desperately for her to be happy. I knew that only something extraordinary would accomplish that. We were dirt poor. She was not very beautiful but she had a galvanizing personality, an extremely assertive personality. She was a highly articulate person.

Eventually George got back into town from his tryouts for *Funny Face* in Philadelphia. She reached him. He invited her up. He sensed a kindred spirit. She sensed she understood him, his mind, his soul, in a way nobody ever had. The thing went on. They had appointments. They talked and talked and talked. He found someone he could talk to about many things. Julia continually bemoaned our poverty. At the beginning she received an autographed picture from him and later [in 1932] he gave her an autographed copy of his *Songbook*. But there were never any gifts.

Gershwin had a very dark side. He griped to her about his deep unhappiness with people in show business and the fact that he never felt well. He complained about headaches a great deal and said that, as a kid, he had been kicked in the head by a horse. That was his explanation for the headaches he was suffering. He complained he had to write shows for the money instead of being able to concentrate on serious music. He explained he was invited to the homes of the richest people in the United States and had to be able to reciprocate properly.

Van Norman does not believe Gershwin and his wife engaged in an intimate sexual relationship, despite the fact they continued to be close for ten years. But Nancy Van Norman Bloomer Deussen, a third child, who is a composer living on the West Coast, disagrees. Born in 1931, Nancy Bloomer Deussen thinks she is Gershwin's child.

. . .

In a conversation in 1990, Stanley Adams, the former president of ASCAP repeatedly referred to Gershwin's virile characteristics, both as a man and composer. During Adams's presidency, Albert Schneider, using the name Alan Gershwin, tried to join ASCAP as a songwriter. Identifying himself as Gershwin's son, he was repudiated by the Gershwin family as well as by ASCAP. When this event was brought to Adams's attention in 1990, Adams said that a spokesman for the Gershwin family, which collects millions annually from ASCAP, said that Alan was nothing but a fraud, an imposter, that no credence should be given him.

When Adams was reminded of his own characterization of George as being intensely masculine, and was asked if he thought the composer had used condoms whenever he had sexual intercourse, Adams laughed. He dismissed the notion, saying that in those days men used to joke that wearing a condom was like taking a bath with your socks on. Asked, then, if it were not possible that Alan was speaking the truth, Adams paused, reflected, and said yes, he guessed it was possible. Isn't it also possible that five years after Alan was born, Gershwin fathered another child, a daughter who, like Alan, is also deeply involved with music?

In his discussion of the events of 1927, Horace Van Norman mentioned Gershwin's first letter to his wife in which Gershwin referred to the City College Stadium summer concert at which he was going to appear. Van Norman himself spoke of the tryouts in Philadelphia of *Funny Face*. Between these two events there was *Strike Up the Band*, which opened on August 29 at Long Branch, New Jersey, and ran two weeks in Philadelphia before closing.

The Stadium concert took place on July 26. It was Gershwin's first appearance there. The summer quarters for the New York

Philharmonic, Lewisohn Stadium was an open-air theater also used as an athletic field for City College during the academic year. On this particular occasion Willem van Hoogstraten, a Dutch conductor, led Gershwin and the orchestra in a performance of *Rhapsody in Blue*. The concert drew eighteen thousand people, the largest audience until then and a particular source of pride for Gershwin. Apparently Julia Van Norman, despite her rush to move to the city, did not make it for this particular event.

Strike Up the Band did not present adorable women and men singing and dancing their way through a lightweight script. It was, in fact, the first serious book musical on Broadway and anticipated Kern's *Showboat*. The Gershwins began work on it during the spring. They rented a house in Ossining in Westchester County, less than an hour's drive from Manhattan. House guests included Robert and Mabel Schirmer, Lou and Emily Paley, Bill Daly, George S. Kaufman, Franklin P. Adams, the columnist, and Howard Dietz. Obviously whatever bad feelings he had about his failure to be included in the credits for the lyrics of *Oh, Kay!* did not prevent Dietz from showing up as a guest.

Strike Up the Band was produced by Edgar Selwyn—this was hardly material for Aarons and Freedley or Flo Ziegfeld. It was conducted by Bill Daly. But the public was not ready for its cynical illumination of man's corrupt spirit and self-serving reasons for going to war. Kaufman's plot: The Swiss protest an American tax on their cheese. Horace J. Fletcher, an American cheese manufacturer, suggests the matter is sufficiently important to warrant a U.S. declaration of war on Switzerland. Fletcher says he will underwrite the war himself if he can be assured it will go down in history as the Horace J. Fletcher Memorial War.

However, when his daughter's fiancé threatens to reveal Fletcher's use of Grade B milk in his cheese products, Fletcher does an immediate about-face and becomes an impassioned pacifist. His change of heart comes too late; war fever has been unleashed throughout the land and there is no stopping it. After Fletcher is discovered wearing a Swiss watch, he himself comes under suspicion. The war delights everyone, including all the Swiss hotel owners who are housing idle American troops at exorbitant rates. The conflict ends when secret Swiss yodeling signals are decoded. But the war has been such good fun that when a tax is imposed on caviar, the United States and Russia cheerfully prepare to fight matters to the end.

"The Man I Love" was written into *Strike Up the Band*, but because the show closed before coming to New York, the song disappeared from the theater again. The Gershwins also distinguished themselves with a number of new songs. These included "Oh, This Is Such a Lovely War," "The War That Ended War," "Fletcher's American Cheese Choral Society," and "Strike Up the Band."

Ira Gershwin's description in his *Lyrics on Several Occasions* of the composition of the title song testifies to the importance George gave to his first serious, full-length Broadway show:

> The Fifth Try. Late one weekend night in the spring of 1927, I got to my hotel room with the Sunday papers. I looked for a slit of light under the door of the adjoining room—but no light, so I figured my brother was asleep. (We were in Atlantic City for *Strike Up the Band* discussions with Edgar Selwyn.) I hadn't finished the paper's first section when the lights went up in the next room; its door opened and my pajamaed brother appeared. "I thought you were asleep," I said. "No, I've been in bed thinking, and I think I've got it. Come on in." It was off season and with no guests to disturb within ten rooms of us, the hotel sent up a piano. I sat down near the upright and said, "I hope you've finally made up your mind." He played the refrain of the march practically as it is known today. Did I like it? Certainly I liked it, but—"But what?" "Are you sure you won't change your mind again?" "Yes. I'm pretty sure this time." "That's good. Don't forget it." By this last remark I meant not only the new tune but also the implied guarantee that he wouldn't try for another.
>
> The reason I wanted assurance was that over the weeks he had written four different marches, and on each occasion I had responded with "That's fine. Just right. O.K. I'll write it up."

And each time I had received the same answer: "Not bad, but not yet. Don't worry. I'll remember it; but it's for an important spot, and maybe I'll find something better." This fifth try turned out to be it. Interestingly enough, the earlier four had been written at the piano; the fifth and final one came to him while lying in bed.

The show's devastating failure out of town moved the Gershwins to return to a more traditional form for their next effort. *Funny Face* opened at the Alvin Theater on November 22, 1927. It was the first show to be mounted in the theater owned by producers Alex Aarons and Vinton Freedley and named for them. The musical starred the Astaires, Victor Moore, Allen Kearns, and Betty Compton. Ohman and Arden were at the two pianos in the pit. Bill Daly conducted. The score included "Funny Face," "High Hat," "My One and Only," "He Loves and She Loves" and " 'S Wonderful." It pleased both critics and public and ran 244 performances.

Still unwilling to face the risk of another high-falutin' show, the Gershwins followed *Funny Face* with *Rosalie*. While *Funny Face* showed unity of conception and execution, *Rosalie* was a potpourri. One wonders why Gershwin, as busy as he was, agreed to work on the show. Ziegfeld had, after all, turned his back on him when he was on his way up. And now that he was a giant in his field, Ziegfeld had him not only collaborating with Sigmund Romberg, whose aesthetic was far from Gershwin's own, but also taking second billing behind Romberg.

In any event the result was a hodgepodge—the Viennese operetta style invaded by a hard-edged jazzy sound. The Viennese operetta won. Once before, in *Song of the Flame*, which Gershwin composed with Herbert Stothart, the result was a Stothart operetta, not a Gershwin show. Still, in an era when everyone's goal was to get shows fast, *Rosalie* ran 355 performances, longer than any Gershwin show. Marilyn Miller, whom Ziegfeld had introduced to the public in his *Follies* of 1918 and who had been the producer's mistress, was the star. In a 1990 letter Horace

Van Norman wrote that Gershwin had told Julia that, during the show's run, he was having an affair with Miller.

According to his biographer, Martin Gottfried, producer-director Jed Harris was one of the most feared and hated men in show business. He was also something of a prodigy. By the age of twenty-eight, he had had four straight hits on Broadway in the space of two years. In *Jed Harris: The Curse of Genius*, Gottfried writes of an incident that Harris liked to talk about. It happened in 1926 during

> a stroll along 41st Street when he was stopped by a young man very much like himself, dark, wiry, and unmistakably Jewish.
>
> "You're Jed Harris, aren't you?"
>
> "Yes," Harris whispered with a smile.
>
> "I'm George Gershwin."
>
> "I know. I've seen you in theater lobbies, Mr. Gershwin. I think you're a wonderful song writer."
>
> "I am," Gershwin said, "aren't I?"
>
> "The best."
>
> "There's a question I've been wanting to ask you. How old are you, Mr. Harris?"
>
> "I'll be twenty-seven in February."
>
> "Shit," Gershwin said. "I'm twenty-eight."
>
> "In a philosophical sense," Harris later mused. "Gershwin was much older than that, for he was only going to live another twelve years."

For Gershwin "living" meant continually working and not producing flops. In that sense Harris's life did not last much longer than his own. The subtitle of Gottfried's biography relates to that extended period of sterility and despair that characterized Harris's middle and late years.

Harris's decline began when he was twenty-eight. The following year he and actress Ruth Gordon had an illegitimate son. They never married. They called him Jones, Ruth Gordon's maiden name. Jones Harris went on to a life in which he spent almost as little time with his parents as Alan Gershwin spent with his. "In 1929," Gottfried writes, "having or being an illegitimate child was more than scandalous. News of the event would have destroyed Ruth's career, or so Jed Harris had feared, and considering the devastation such a birth visited twenty-five years later on the career of Ingrid Bergman, the fear was not unfounded. The babe was hatched in secret . . ." similar to the arrangements that concealed from the public the birth of Alan Gershwin a few years before.

The story of Harris's meeting with Gershwin on Forty-first Street suggests the composer felt the pressure of time from his early years. When *Half-Past Eight* failed he was only twenty, but he told friends he did not have the time for flops. Perhaps he accepted the assignment for *Rosalie* because it would give him another credit. With Ziegfeld's imprimatur, the chances were good that it would be a hit. This seems to be the story accepted by Charles Higham, Ziegfeld's biographer. During the early stages of *Show Boat*, Higham writes, an exhausted Ziegfeld went to Palm Beach for a rest. While there he received a forty-two-page telegram from book writer William Anthony McGuire. McGuire suggested a silly plot inspired by the famous visit of Queen Marie of Romania to the United States. It dealt with a romance between a Ruritanian princess and a lieutenant at West Point.

At first Ziegfeld thought little of this scenario, but what seduced him into producing it was the fact that the heroine's name was Rosalie, the same as his mother. Ziegfeld was prone to the same kind of mystical connection as Schoenberg and Gershwin. As malevolent as the number 13 was to the father of twelve-tone music, it guaranteed success for Ziegfeld. When he put on his first extravaganza, he spent time and energy coming up with a title—*Follies of 1907*—that contained exactly thirteen characters.

Ziegfeld went to work immediately. He engaged the dependable British writer Guy Bolton to work with McGuire on the book. McGuire was a heavy drinker who could not be counted on to finish what he began. So Ziegfeld engaged Wodehouse to write the lyrics. He signed Marilyn Miller, although their affair had burned out by this time. In fact, to get her to do the show, he engaged Jack Donahue, her lover at that time, as the male lead.

Here is Higham describing the arrangement in which Romberg and Gershwin created separate songs and Wodehouse and Ira worked independently on some lyrics and together on others:

> Several attempts to acquire European composers for the score failed, and Ziegfeld decided to engage Sigmund Romberg. Romberg turned him down flat; he was, he said, just about to go into rehearsals for *New Moon*. Ziegfeld was adamant. Finally Romberg scratched his head thoughtfully and suggested to ease the workload he should collaborate with George Gershwin. Ziegfeld snatched up his famous gold telephone and called Gershwin. When Gershwin arrived at his office, he said that he was too busy also—he was preparing to present *Funny Face*.
>
> According to Elliot Arnold, Romberg's biographer, Ziegfeld looked at the two men and said, "Gentlemen, it is hopeless to argue with me. Both of you better agree now. It will save a world of argument." When the two men reluctantly agreed to this hurricane force, he added a characteristic afterthought: "And remember, gentlemen, I have to have the music in three weeks. Not a day later."

The question is this: why did Gershwin work on this show when there seemed to be so many things working against it for him. Higham prefaces his biography with an anecdote indicating that he believes it reveals an essential characteristic of his subject:

> One day Ziegfeld received the news that his great friend and backer, wealthy Jim Donahue, had been ruined by the stock market crash and had thrown himself out of a window. Immediately after he heard the news he wrote the following words to Donahue's widow: "Your late husband promised me $20,000 just before he fell." The money arrived two days later.

Broadway historian Miles Kreuger describes Ziegfeld as a lecherous despot. He did not pay his debts. He withheld royalties. Each day four or five showgirls would come out of his office —separately—disheveled for all the staff to see. In 1924 he refused his father permission to go backstage to visit one of his "girls." And he forced Anna Held, the French star who was his first wife, to have an abortion because her pregnancy interfered with his rehearsal schedule.

One of those for whom Ziegfeld had contempt was George White, who had started as a dancer in Ziegfeld shows and then created his own *Scandals* to compete with Ziegfeld's *Follies*. White, in fact, went further than Ziegfeld in adorning his chorus girls in revealing costumes, often by Erté, the renowned Deco designer. Still, every time Ziegfeld had the chance, he would humiliate White in print, calling him a "mere imitator."

It could not have helped Gershwin's standing with Ziegfeld to have been the sole composer of the *Scandals* from 1920 through 1924. If he had not behaved decently to Gershwin years before, Ziegfeld certainly would not go out of his way to be generous to him then. Why then did Gershwin agree to work for him? In a 1930 letter, Gershwin wrote that "Flo Ziegfeld had a way of getting what he wanted."

Bennett Cerf once devoted a column to anecdotes about Ziegfeld. Although he invested the stories with humor, they reveal a ruthless man who brooked no obstacle in getting his way. He ended the column with this story:

> A would-be dramatist, who had been pestering Ziegfeld to read his new play for weeks, was struck by a hit and run driver one afternoon, directly in front of the Ziegfeld Theater, with the manuscript tucked tightly under his arm. When the man was carried into the theater, Ziegfeld reluctantly produced a bottle of brandy from his private stock and suggested a headline for the newspaper account: Foul Play Suspected.

Foul play was Ziegfeld's oxygen. It could be that Ziegfeld knew about Gershwin's child with Margaret Manners, a dancer in his rival's show, and threatened to expose him. Or it could have been nothing more complicated than the fact that *Rosalie* offered Gershwin another marquee credit and some money. His only important song from that score is "How Long Has This Been Going On?" and that had been written for but not used in *Funny Face*. (Even in *Rosalie* it did not stand out. The song did not attract attention until years later when Peggy Lee recorded it with Benny Goodman's band.) Gershwin's own title song for *Rosalie* is not the hit song we know now as "Rosalie"; that was written by Cole Porter for the movie version of the show.

Edward Jablonski, author of two books on the Gershwins, writes that *Rosalie* is "generally dismissed as one of Gershwin's lesser efforts, a mere collection of scrapings from the trunk." From *Primrose* he took "Wait a Bit, Susie," and called it "Beautiful Gypsy." From *Oh, Kay!* he lifted "Show Me the Town," and from *Strike Up the Band* "Yankee Doodle Rhythm." "Dance Along with You," unused in *Funny Face*, became "Ev'rybody Knows I Love Somebody." He did write a few new songs: "Oh, Gee! Oh, Joy!" was probably the best of them.

If Gershwin unconsciously was trying to sabotage Ziegfeld because he really did not want to be there, he did not succeed. While the music left something to be desired, Marilyn Miller and the Ziegfeld treatment made the show a major hit. In a review in the *World*, Alexander Woollcott described Miller's entrance: "Fifty beautiful girls in simple peasant costumes of satin and chiffon rush pell mell onto the stage, all squealing simple peasant outcries of 'Here she comes.' Fifty hussars in a fatigue uniform of ivory white and tomato bisque march on in columns of four and kneel to express an emotion too strong for words. The house holds its breath. And on walks Marilyn Miller."

Miller's accompanist for her coaching sessions was Ann Rosenblatt, a songwriter and recent graduate of Radcliffe College who met Gershwin late in 1926. Later Gershwin suggested that she change her name to Ronell. He also led her to her first job in New York, helping Miller with the songs for *Rosalie*. One of

Ronell's first comments about that show was that Romberg, with whom she later worked frequently, who always was present at rehearsals, was absent from the preparations for this particular show. Romberg was either busy with another show or felt as ambivalent about *Rosalie* as George did. When she first met Gershwin, Ann Rosenblatt was a critic for a Radcliffe music magazine. In that capacity she interviewed composers who were visiting the Boston area because their works were being presented by the Boston Symphony Orchestra under the direction of Koussevitzky. Rosenblatt interviewed Copland, Vladimir Dukelsky, and now was intent on getting through to Gershwin. In March 1989, she recalled this sequence of events:

> On a vacation from college, I went to New York and called Gershwin at the 103d Street house. Ira answered and I asked for George. George had picked up the extension and when he heard Ira tell me he was too busy to see me, George interrupted and told me to come over.
>
> A white-coated butler answered the door. The elevator took me up to the fifth floor where George had his studio. I told him I was an admirer. He asked me what I was studying. I answered orchestration and counterpoint, with a major in English literature. Soon he was interviewing me. He asked me what I was writing. I told him of my interest in musical comedy and he suggested I get in the dancing chorus of a show or work as a rehearsal pianist. He played for me and I danced the Charleston. He kept asking questions like when was I coming back to New York. I told him I had made an arrangement to play a two-piano concert with Elizabeth Hayes, a black girl at school. "If you come to New York with her," he said, "I'll try to help you."
>
> When we came to New York, George brought us to H. S. Kraft, an agent who was then involved in *The Front Page*, a Jed Harris production. After we auditioned, George suggested to Kraft that he should try to book us at the Roxy and call the act "Black and White Keys." George advised us to keep in touch with him but nothing came of this particular idea.
>
> George told me he was coming to Cambridge with Marguerite d'Alvarez and invited me to the concert. I went with a

friend. I remember her singing "The Man I Love." George invited me to join them in the green room of Paine Hall. I was sure that between Gershwin and d'Alvarez nobody would let me in, but George saw us approach the door and took us in himself, introducing us to everyone there. Then he talked to me quietly. He told me about the Viennese and German scores he had seen since our last visit. During my interview with him I had told him about an article I had read about Webern, Berg and Kurt Weill, who was having a big success in Germany then. So it was natural for him to pick up on this.

George also told me his family had taken a summer house in Ossining, New York, and suggested I take the train from Cambridge to Yonkers where he would pick me up and drive me to Ossining. When I went, I found his mother in the kitchen making borscht. Frankie and Arthur were there. Upstairs Ira and Leonore had a suite. I sang and played a jazz spiritual I had written, "Down by de Ribber."

After I graduated, I went back to Omaha, Nebraska. Then I got a letter from George. He wanted to see me, he said. Very little news from New York ever reached Omaha, Nebraska. My parents had never heard of Gershwin. But my brother had graduated from Harvard Law School and was living in Manhattan so my father, who had taken me to concerts all my life and had given me dancing lessons, said, "If you have a contact you say is so good, maybe he will get your songs published."

George was a generous and helpful person. I was a nineteen-year-old amateur when we met and he was twenty-nine and world renowned.

When Rosenblatt arrived in New York, Gershwin took her to a rehearsal of *Funny Face* and asked if she would like to be in the chorus. She said she could not dance well enough for that, so he found her a job in the Capitol Theater rehearsing its chorus. When he began working on *Rosalie*, he introduced her to the show's conductor, who gave her the job working with Miller. "I'd report to George what I was doing. George introduced me to Dreyfus and I played 'Down by de Ribber' for him. Mr. Dreyfus asked me for the verse. When he discovered I had written no verse he said, 'You have to know much more about the song business before you come here.' George stepped in. He told me Dreyfus was always hard and I should not be discouraged by him." As Ann Ronell, Rosenblatt went on to write "Baby's Birthday Party," "Willow Weep for Me," and "Rain on the Roof" among others. Ronell was the name she used for the rest of her life.

In New York, Gershwin invited Ronell to dinner at the 103d Street house. As in most single-family houses in Manhattan, the kitchen was on the ground floor and the dining room on the first floor, so a dumbwaiter carried the food up from the kitchen to the dining room. Rose and Morris were seated at the opposite ends of the table. Ann was next to Frankie, who talked of her studies to become a dancer. Arthur said he wanted to be a lyricist. At this moment in his life George was not only an icon on Broadway and the first songwriter to have become a "composer"; he had played piano for eighteen thousand people at the Lewisohn Stadium concerts.

"George was sacred to me," Ronell continues. "He was my idol. I became like a sister to the family and was his protégée. I remember him visiting me once and playing Beethoven's 'Moonlight' Sonata. Someone who was staying in the house complained. There was too much noise, he said. George stopped his performance right away. George sent me to Bill Daly to study and that was a wonderful gift. Daly was a marvelous man and a brilliant musician."

During the preparation for *Rosalie*, Ronell went up to the Gershwin house with a new song she had written. She laughed when she recalled the beginning lyric: "Oh I'm so lonesome, all by my ownsome. Why don't a handsome man come along?" George took the sheet music and played it through. "He told Ira he thought it was good and that he wanted to interpolate it into the score. Ira asked why he was bothering about it and said it wasn't worth his time. Ira always reined George in. He was the businessman. He made the decisions about everything. George was so giving, so spontaneous. It was Ira who always pulled him back."

. . .

Throughout 1927, *Show Boat* dominated show-business news. The flood of press releases began soon after October 12, 1926, when, at the opening of Kern's *Criss Cross*, Alexander Woollcott, at Kern's request, introduced him to Edna Ferber, *Show Boat*'s author. Even as early as this, Kern and Hammerstein were engaged in transforming her novel into a musical. All they needed was her permission to go ahead. Although she thought the work was unsuitable for musical treatment, she gave her permission because she believed that, according to Gerald Bordman, the project would never get off the ground.

From the start both authors wanted Ziegfeld as producer. On Saturday, December 11, they signed a contract with him. It held that they would deliver a first draft on January 1, 1927, and that he would have something on stage by April 1. Early in 1927, *Variety* noted on three different occasions that the show was in active rehearsal. Each time *Variety* was wrong. The serious problems that postponed the production for another nine months can be sensed by the following telegram Ziegfeld sent Kern from Palm Beach during that same vacation period he received the lengthy plot scenario for *Rosalie:*

> I feel Hammerstein not keen on my doing *Show Boat*. I am very keen on doing it on account of your music but Hammerstein book in present shape has not got a chance except with critics but the public no, and I have stopped producing for critics and empty houses. I don't want Bolton or anyone else if Hammerstein can and will do the work. If not, then for all concerned we should have someone help. How about Dorothy Donnelly or anyone you suggest or Hammerstein suggests. I am told Hammerstein never did anything alone. His present lay-out is too serious. Not enough comedy. After marriage remember your love interest is eliminated. No one on earth, Jerry, knows musical comedy better than you and you yourself told me you would not risk a dollar on it. If Hammerstein will fix the book I want to do it. If he refuses to change it or allow anyone else

> to be called in if necessary you and he return the advances. You yourself suggested you would and let someone else do it. If Hammerstein is ready to work with me to get it right and you and he will extend the time until October first let's do it together. I really want to if O.H. is reasonable. All we want is success. Answer.

Show Boat gave its first public performance at Washington's National Theater on November 15, ran between four and four and a half hours, and although there was a consensus that the work would have to be cut, the show was generally recognized as a masterpiece.

The reaction was the same in Cleveland and Philadelphia and was confirmed when *Show Boat* opened in New York at the new Ziegfeld Theater on December 27, 1927. A chorus of 96 included 36 white women, 16 white men, 16 black men and 12 black women. The story is about a romance between a river gambler and the daughter of a show boat's captain.

The circumstances surrounding *Show Boat* were probably painful for Gershwin, whose half-baked *Rosalie* opened in New York only two weeks later. For one thing he had believed some time before that he had outdistanced Kern, yet here was Kern doing something like what he had dreamed after he read *Porgy*. Not only that, but even the plot of *Show Boat*, touching as it does on miscegenation, anticipated his own intention to set a work that dealt with the oppression of the blacks.

Finally a curious note was interjected by *Variety*'s critic who panned Kern's "Bill," sung by Helen Morgan sitting on top of a piano, and wrote that it would have been a wise decision to have interpolated "The Man I Love," still not heard on Broadway, at that moment in the Kern show. The critic noted that the Gershwin song had been intended for *Strike Up the Band*, but that this Gershwin show had been a flop out of town. And so Gershwin saw in print that *Strike Up the Band*, which, like *Show Boat*, was a musical with a serious book, had been reduced to the status of "flop."

When his youthful *Half-Past Eight* failed out of town, Gershwin said that he had no time for flops; he surely had no time for them now that an essay in *Modern Music* elevated Kern to the position of a composer of high art. After the essayist discussed how the score heightened the book's emotional impact, he wrote, "Themes are quoted and even developed in almost Wagnerian fashion. . . . An examination of the full score will reveal dozens of interesting passages which testify to the composer's skill. They may not be apparent to the casual customer, who does not know what it is that is gripping him, but the musician will find much to admire."

Then the writer predicts something that probably mobilized Gershwin's competitive drive: "Kern seems to be at the turning point of his career. If he makes the transition from a sort of opéra comique—and *Show Boat* is exactly that, in the classic sense of the term—to 'leit-opera,' we may finally have opera that is thoroughly and indigenously American."

Ten years later, after Gershwin died, Kern submitted these observations to a collection of essays about Gershwin published by Merle Armitage, who produced Gershwin's concerts on the West Coast.

> There was never anything puny or insignificant about the life, work or opinions of George Gershwin. He lived, labored, played, exulted and suffered with bigness and gusto. It was some other contemporary, definitely *not* George, who was the subject of Thomas Mann's observation, "Why does he make himself so little? Surely he is not that big." There is so much that this unpracticed pen can add to the volumes already written in critical survey of George's work; yet one utterance may be recorded which came from the heart of the man and is illustrative of his stature. It came at the crossroads of his career, long after his dissatisfaction with Broadway musical comedy; even after he had unfolded his pinions and lifted himself into the realm of serious music: "Do you think," he asked with

naivete, "that now I am capable of grand opera? Because, you know," he continued, "all I've got is a lot of talent and plenty of *chutzpah*."

It was then that these ears realized that they were listening to a man touched with greatness.

Frankie Gershwin was not only a talented dancer; her voice and singing style were well suited to her brother's songs. In later years she went on to become an abstract expressionist painter. Arthur, according to his son Marc, played piano well. Ann Ronell reports that he wanted to be a lyricist. But after World War II, he and Fred Spielman composed the music for *A Lady Says Yes* for Broadway.

Still, the accomplishments of the Gershwin family did not include the ability to see their famous brother with clarity. All of them have portrayed him as a cheerful, self-involved man who went from success to success and then died. Despite the recognition by others, including Jerome Kern, that he suffered, his family chose to believe that he led an unrelievedly charmed life. Nor did his relatives ever get involved enough in his inner life to question the reasons for his choices: The decision to collaborate with Romberg provoked critic Alexander Woollcott to write that the pairing of Gershwin with Romberg was like a collaboration of Hemingway and Harold Bell Wright, an author of all-but-forgotten romance novels. Yet Ira and Leonore seem never to have remarked on this incongruous coupling.

Even after George was dead many years, Judy Gershwin, according to relatives and friends, divorced Arthur because "he was still living in George's shadow." Leonore also seemed to be consumed with envy. Her biggest problem, according to her sister-in-law Frankie, "was that she was not Mrs. George Gershwin." While his family seemed to be insensitive to George's feelings, George appeared equally insensitive to others. Barbara Barondress MacLean, an actress, reported in 1991 that she met Gershwin in 1927 at a party at the Strunskys. George invited her to be his "date" at the first Lewisohn Stadium concert that presented *Rhapsody in Blue* where he was the soloist. Then he asked her to accompany him to a party. She says that when they arrived he went straight to the piano and did not look for her after that. Because she was not fluent in English (she had grown up in Russia), she could not converse with the other guests, so she left by herself and took the subway home.

The next day Gershwin called and asked what had become of her. She told him that if all she had wanted was to hear him play, she could have bought the Victor record. Gershwin replied by promising her that at the next party he would allow her to sit next to him on the piano bench.

This behavior did not endear him to women. Nor did it enhance his position with musicians. Dick Sudhalter, a trumpeter and jazz historian, repeats a story Bud Freeman, the tenor saxophonist, told him: "Gershwin arrived at a party. He went to the piano and compulsively entertained. He played and played with a driven quality. The acolytes surrounded him but the great musicians in the room were contemptuous. As soon as he finished playing he left."

Books about Gershwin usually quote a remark made by John O'Hara, the novelist, at a memorial concert for Gershwin three years after he died: "George Gershwin died on July 11, 1937, but I don't have to believe it if I don't want to." No biographer has included the entire O'Hara statement, which gives it an entirely different meaning: O'Hara began his reminiscence by speaking of his memories of parties at the Ira Gershwins' on East Seventy-second Street, "with George playing Gershwin endlessly." And after saying he did not want to believe that Gershwin had died, he goes on to say, "I am sorry now that I did not like George, that I was not his friend."

One probable reason why Gershwin did not like to talk to others was that it demanded an intimacy he was not able to give. But even more important could have been his need to have the spotlight to himself. This may well have come from his sense that his parents preferred his older brother, Ira, to him. Ira was the first born. He always behaved himself. He understood the value of money and never squandered it on movies or clothes. Ira went to synagogue, passed the competitive examination and got into Townsend Harris and spent a year in college. Ira even helped his father in Morris's many business ventures. George, on the other hand, was a boy both parents assumed would end up as a bum.

Very early George reacted against this by competing aggressively with Ira. Everything Ira did, he did better. His aunt Kate Wolpin said, "Ira began to paint before George ever picked up a brush. But as soon as George began painting, Ira just about dropped it."

Apparently the pattern was repeated with Leonore. "Did you know," Wolpin said, "that Lee was infatuated with George? And why not? He was so attractive, so dynamic. There were columns in the papers linking Lee and George romantically. I asked George how he could stand such things. He said that some awful things were written about him and some wonderful things were written about him and that a person should always take the large view."

It was easier for George to take the large view than it was for his brothers and sister to deal with their feelings for their brother when he was constantly outdistancing them in every possible arena.

Marc Gershwin owns a still life by George dated April 25, 1927, sixteen months after the first performance of the Concerto in F. George had the time and the energy for serious music, but he chose instead to paint. The pattern continued. His next orchestral score, *An American in Paris*, was first performed in December 1928, twenty months after that painting. Between the two works, he composed a fine score for *Treasure Girl*, which failed on Broadway (sixty-eight performances) even though it starred Gertrude Lawrence. He was planning to go to Europe with Ira and Leonore and visit Mabel Pleschette, who was by then married to Robert Schirmer. Frankie remembers one evening when she and George were returning from Lindy's delicatessen, a Broadway hangout for theater and sports people. She told her brother that she wanted to go with them to Europe to avoid a man who was hounding her. George told her that he was trying to get away from a woman.

It is difficult to identify the woman. Although his affair with Kay Swift had begun, she was still Mrs. James Warburg and therefore not free to be with him. In fact, the night before the Gershwins left on their voyage, the Warburgs gave them a party that lasted until the ship sailed. The woman George was fleeing could have been Margaret Manners. Questions undoubtedly were being asked then about George's responsibilities to their two-year-old son. She could have been Julia Van Norman, who, by this time, was obsessed with Gershwin and needed frequent contact. Or any number of other women, for there were always dozens around. But Gershwin kept turning toward more motherly figures, somewhat older than he, married, generally with children, who saw him as someone they could appropriate.

This did not put him off, because his model at home, his rejecting mother, used him in much the same way for her needs. He seemed unable to connect with women who were capable of love. When you have a disapproving mother, you can come to believe that rejection is love.

Whatever woman was driving Gershwin from New York, she did not interfere with his pleasures in Paris. Frankie says George had an affair with the Countess de Granny, who was played by Alexis Smith in the Gershwin biographical movie, *Rhapsody in Blue*. Some of the women Gershwin courted say he talked about marriage to them. Frankie said, "George was always looking for a woman to marry. He talked about marriage a lot. Even as far back as when we were living on 110th Street, he would say how he wanted a beautiful home with beautiful dishes and beautiful glasses. He wanted everything to be beautiful. But when you don't have nurturing parents you don't know how to give love."

Women generally don't like to talk about proposals that do not lead to marriage. But Gershwin's women friends appear to have understood that he was never serious about his proposals. He asked women to marry him in much the same way that he asked famous European composers to teach him; he was respectful but finally not serious. It is unlikely that Gershwin would have gone to the Soviet Union to study orchestration with Glazunov, as he told the Russian composer after the Concerto in F premiere. In the same way, he went to Nadia Boulanger with a letter of reference from Ravel asking to study with her.

He seemed really to believe that just as marriage would bring beautiful things to his home, so study with Stravinsky, Ravel, Glazunov, or Boulanger would bring beautiful techniques to his scores. But being a student of an established figure implied a kind of surrender he was unable to make. To say this is not to suggest that Gershwin never called on anyone to help him with the technical disciplines he lacked. In 1927 Gershwin studied with Henry Cowell, the idiosyncratic composer who introduced the device of tone clusters, a group of notes played with the fist instead of the fingers.

In 1990 Sidney Cowell, Henry's widow, said, "Gershwin was a bona fide student of Henry's. Henry told me of times in his apartment when Gershwin was wearing a dressing gown and had three or four secretaries in attendance." Such a setting was not calculated to endear Gershwin to the community of serious composers. Nor did it. "Nobody thought of him," she said, "as belonging to the 'long-haired' composers. Gershwin was a popular composer. That set him apart. There was a justified snobbism on the part of people like Henry who had worked hard at their music, who had studied and mastered sixteenth-century counterpoint. Gershwin studied sixteenth-century counterpoint with Henry and they met several times a week. Then they would go for months without seeing one another because one of them was away. Henry did not believe Gershwin learned enough from him to make big public claims that he had been his student."

Mrs. Cowell also said that her husband sent Gershwin to study with Joseph Schillinger, the originator of a mathematical basis for composition with whom Gershwin worked in the early 1930s. He may well have suggested Schillinger to Gershwin, but many others, including Glazunov, claimed they did too. This was one of the many events in Gershwin's life for which an army of people took credit.

By this time it seemed that just about everyone who ever met Gershwin claimed a piece of him. Early in 1928, after the lessons with Cowell stopped, Gershwin met Ravel at a birthday party Eva Gauthier gave for the French composer. Ravel had asked Gauthier to invite Gershwin. Gershwin responded by bringing Ravel to the nightclubs in Harlem. Months later, while Gershwin was in Paris, Ravel told an audience in Houston that he hoped the American school of music would "embody a great deal of the rich and diverting rhythm of your jazz and a great deal of sentiment and spirit characteristic of your popular melodies." He was speaking to deaf ears. The "long-haired" composers in the United States had by then given up the American vernacular.

But Gershwin had not. On March 10, 1928, he left for his fifth and last trip to Europe. Even before he left New York, he sketched out plans for *An American in Paris*. In Paris he composed the blues section and realized the plans for most of the rest. Two years earlier in Paris, he had bought the taxi horns that gave him the timbre as well as the precise off-key pitches he wanted. This is another of those decisions for which a number of people take credit. Mabel Schirmer reportedly helped him make his choices. This could be true. She had, after all, studied with Hambitzer and served as the model for *Dere Mabel*, and he continued to rely on her in many ways.

Before leaving New York, Gershwin wrote asking her to engage a multilingual valet because he hoped to take a house outside Paris where he would immerse himself in his work. He never managed that. His trip was frenetic from start to finish. It began in London, where he and the family attended a show for which Ira wrote some lyrics. They also went to the British performance of *Oh, Kay!*, with Gertrude Lawrence again in the leading role. George's self-enforced absence from New York at this time—he was not in Europe for any professional reason—suggests that the separation from Kay Swift, the woman behind the choice of "Kay" two years before, was not in the least painful to him. During this trip his sister, Frankie, met Leopold Godowsky, Jr., son of the concert pianist and legendary teacher. Two years later she married him.

In 1989 she talked about her experiences in show business in

Paris and about her sister-in-law Leonore. "On the ship going over," she said, "a man fell for me. Leonore became furious at the attention I was getting. She kept telling me I would not do as well in Paris. She was cruel, really abusive. I told George how Leonore was treating me and he was very sweet. 'That is the way she is,' he said. 'Don't pay any attention to her.' "

In Paris the Gershwins went to a party at Elsa Maxwell's, where they met Cole Porter, the multimillionaire expatriate who had written "Night and Day." He had not yet become a renowned show composer. Frankie sang for him and he was so taken with her that he suggested she have a spot of her own in his *Revue des Ambassadeurs*. Frankie stayed in Paris while the others spent the next weeks traveling. George returned in time for her opening on May 10, but Lee and Ira did not. Lee claimed illness.

Porter wrote a verse with which Frankie introduced her act:

I happen to be the sister
Of a rhythm twister,
No doubt you know him as Mister
George Gershwin.

Then, after some lines in which Porter coupled "Georgie" with "orgy," Frankie announced her intention to sing some favorites of "the man I love."

On opening night George accompanied her. They performed not only "The Man I Love" but also "Embraceable You" two years before it was heard in *Girl Crazy*, "Do, Do, Do," and "Oh, Gee! Oh, Joy!" Frankie says she received offers from producers but George would not let her stay after he had gone back to New York. In this instance George took over and "reined" Frankie in.

George did permit Frankie to remain in Paris to rehearse the Porter show while he went to Berlin and Vienna. In Berlin he met Kurt Weill. This was before Weill's *Die Dreigroschenoper* but after *Das klein Mahagonny*, a jazz-influenced song cycle. In Vienna he attended the world premiere of Ernst Krenek's *Jonny spielt auf*, an opera with a jazz base that the Metropolitan Opera

Broadway caricaturist Al Hirschfeld's drawing of George and Ira Gershwin, 1981.

Edward Steichen photograph of George Gershwin, 1927.

Gershwin self-portrait, 1934, based on Steichen's photograph.

3

Profiles of father (front) and son, Alan Gershwin (Schneider), photographed when each was in his mid-thirties.

5

James Reese Europe, leader of the Clef Club Band, 1914.

6

Luckey Roberts, a pioneer stride pianist and major influence on Gershwin.

7

James P. Johnson, influential composer, pianist, stylist, late 1920s.

8

Eubie Blake (left) and Noble Sissle in 1919, before their *Shuffle Along* appeared in one of the better Broadway theaters.

Gershwin in his piano roll days, c. 1916.

The Favorites of Broadway Play Dance Music Exclusively for

The DUO-ART

Reproducing Piano

GEORGE GERSHWIN

THE latest, most entrancing jazz music! The tunes that Broadway is dancing to this minute in her smart cabarets, hearing in her most popular musical shows. .

Have them in your own home on the Duo-Art, played by the dance pianists whom knowing Broadwayites acclaim.

EDYTHE BAKER

The Duo-Art is obtainable in the

STEINWAY · STECK · WEBER

WHEELOCK · STROUD · AEOLIAN

Grand and Upright Pianos

Uprights from $695 Grands from $1750

Convenient Terms

PHIL OHMAN

The AEOLIAN COMPANY

Foremost Makers of Musical Instruments in the World

IN FORDHAM—270 E. Fordham Road

10

Advertisement for the Duo-Art Reproducing Piano with George's photograph.

Will Vodery, arranger, composer, and conductor, who orchestrated Gershwin's early opera *Blue Monday Blues.*

11

Will Marion Cook (standing), distinguished black composer and violinist, with (left to right) unidentified saxophone player, Harold Arlen, Fletcher Henderson, Bobby Stark, Lois Deppe, and Rex Stewart, June 1929, Atlantic City.

12

Pauline Heifetz, Jascha's sister and Gershwin's first important romantic interest.

Gershwin with first edition copy of *Rhapsody in Blue*, 1924

13

14

15

Paul Whiteman in 1925 with participants in his Carnegie Hall performance of *135th Street,* the retitled *Blue Monday Blues.* Left to right: Ferde Grofé, who arranged it, Deems Taylor, composer and commentator, Blossom Seeley, vocalist, and Gershwin.

16

Gershwin with Whiteman band, May 21, 1924, *Rhapsody in Blue* tour, St. Louis railroad station.

On tour with Paul Whiteman, Gershwin played in Rochester, New York, where he visited the Eastman School of Music.

17

To the most wonderful Music School in America. Long may its flag wave.

George Gershwin

Clar.

18

Julia Van Norman, whose fan letter to Gershwin in 1927 began a relationship that lasted the rest of his life.

Gershwin with conductor Walter Damrosch at work on the *Concerto in F*.

19

Margaret Manners (right) in George White's *Scandals,* 1927.

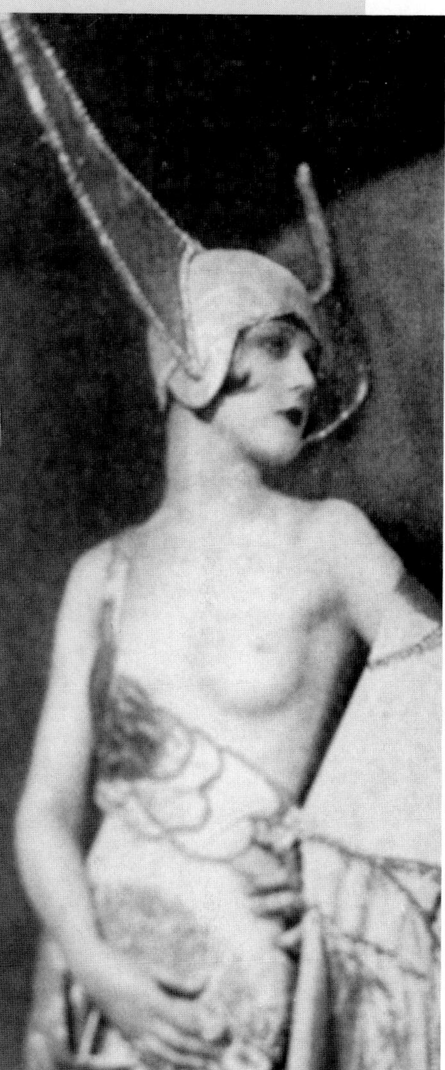

Beauties of the New "George White's Scandals," Now at the Apollo Theatre.

ELISE GERNON.

MAR-GARET MANNERS.

PEARL BRADLEY.

(All Photographs by The New York Times Studios.)

JAC-QUELINE FEELEY.

MAE SLATTERLY.

LA VERTA McCORMICK.

Young actresses with Margaret Manners, born Mollie Charleston, the mother of Gershwin's son.

SOMEBODY LOVES ME

George White's Scandals

Lyrics by B.G. De Sylva and Ballard McDonald Music by George Gershwin

HARMS NEW YORK

22

Gershwin with Alex Aarons, producer of George and Ira's most successful Broadway musicals, beginning with *Lady, Be Good!* and ending with *Girl Crazy*.

(Left to right) Buddy DeSylva, Lew Brown, Ray Henderson, and George White, working on the *Scandals* after George left the show.

23

24

At Eva Gauthier's birthday party for Maurice Ravel. Left to right: Oscar Fried, conductor; Gauthier, who presented some Gershwin songs at a recital of serious music a few months before Whiteman's famous "experiment"; Ravel; unidentified man; and Gershwin.

Ann Ronell during her Radcliffe days.

25

26

Max Dreyfus, the Gershwins' music publisher, with Ira in a photograph inscribed to Dreyfus's associate, Irene Gallagher.

27

Florenz Ziegfeld, his wife, actress Billie Burke, and their daughter.

Gershwin with colleagues from *Rosalie:* Left to right: Jack Donahue, the male lead; Sigmund Romberg, Gershwin's collaborator; Marilyn Miller, the star; and Ziegfeld.

28

Kay Swift,
the inspiration
for *Oh, Kay!*

30

Gershwin with Swift at the Warburg home in Connecticut.

In Belmar, New Jersey, around 1929: Left to right: Ann Ronell, Gershwin, family friend Elsie Schloss, Emily Paley, Yip Harburg, Lou Paley.

31

Gershwin's Art Deco dining room at 33 Riverside Drive, the first home he inhabited without his parents.

Gershwin's favorite corner of his living room. Kay Swift decorated the apartment.

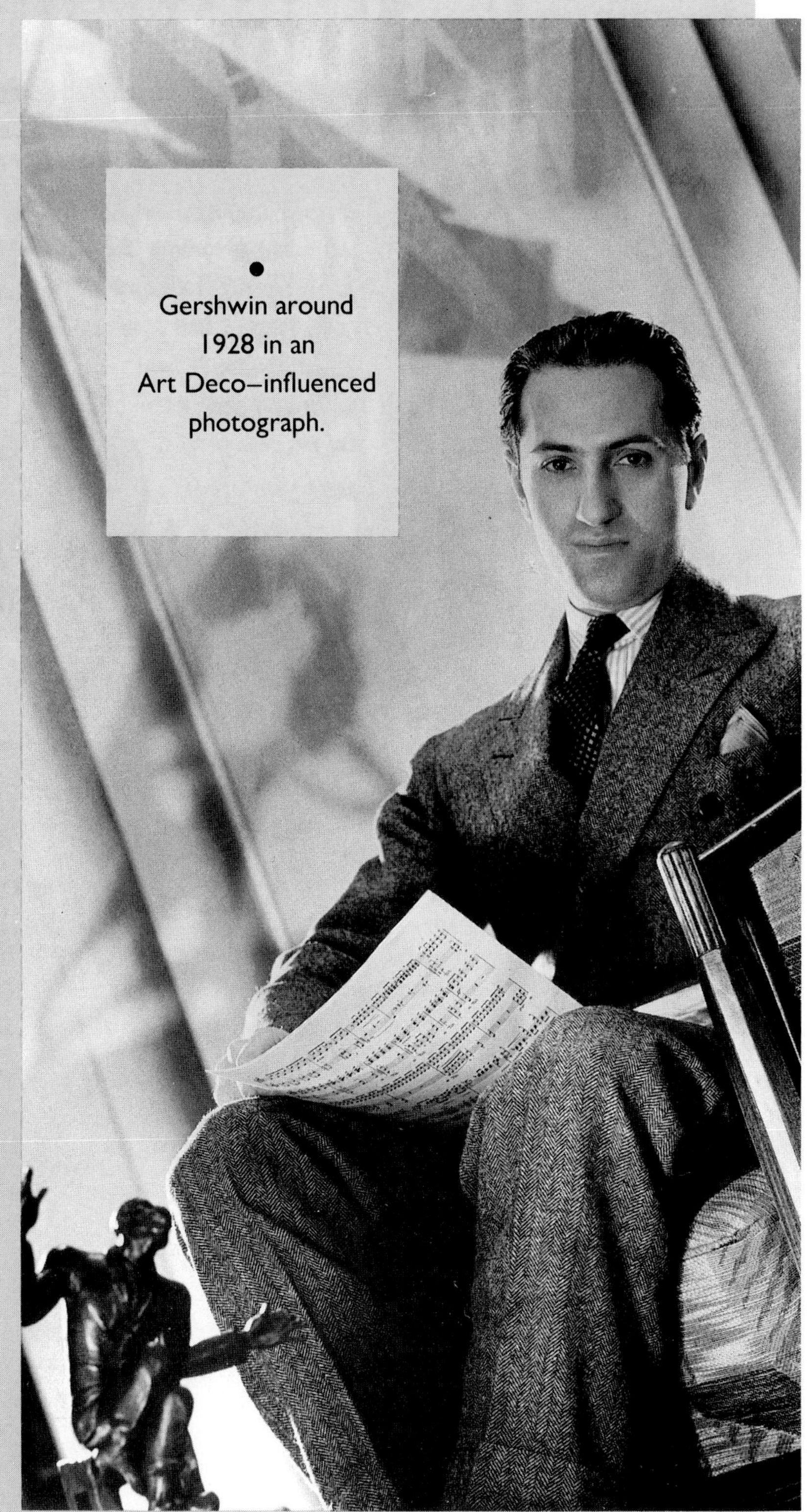

Gershwin around 1928 in an Art Deco–influenced photograph.

35

Arthur Gershwin, two years younger than George. He composed the Broadway show *A Lady Says Yes* (1945) with Fred Spielman as well as a number of pop songs including "Invitation to the Blues," "Slowly But Surely," "After All These Years," and "No Love Blues"—songs that never enjoyed the success of George and Ira's.

36

Leopold Godowsky, Jr., with his wife, Frances Gershwin Godowsky, the youngest of the Gershwin children.

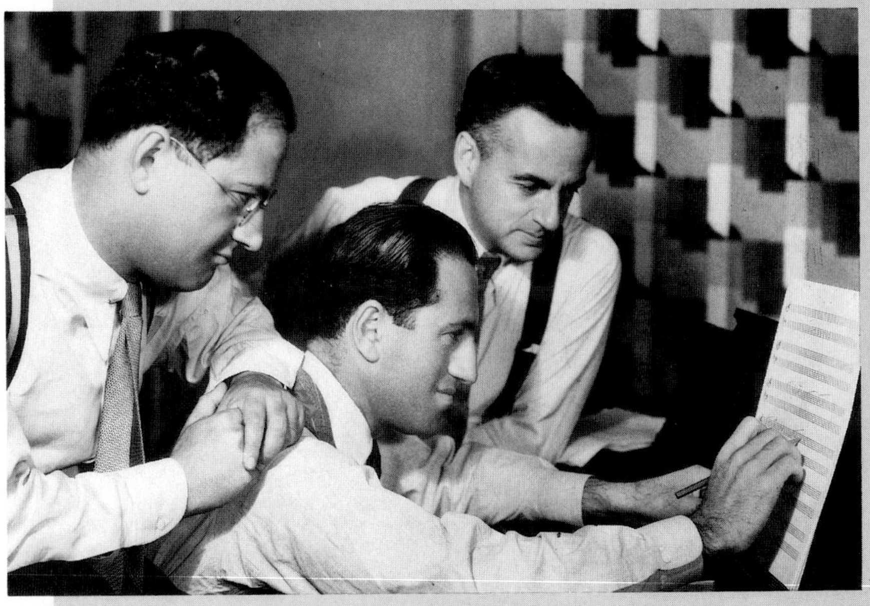

37

Ira and George with Guy Bolton, at work on *Delicious,* 1931.

ALVIN THEATRE

GIRL CRAZY

38

Program for *Girl Crazy*, the first show four-year-old Alan attended.

Gershwin with conductor Arthur Rodzinski in Hollywood house formerly occupied by Greta Garbo, 1930.

40

Gershwin in Hollywood working on the score for *Delicious*, a film starring Charles Farrell and Janet Gaynor.

George Pallay, an old friend, with Gershwin and unidentified women, Palm Springs, 1931.

41

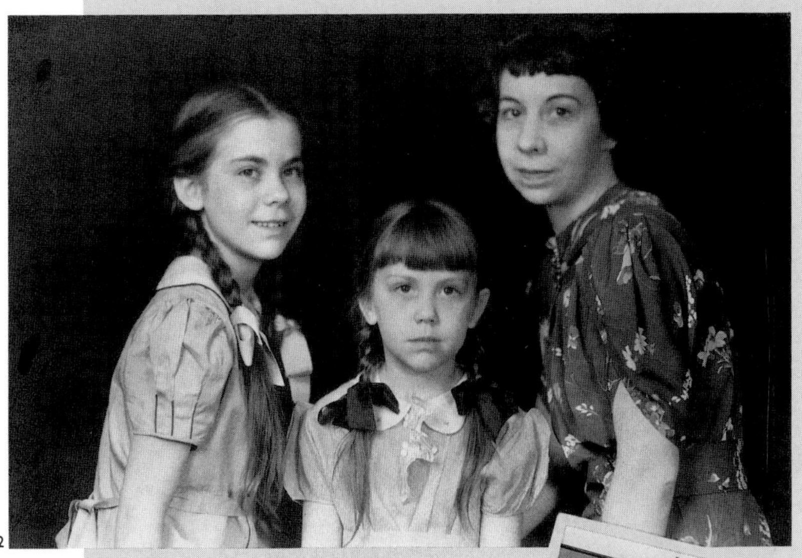

42

Julia Van Norman, with daughters Barbara and Nancy.

43

Gershwin before an all-American concert at Lewisohn Stadium, 1931, with, left to right: Fritz Reiner, Deems Taylor, Robert Russell Bennett.

44

Gershwin with conductor Serge Koussevitzky, 1932, when Koussevitzky was preparing the *Second Rhapsody*, an arrangement and orchestration of some of Gershwin's score for *Delicious*.

Samuel Chotzinoff, who married Pauline Heifetz, with Arturo Toscanini. Chotzinoff invited Gershwin to meet Toscanini at his apartment, hoping the great Italian conductor would be moved to conduct a Gershwin work. The plan failed.

45

46

Gershwin with his close friend, Bill Daly, a Harvard-educated musician.

47

Joseph Schillinger, the inventor of a mathematical system of composition with whom Gershwin studied in the early 1930s.

48

•

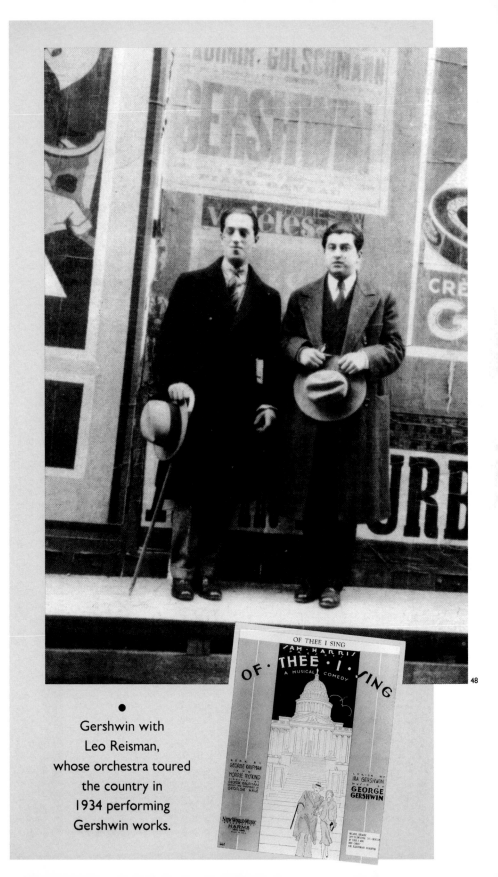

Gershwin with
Leo Reisman,
whose orchestra toured
the country in
1934 performing
Gershwin works.

49

An advertisement for a Gershwin concert in Milwaukee.

The Reisman orchestra with Gershwin at the piano and Mitch Miller, oboe, first row, second from right.

Gershwin with his cousin Henry Botkin, a painter, who helped him acquire a major art collection.

51

52

George used the financial security of his CBS radio show, "Music by Gershwin," 1934, to support him during the strenuous composition period of *Porgy and Bess.*

Gershwin with Harold Arlen on "Music by Gershwin," a radio show on which Gershwin presented music of his colleagues, refuting the claim he only played his own songs.

I GOT PLENTY O' NUTTIN'
THE THEATRE GUILD PRESENTS
PORGY and BESS
MUSIC BY
GEORGE GERSHWIN
LIBRETTO BY
DuBOSE HEYWARD
LYRICS BY
DuBOSE HEYWARD and IRA GERSHWIN
PRODUCTION DIRECTED BY
ROUBEN MAMOULIAN
GERSHWIN PUBLISHING CORP.

The brothers Gershwin with DuBose Heyward, author of the novel *Porgy*, playwright of the drama *Porgy*, and librettist as well as co-lyricist (with Ira) for the opera *Porgy and Bess.*

54

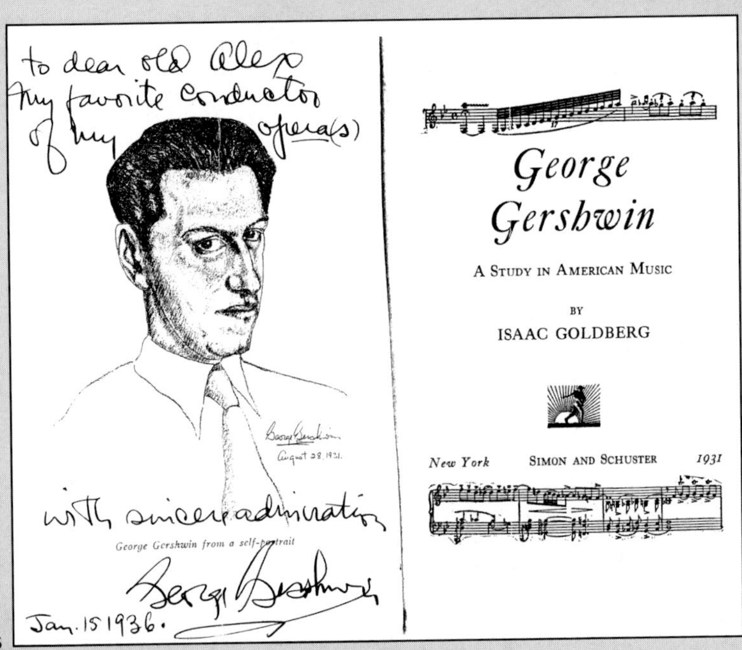

to dear old Alex
my favorite conductor
of my opera(s)

George Gershwin
August 28, 1931.

with sincere admiration

George Gershwin from a self-portrait

George Gershwin
Jan. 15 1936.

George Gershwin

A Study in American Music

BY

ISAAC GOLDBERG

New York SIMON AND SCHUSTER *1931*

55

Gershwin gave a copy of Isaac Goldberg's biography to Alexander Smallens, conductor of *Porgy and Bess.*

George's painting of his mother, Rose.

56

57

George embracing Rose.

George and Ira at Newark on August 10, 1936, leaving for California.

58

Simone Simon, the actress whom George had met in Europe and who became his first romantic partner in Beverly Hills.

Ira and George at work in their customary manner—bridge table and piano—in California, 1936.

Gershwin conducting the Los Angeles Philharmonic in February 1937. At a rehearsal he lost his balance and almost fell off the podium.

62

Gershwin and Ginger Rogers on the set of *Shall We Dance.*

Two drawings by Gershwin. Above: Gregory Zilboorg, his psychoanalyst, on the analytic couch. Below: Leonore Gershwin, his sister-in-law, a drawing that relatives found hostile.

Oscar Levant, cruel to everyone, including Gershwin, and the foremost interpreter of Gershwin's music.

64

65

66

Paulette Goddard: Levant said she was the only love of Gershwin's life.

Gershwin's painting of Arnold Schoenberg, his last. It was based on photographer Edward Weston's portrait.

67

The last photograph of Gershwin, June 19, 1937, three weeks before his death, at an RKO Radio Pictures Convention.

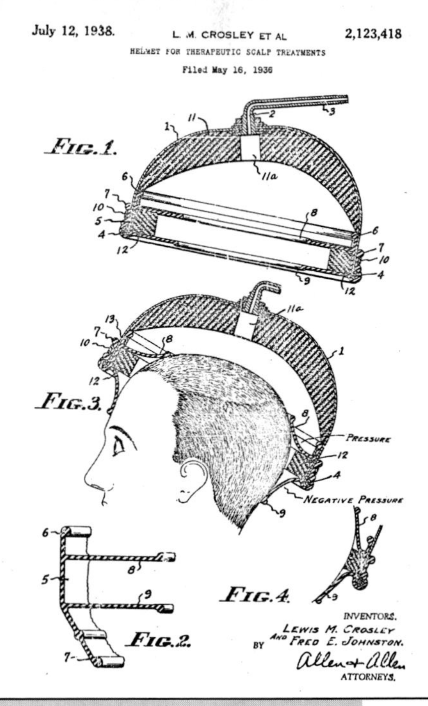
July 12, 1938. L. M. CROSLEY ET AL 2,123,418

HELMET FOR THERAPEUTIC SCALP TREATMENTS

Filed May 16, 1936

FIG. 1.

FIG. 3.

PRESSURE

NEGATIVE PRESSURE

FIG. 4.

FIG. 2.

INVENTORS.
LEWIS M. CROSLEY
AND FRED E. JOHNSTON.
BY Allen & Allen
ATTORNEYS.

68

The patent registering the helmet Gershwin began using in April 1939, initially to impede baldness, later to lessen the pain of his excruciating headaches.

Gershwin funeral at Temple Emanu-El in New York with Mayor Fiorello La Guardia in foreground at left. Gershwin's death marked the beginning of the end of the great era of American songwriters.

Vernon Duke, the American songwriter who had been Vladimir Dukelsky, a Russian composer. He completed Gershwin's score for *The Goldwyn Follies.*

70

71

On the set of the movie *Rhapsody in Blue,* 1945. Left to right: Levant, producer Jesse Lasky, Ira and Leonore, and actor Robert Alda as Gershwin.

Alan Gershwin, in a recent photograph.

72

Nancy Bloomer Deussen, in 1988, composer and daughter of Julia Van Norman.

73

presented the following year. But more important than any other encounter was his meeting with Alban Berg before Berg had become known in the United States. Berg, a Schoenberg pupil, was a remarkable composer, producing elegantly structured, complex works.

After the initial meeting, Berg and Gershwin got together again at the home of Rudolf Kolisch, Schoenberg's brother-in-law. Kolisch, a violinist, and three other string players performed Berg's recently composed quartet. Then, in response to a request, Gershwin sat down at the piano. He played some show tunes, then a few bars of the *Rhapsody*. Then he stopped, explaining he felt uncomfortable with this music after listening to the Berg work. Berg is reported to have responded courteously: "Music is music, Mr. Gershwin." Still, George later confided to Ira he felt Berg had treated him in a patronizing way.

When Gershwin arrived in New York, he brought with him an eight-volume set of Debussy's piano works, a pocket score of the Berg quartet, and an autographed excerpt from Berg's *Lyric Suite*, which he hung on the wall of his study. He also brought back two versions—neither of them completed—of *An American in Paris*.

An American in Paris was the first concert piece Gershwin composed without a commission. Gershwin had begun to think about *An American in Paris* when he was in Europe in 1926. Because some of the music in *An American in Paris* came from the opening measures of the last movement of his Concerto in F, it is logical to assume the germ of the later piece took hold at the completion of the concerto.

He proceeded with the writing without a financial or performance commitment, although he probably knew by then that he could find an orchestra to play it. It was also his first concert work written without a piano part. Gershwin may have set this goal to test his skill in orchestration in contrast to the image he had of himself as a composer with tunes "oozing out of [his] fingers." It probably was not easy for him. In fact, the facsimile edition of the score indicates that more than once he included a piano part and then took it out; pages 45 and 47 show piano staves with notes the composer later crossed out.

Gershwin's script is elegant. The title page of the facsimile edition reads:

AN AMERICAN IN PARIS
A Tone Poem
for
Orchestra
Composed and Orchestrated
by
George Gershwin
Begun early in 1928
Finished November 18, 1928

Here Gershwin specifies that he "composed and orchestrated" the piece. Ordinarily one assumes the orchestration is the composer's own. That Gershwin spelled it out in this way shows his frustration at the charges he relied on someone else to do this work as well as his desire to be accepted by the symphonic world. The score reveals other signs of that wish. Musical directions still appear in Italian: *subito con brio*, *tranquillo*, *giocoso*. Then he scores the rhythm section not for a jazz drummer, who would have been better suited for the work, but for the traditional symphony orchestra array of three percussionists.

Torn between the two worlds, Gershwin never eliminated one for the other. Despite his concessions to Carnegie Hall, touches of jazz permeate the whole piece. While he dropped the saxophones that gave a blues color to the *Rhapsody* for his Concerto in F, he brought them back for *An American in Paris*. In addition, he weaves the jazz-derived textures throughout the work. As much as Gershwin wanted to be part of the high art universe, whenever it seemed possible that he was arriving, he sabotaged himself. While Gershwin was working on this tone poem, Stokowski looked at the score and told him he would like to premiere it. Gershwin said no; it was going to Damrosch. By the time Stokowski made his offer, Gershwin and Damrosch were corresponding about the piece. Still, his rejecting a Stokowski performance when he was not yet tied down by a formal commission suggests that Stokowski intimidated him and that he was more at ease working with such work-a-day musicians as Shilkret and Damrosch.

By the fall of 1928, Arturo Toscanini had become principal conductor of the New York Philharmonic. That orchestra had merged with Damrosch's New York Symphony Society, and Damrosch got the title of principal guest conductor. While Toscanini showed no interest in Gershwin until years after he died, Damrosch actually made suggestions about the *American in Paris* score.

On his own, Gershwin had cut part of the work before he began to score it. The original manuscript reveals minor suggestions from Daly. But Damrosch tightened the work considerably, deleting 108 measures in all. Gershwin finished the two-piano sketch on August 1. Because he was still writing *Treasure Girl*, he did not complete the orchestration until November 18.

After the first performance, on December 13, at which the audience cheered, Chotzinoff gave high praise to the piece. There were scattered kind remarks from a few others but the majority of critics wrote harsh reviews. In the New York *Times* Olin Downes said Gershwin "gets no farther than the earlier works; it reveals no new artistic or emotional ground." In the *Telegram* Herbert Francis Peyser called *An American in Paris* "long-winded and inane." In the *Post* Oscar Thompson held it to be "very pedestrian indeed."

Nor did Gershwin's title page stop rumors of his having others orchestrate for him. The chorus of accusers grew until it erupted into print in 1932 after a performance of *An American in Paris* at the Metropolitan Opera House. Allan Langley, a violist in that orchestra and a failed composer and conductor who had been attacking Gershwin since 1926, wrote an essay, "The Gershwin Myth," published in the *American Spectator*. Langley claimed that during rehearsals it was clear to him that Daly knew the piece better than Gershwin and that it was obvious that Daly had scored it. Daly responded in the New York *Times:* "I have never orchestrated one whole bar of any of his symphonic works."

Recently Morton Gould said, "*An American in Paris* has some messy orchestration but it also has something else that is much more difficult to find than skillful arranging. It has musical personality and character. It comes off. I remember a competition for composers when Robert Russell Bennett, the orchestrator, said: 'These guys can beat Gershwin any day in technique and form. But where are those four bars of a Gershwin score that can sear your heart as no other music will?' "

Many an artist who receives ten good reviews and one bad one will say that the one bad one carries more weight than the ten good ones, and the bad one haunts him. That is because it is the one that confirms what he most fears about himself. Despite the approval of the audience for his latest effort, Gershwin was being worn down by the persistent and growing critical attacks on his craftsmanship. Rose Gershwin did nothing to counteract this. Burton Lane, composer of *Finian's Rainbow* and *On a Clear Day*, was at the Gershwins' in 1928 when Rose asked George why he couldn't write hits like those by DeSylva, Brown, and Henderson. George became enraged but said nothing and just left the room.

In 1990, in response to a request to sum up Gershwin, conductor, composer, and music lexicographer Nicolas Slonimsky said, "Gershwin was extremely uncertain of himself, of his accomplishments. He constantly defended himself against accusations of not being knowledgeable enough to compose his own music. He was a man completely free of self-aggrandisement."

But at least a bit self-protective. In a letter dated August 18, 1928, to an ASCAP official Gershwin wrote: "Mr. Kern at lunch the other day brought to my attention that Ferde Grofé had listed among his compositions 'The Rhapsody in Blue.' Mr. Kern said he objected to this at the last meeting and he advised me to write to you about it. Mr. Grofé made a very fine orchestration from my completed sketch but certainly had no hand in the composing. . . . Hoping you will straighten this out. With best regards."

. . .

Adolph Lewisohn, for whom the stadium at City College was named, was a member of the community of German Jews who settled in New York in the nineteenth century. Their origins were often as humble as those of the eastern European Jews who began arriving in the United States decades later and settled on New York's Lower East Side. But by the end of the century, several of these German-Jewish families had grown wealthy as merchants and bankers and owned mansions on Fifth Avenue, large estates on Long Island, rambling properties in the Adirondacks, and elegantly landscaped grounds on the Jersey shore. They also owned vast art collections and gave millions to museums and hospitals. Loeb, Lehman, Schiff, Straus, Seligman, Guggenheim, Kahn, and Warburg are among the names of the most prominent of these families.

Otto Kahn, an investment banker, presided over a chateau on upper Fifth Avenue where he frequently hosted dinners with as many as sixty seated guests. In *Our Crowd*, Stephen Birmingham writes that Kahn had a taste "for high life, and, of all things, Bohemia." Although he dreamed of being a poet when he was growing up in Mannheim, his mother ended that career when she destroyed all of his poems. Kahn went on to become one of the most successful financiers in the United States. He spoke with a British accent, had his clothes made in Savile Row, peppered his speeches with quotes from great writers, and considered Felix Warburg, another German-Jewish investment banker, his closest friend. Invited to become a member of the board of directors of the Metropolitan Opera Company, Kahn accepted and performed his duties so well he was named chairman in 1907. At that time Jews were not permitted to hold boxes at the Met. Despite his chairmanship, that rule applied to Kahn.

Gershwin gravitated to people who were rich and well connected. Because Warburg and Kahn were both Jews, Gershwin was particularly comfortable with them, even though German Jews tended to look with contempt on eastern European Jews, who began to arrive in the United States in large numbers in

1881. (After all, Emma Lazarus, a German-Jewish poet from Baltimore, wrote the lines that appear on the Statue of Liberty about "the wretched refuse of your teeming shores."

At the premiere of *An American in Paris* in 1928, Kahn was in the audience. He was also present at the reception afterward hosted by Jules Glaenzer. An inscribed sterling silver humidor was presented to Gershwin. Then Kahn delivered a speech. He started by comparing Gershwin and Lindbergh, saying they were alike in "the same engaging and unassuming ways, the simple dignity and dislike of show, the same absence of affectation, the same uncomplicated, naive, 'Parsifalesque' outlook on life." After complimenting the "raw material" in Gershwin, Kahn said that what he believed Gershwin needed to turn his talent into art was a dose of sadness. First he quoted Thomas Hardy:

> I shrink to see a modern coast
> Whose riper times have yet to be;
> Where the new regions claim them free
> From that long drip of human tears
> Which people old in tragedy
> Have left upon the centuries' years.

Then he went on: "My dear George, they have great and strange and beautiful power, those human tears. They fertilize the deepest roots of art, and from them flowers spring of a loveliness and perfume that no other moisture can produce. I believe in you with full faith and admiration, in your significance in the field of American music, and I wish you well with all my heart. And just because of that I could wish an experience—not too prolonged—of that driving storm and stress of the emotions, of that solitary wrestling with your own soul, of that aloofness, for a while, from the actions and distractions of the everyday world, which are the most effective ingredients for the deepening and mellowing and the complete development, energizing and revealment, of an artist's inner being and spiritual powers."

In addition to being pompous and presumptuous, Otto Kahn was wrong. Gershwin had suffered. As a child he was afflicted with rejecting parents. As an adult he had fathered at least one illegitimate child and must have realized that he was not behaving much more fatherly than his own father had. Finally, as the most successful member of his generation of Gershwins, he was burdened with responsibility not only for his parents' support but for Ira's and Leonore's as well. And Leonore was expensive. Still, Gershwin reportedly smiled courteously as Kahn delivered his remarks.

Soon afterward, Gershwin approached him as the chairman of the Met's board with an idea for an opera for the Met. It was, he said, to be based on *The Dybbuk*, a play by S. An-Ski, a Russian-Jewish playwright who wrote the work in Yiddish. It is about the demon of a dead person that enters the body of a living being.

In the fall of 1929 the Met signed a contract with Gershwin for an opera that would include a piano-vocal score, a full orchestral score, all orchestra and choral parts as well as the supervision of the correction of those parts. The work was to be completed by April 1, 1931, and Gershwin would have to share his fee, which was to be $1,000, with the librettist, Henry Alsberg, who had translated the An-Ski play into English.

If Gershwin's goal had only been money, he would never have bothered with such a paltry fee. But he accepted it and then planned to spend several months abroad to study Jewish folk and liturgical music. He also began jotting down musical themes in a notebook. He played some of them for his biographer, Goldberg, who wrote of their resemblance to Hasidic melodies. But in 1930 Ludovico Rocca, an Italian composer, informed the Met that he had secured the rights to the play and would sue if the company went ahead with its plan.

This must have been a disappointment for Gershwin, whose experiences on Broadway were also turning bad. First he was committed to a show, *Ming Toy*, based on the play *East Is West*. Then Ziegfeld dropped it to do *Show Girl*. Here is Gershwin in a letter:

> I'll never forget *Show Girl* because it was the greatest rush job I've ever done on a score. I was working on another show for Mr. Ziegfeld, when he suddenly decided to drop that one and produce *Show Girl* immediately. He often did those things. Mr. Ziegfeld called me down to his office one day and said, "George, I'm going to produce J. P. McEvoy's *Show Girl* and you must write the score for it. We go into rehearsal in two weeks." I said, "But Mr. Ziegfeld, I can't write a score in two weeks. That's impossible." Mr. Ziegfeld smiled up at me and said, "Why, sure you can—just dig down in the trunk and pull out a couple of hits." . . . Well, the show went into rehearsal with half the score finished and about one-third of the book completed. Mr. Ziegfeld said, "I would like to have the minstrel number in the second act with one hundred beautiful girls seated on steps that cover the entire stage." This minstrel number was to be sung and danced by Ruby Keeler. So we went to work on a minstrel number and wrote "Liza." The show opened in Boston and I think the last scene was rehearsed on the train going up. The first act went along fine. The second act came and the attractive and talented Ruby Keeler appeared to sing and dance "Liza." Imagine the audience's surprise and mine when, without warning, Al Jolson who was sitting in the third row on the aisle, jumped up and sang a chorus of "Liza" to his bride. Miss Keeler and he had just been married. It caused a sensation, and it gave the show a great start.

A great start, perhaps, but an ignominious end; it was a critical and box-office disaster. The opening—to which Gershwin escorted Barbara Barondress MacLean, a woman he once ignored to play the piano at a party—was on June 24, 1929; the closing 111 performances later. The failure must have been Ziegfeld's own, because a lot of talented people worked on the show. The Gershwins plus lyricist Gus Kahn wrote twenty-seven songs. Among them were "Do What You Do," "So Are You," "Harlem Serenade," and "I Must Be Home by Twelve O'Clock," all up to Gershwin standards. Bill Daly conducted. Duke Ellington led his band in a scene and the comedy team of Lou Clayton, Eddie Jackson, and Jimmy Durante were in the cast. On top of all this, Ziegfeld appropriated *An American in Paris* and cut it to suit his needs as music for a ballet sequence at the opening of the second act.

Gershwin started to conduct when he was having difficulties with his work for Broadway. His last four shows—*Rosalie*, *Treasure Girl*, *Ming Toy*, *Show Girl*—had either been aborted before opening or failed. Three had been produced by Ziegfeld, but *Treasure Girl* had been mounted by Alex Aarons and Vinton Freedley, who had overseen such gems as *Lady, Be Good!*, *Tip-Toes*, *Oh, Kay!*, and *Funny Face*. To make matters worse, *An American in Paris* received mostly hostile reviews.

In August 1929, two months after *Show Girl* opened, Gershwin for the first time conducted a concert work with a symphony orchestra when he led members of the Philharmonic at Lewisohn Stadium in a performance of *An American in Paris*. On the same program he appeared as soloist in *Rhapsody in Blue* under the direction of Willem van Hoogstraten, the regular conductor for the Stadium concerts and the man under whom Gershwin had first appeared there in 1927. Gershwin attracted an overflow crowd.

To prepare this conducting debut, he went to Bill Daly and Edward Kilenyi, his former teacher, for help. In individual sessions with each of them, Gershwin stood in front of a mirror conducting the work to the recording Shilkret had made for Victor. In a magazine article in 1950 Kilenyi wrote, "We spent hours in practice-conducting. I tried to give him all the practical and helpful hints I could give as a result of my experience in conducting theater orchestras. His concert was a triumph."

Three months later Gershwin conducted the same work again, this time at the Mecca Temple (now the New York City Center) with the newly formed Manhattan Symphony, which was under the direction of the American Henry Hadley. By this time Gershwin had apparently become intoxicated with conducting and decided to get into the pit for the opening performance of

Strike Up the Band. In the pit with him was an all-star jazz band led by cornetist Red Nichols, that included Benny Goodman, Glenn Miller, Jimmy Dorsey, Gene Krupa, and Jack Teagarden.

Goldberg, who was writing his biography at the time, offers this description of Gershwin's work on the show: "To watch him at rehearsals is to see with what ease he gets the most out of his men under his baton. Baton, did I say? George conducts with a baton, with his cigar, with his shoulders, with his hips, with his eyes, with what not. He sings with the principals and the chorus; he whistles; he imitates the various instruments of the orchestra; nothing but a sense of propriety . . . keeps him from leaping over the footlights and getting right into the show himself."

Obviously Gershwin loved what he was doing then. But unlike Boulez and Bernstein, who also started their conducting lives by directing their own works, he did not move into conducting other composers' works. The revised *Strike Up the Band* opened in January 1930. The stock market crash in October 1929 had devastated Ziegfeld. Now Gershwin was free to operate again on his own terms, and *Strike Up the Band*, despite the bad economy, managed to flourish. Kaufman allowed Morrie Ryskind to work on his 1927 book. George rewrote more than half of the score. In some respects the new show was a typical old-fashioned Gershwin piece with great songs and lively comedy. But it managed to retain its original purpose—the lampooning of war, big business, and politics.

This time, though, the show did not quite have the Kaufman bite. While the original had the final curtain go down on the United States preparing to go to war with Russia over caviar, the revised version has the whole plot turn into a dream. The central figure awakens; only the music remains.

While most of the songs are obvious tributes to Gilbert and Sullivan, the Gershwins add enough of their idiosyncratic touches to make the score entirely their own. They borrowed "I've Got a Crush on You" from *Treasure Girl* and added thirteen numbers to the original *Strike Up the Band* musical. Many are as good as anything Gershwin had written to that time, but because they are so intimately tied to the plot, they made little sense performed on their own.

The Warburgs gave Gershwin an opening-night party to celebrate his triumph. Vernon Duke told this story of an incident at the Warburg party: "On Tuesday, January 14, 1930, Prokofiev and I went to the *Strike Up the Band* opening and later to a midnight party in Gershwin's honor at the Warburgs, where there was no room for nostalgia but where the music was better: George didn't leave the piano until the notices—all excellent—arrived, then resumed his recital with renewed vigor. At the party Pop Gershwin distinguished himself: when Russell Crouse asked him how he liked the show, he parried with: 'What you mean how I like it? I *have* to like it.' " While many writers report it as another example of Morris Gershwin's wit, it is a hostile response by an uninformed and jealous man.

On August 28, 1930, Gershwin made his third appearance at Lewisohn Stadium. Van Hoogstraten conducted Weber, Debussy, and Tchaikovsky, as well as *Rhapsody in Blue* and the Concerto in F with Gershwin at the piano. Gershwin himself led a performance of *An American in Paris.* Again there was an overflow crowd. But that was not typical of the entertainment industry that year.

In a brochure enclosed with a 1990 recording of the Gershwins' show *Girl Crazy,* which opened on October 14, 1930, Robert Kimball describes how the collapse of Wall Street and the coming of talking pictures affected those in the theater at the end of that year, well before the depths of the Great Depression were reached:

> More than 70 percent of the 15,000 hotel rooms in the Times Square area, which catered largely to theatrical people, were unoccupied and many actors were delinquent with their rent. Close to 1,000 vaudeville actors had quit show business during the first seven months of 1930. All walked, according to *Variety,* "on account of eating."

Ballrooms and dance halls were suffering. "From the most spacious halls on Broadway to the smallest in the jerkwater road stands," reported *Variety*, "the stepping spots are limping through the worst season they have experienced since the war." New York's 405 dance halls were 105 below the previous year's.

Empty stores lined Broadway. From 42nd to 59th streets there were 54 vacant street locations on the Main Stem, an average of three empty stores per block. Real estate companies reported at least a 25 percent vacancy rate in office space in the area and rentals tumbled about 30 percent lower than they had been ten years earlier when the Broadway real estate boom began.

Some aspects of show business, however, continued to thrive. Among the performers on Broadway at the beginning of 1931 were the Astaires, Fanny Brice, Melvyn Douglas, W. C. Fields, Helen Hayes, Katharine Hepburn, Libby Holman, Eva Le Gallienne, Clifford Odets, Walter Slezak, Rudy Vallee, and Clifton Webb.

Ethel Merman and Ginger Rogers were playing in *Girl Crazy*. Neither was yet a household name. Vinton Freedley discovered Ethel Zimmerman, a secretary from Queens, singing at the Brooklyn Paramount. After she dropped the "Zim," she became an overnight star in the role of Frisco Kate. Her big moment came when, on the second chorus of "I Got Rhythm," she held a single C for sixteen bars while the band continued working around her long note. Ginger Rogers, appearing in her second Broadway role, played the postmistress of a western town.

But it was the score that made the show memorable. In addition to "I Got Rhythm," there were "Biding My Time," "Embraceable You," "Sam and Delilah," "But Not for Me," songs that made *Girl Crazy* even more exhilarating than *Lady, Be Good!*, *Tip-Toes*, *Oh, Kay!*, and *Funny Face*, all hits and all Aarons and Freedley shows.

Aware of the value of the musicians in the pit in *Strike Up the Band*, Gershwin asked Red Nichols to pull together another first-rate group for *Girl Crazy*. When the show opened at the Alvin, the line-up included Nichols on cornet, Charlie Teagarden on trumpet, Glenn Miller on trombone, Benny Goodman on clarinet and saxophone, and Gene Krupa on drums. During intermissions, these men took off on jam sessions, thrilling audiences.

Robert Russell Bennett was the prime orchestrator of the score. When he was given the assignment, he had just returned from Paris, where he had been studying with Boulanger. Apparently he was stunned to discover how the fashion in orchestration had changed. Herbert Warren Wind, in a 1951 profile of Bennett in *The New Yorker*, writes, "Beginning with such DeSylva, Brown and Henderson musical comedies as *Good News* [1927] and *Hold Everything!* [1928] the jazz band had solidly entrenched itself in the pit. It took Bennett a couple of shows to learn how to give the producers the crooning saxophone ensemble and three screaming trumpets, but after doing *Girl Crazy* he was on easy terms with the lick, rip, and break."

Before he went to work on *Girl Crazy*, though, Bennett got some help. Sudhalter writes, ". . . certain of the hotter numbers, notably 'I Got Rhythm,' seemed to cry out for an arranger who understood swing and could write comfortably in a more rhythmic vein. [Glenn] Miller, Nichols said, would be in the new band, so why not let him do some scoring as well? . . . reports persist that Miller wrote at least the rideout chorus to 'I Got Rhythm' and some of the incidental music. He received $800 for this work."

A few years before his death, Goodman talked to Loren Schoenberg, whose orchestra Goodman later took over for his last performances. Goodman said that when Gershwin heard him playing in rehearsals, he composed an interpolated clarinet solo in the overture to showcase Goodman briefly. Goodman was proud of Gershwin's attention. Sometime afterward, when Goodman left the band during the run of the show, Gershwin deleted that passage. Goodman told Schoenberg that Gershwin conducted the band throughout the opening week's performances.

As attentive as George always was to the music and the details of its performance, Ira, who could barely read music, remained oblivious to everything but his words. In *Lyrics on Several Occasions*, he writes: "I am told the hep [*sic*] pit orchestra, conducted by Red Nichols, included many instrumentalists who later became famous in the jazz world." On the same page, separated by three asterisks, there appears the following: "*Additional Notes Written about a Year Later*. As lyricist I had nothing to do with the pit orchestra except to listen and take for granted their excellence—concerned only that the playing wouldn't be too loud. (From an unfinished lyric: 'When the orchestra drowns the singers, And the singers drown the words. . . .') The musicians were usually selected—still are, I imagine—after discussions among composer, conductor, producer, and the union contractor. Recently I have been able to obtain the names of some of the *Girl Crazy* pitmen from film producer Roger Edens who was on-stage pianist for Miss Merman in the Western bar scene. Among them: Benny Goodman, Gene Krupa, Jack Teagarden, Jimmy Dorsey."

Roger Edens, Ira's informant, took over from Al Siegel, Merman's regular accompanist, when Siegel was unable to bring himself to play piano in full view of the audience.

Ira, generally meticulous with information (Louis Calhern is reported to have told an encyclopedia salesman he didn't need a set because he had Ira Gershwin as a friend) was uncharacteristically sloppy in his treatment of the *Girl Crazy* musicians. In being so cavalier about the musicians, Ira seemed to imply that the musical matters which so concerned George held no interest for him. In fact, as he wrote in his "unfinished lyric," George's music could be used to drown out his words.

The book for the show, written by Bolton and McGowan, centered on a rich New Yorker whose father sends him to a sleepy western town because he is disgusted with his son's lusting after girls. Again, this Aarons and Freedley show picks up where their others left off in reflecting some aspects of George's own life. While earlier shows had him focused on Mabel or Kay, this one had him "girl crazy." Still, the girl that the boy marries is the postmistress, who is named Molly. This gives weight to the notion that in 1930, Molly, i.e., Charleston, remained an important part of Gershwin's life.

One of Alan Gershwin's earliest memories, when he was four, is going to *Girl Crazy* on opening night and meeting Ethel Merman backstage after the show. It is understandable that his father wanted him to go to this show. The flimsy story would not challenge the boy. The color, the dancing, Merman's high C, and the Red Nichols band playing in the pit would entice his eyes and ears. Most important, the boy would have the chance to hear a score by his father that George must have known was superb.

At the end of 1930, when this show was enjoying its first success, Kay Swift was still the most visible woman in George's life. In a 1987 interview, she said she knew George was going out a lot with showgirls but insisted this did not upset her because she knew they meant nothing to him. More than fifty years after the fact, Swift seems to be censoring her memories. Not only did she know about his closeness to Julia Van Norman but she also knew of a beautiful rival fifteen years younger than she.

Rosamond Walling first met Gershwin when she was seven and attended the wedding of her cousin Emily Strunsky to Lou Paley. She says she was smitten with Emily's brother, English, and hardly noticed Gershwin. But over the years a friendship developed and, in 1928, she joined the Paleys to greet the Gershwins on their return from Europe. George brought two presents for her, a cigarette case in black and white with an eggshell inlay in a cubist design, and a bracelet with emeralds, rubies, and pearls set in old gold. A Swift relative says Gershwin gave Kay costly gifts. But Mueller, the valet, insists it was Kay who gave George presents regularly.

Ann Ronell recalls being in the Gershwin house one day when Leonore brought her into George's room to show her a monogrammed sterling silver comb and brush set. Leonore told her she should stay away from George because she obviously could never afford to give him gifts like this.

Rosamond Walling talked to Robert Kimball for his 1973 book, *The Gershwins.* She told him she was at Lewisohn Stadium the evening in 1929 when Gershwin made his first appearance as conductor of a major orchestra. She also was at the concert at

Carnegie Hall where *An American in Paris* received its premiere. But as with all the other women, nothing permanent materialized: "George's idea of marriage," she said, "held no charm for me. 'Let's have four children to begin with,' George would say, 'and bring them up in the country. Greenwich, if you like. You can teach them to ride. We'll get six horses to start with.'

"This absolutely lacked charm for me: I hoped never to see Westchester County again, and I didn't get around to wanting children for a good ten years."

Despite Gershwin's perfunctory approach to marriage, Walling considered it for some time.

"I nearly married him," she continued, "when he moved to 33 Riverside Drive, because he said we could have the downstairs apartment and we'd make an inside staircase; so I would have privacy and could paint. It was a temptation. But I did not approve of the decorating job in the end. Too finished for me."

The decorating job had been done by Swift in an art deco mode. Kay did a great deal for George, yet during the period that she was helping him in so many ways, he was courting Rosamond Walling and a number of other women.

But Kay received favors from George, too. It was shortly after their affair began that she started to carve out a music-theater career of her own. In 1927, when she was thirty-two, Swift took a job as rehearsal pianist for Rodgers and Hart's *Connecticut Yankee*. Considering that George got Margaret Manners a job in George White's *Scandals* and Ann Ronell a job working in *Rosalie*, it is probable that it was he who arranged for her to get the post she did in *Connecticut Yankee*.

Two years later—after participating in a revue that opened and quickly closed in the Bronx—Swift wrote "Can't We Be Friends?" Libby Holman sang it in a Broadway revue, then recorded it. In "A New Leaf," a short story by F. Scott Fitzgerald that appeared in the July 4, 1931, issue of the *Saturday Evening Post*, Dick Ragland asks Julie to sing it, then sing it again. She says she will sing it all afternoon. The song had moved into the world of popular culture.

In 1930 Swift wrote the score to *Fine and Dandy*, a show that opened on September 23 at the Erlanger Theatre and became a hit. It contained the romantic ballad, "Can This Be Love?" This may have been the first Broadway show ever composed by a woman.

In her conversations about Gershwin, Kay Swift was discreet and unrevealing. Yet the relationship, which lasted from 1926 to 1936, played a crucial role in Gershwin's life. No other woman competed with her for this central position. That is why a story Ben Bagley, a theatrical producer, told in a telephone conversation in 1990 demands attention. According to Bagley,

"I met Fannie Hurst [the novelist] in the late 1950s. She was living at the [Hotel] Des Artistes and was being very amusing one evening at dinner. 'We had a musical theater giant, here,' she said. 'One summer George Gershwin and Kay Swift had sublet someone's apartment in the building. She would tie him up, then hang him from the ceiling and whip him. The windows were open because there was no air conditioning at the time. Everyone in the building complained at the terrible sounds coming from their place. A tenant's committee got together and saw that they were put out.' "

Fannie Hurst was quite capable of imagining such intriguing scenarios. Still, there was enough of the masochist in George, with his attraction to powerful, denying men and women, to suggest there may be some element of truth in what Fannie Hurst is reported to have said.

One of the hits of *Girl Crazy* is "Treat Me Rough," sung by Danny Churchill, the playboy from New York, who tells the woman:

> I'm no innocent child, baby;
> Make me wooly and wild . . .

Ira's lyric echoes a poem written by Kay's husband, "And Then What?"

> Hit her over the head with a hammer
> Lay her to rest with a wreath,

Do as you like with her bones,
God damn her,
For she got lipstick on her teeth.

While one smiles at the Dorothy Parker tone, and is tempted to think it a one-shot joke, another lyric Warburg wrote which Kay set in a torch song, "Nobody Breaks My Heart," suggests sadomasochism was on the Warburgs' minds:

I'd like to be bruised,
Beaten down and badly used. . . .

One person in George's orbit who was neither powerful nor cruel was his sister Frankie. A photograph of her brother hangs in her East Side apartment with the inscription: "To Frankie, who is a darling." Frankie endured the same mistreatment by her parents that George did. According to Marc Gershwin, Arthur's son, "Rose didn't like Frankie at all. She preferred her sons. When Frankie wanted to marry Leo, he wasn't doing anything and Rose was against it because he had no money. Still, the Godowskys looked down on the Gershwins. From their point of view, nobody in the family had any background."

Marc emphasizes that Frankie was really the first of the children to try show business. Rose was transporting her around as a singer and dancer when she was a child.

After a courtship of little more than two years, Frankie and Leopold Godowsky married. The wedding took place two weeks after *Girl Crazy* opened and just before the Gershwin brothers left for Hollywood with Leonore. They were going to produce a score for their first feature film.

In recalling the wedding for author Robert Kimball, Frankie said her parents were scheduled to leave for Florida for the winter on November 2 and that George and Ira had planned to go to California almost immediately after that.

The wedding was very different from Ira and Leonore's. It confirms Marc Gershwin's remarks that Frankie was held in low esteem by her parents. Here is Frankie's description in Kimball's book:

"Leo came back from Europe the night of November 1, and when he heard everyone was leaving, he said, 'Look, let's get married tomorrow.' I said, 'That's impossible. My parents are leaving. My brothers are leaving. It just can't be done.' "

It was precisely because everyone was leaving and would be gone from New York for months that her fiancé insisted it be done right away. He said he did not want it to seem, particularly because of Rose's negative attitude, that they did this behind anybody's back. So he made all the arrangements overnight, even locating a rabbi in the Yellow Pages who said yes as soon as he heard the Gershwin name.

"I was scared to tell my mother," Frankie went on, "because she blamed her asthma a great deal on the fact I was going with Leo. Anyway, we went up to the apartment and told her, and there was really nothing she could do about it, as it was all arranged." Obviously Leopold Godowsky, Jr., had strength and power on his own and was capable of combatting Rose.

"Then George came in. He walked from his penthouse roof into Ira's with a big cigar in his mouth and his pajamas and robe on. A little later these French doors opened and in walked this rabbi whom nobody knew—he had gone through George's apartment by mistake.

"By this time my father had his watch in his hand and he said, 'We've got to leave here, Rose, in a little while.' He was so concerned about missing their train. Kay Swift had sent my mother flowers, so she pinned them on me because I had no flowers. And George played the wedding march with his big cigar in his mouth. And the rabbi quickly started talking about harmony and rhythm, trying to use all the musical terms he could think of.

"My father kept standing there with the watch in his hand, worrying about the train. When the ceremony was over we all rushed out of Ira and Lee's apartment to see them off. Everybody was in such a panic about that train."

Many people have described the Gershwin household to biographers as gemütlich. They generally speak of what a darling Papa Gershwin was. Frankie's detailed description of her wedding day gives the lie to that. It reveals the older Gershwins as so involved with their own interests that they could not put them in perspective on the most important day of their daughter's life.

Fortunately George saved the day for his sister. Bert Taylor, Gertrude Lawrence's lover, gave a farewell party for George and Ira, and Frankie says "the party became almost like a wedding reception for us because George went around saying 'What do you think? My sister just got married.' "

George and Ira signed a contract with Fox studios in April 1930 to write a score for a movie. They agreed to go to Hollywood after *Girl Crazy* opened. The film, *Delicious*, featured Janet Gaynor and Charles Farrell, two major stars. The contract guaranteed $100,000—$70,000 for George and $30,000 for Ira.

This was a monumental sum for those days. George and Ira were not alone among composers and lyricists trying their luck on the West Coast. As Broadway became riskier, Hollywood looked like the answer to their dreams. George told his family and friends he was doing this to earn enough money so he could take the time to compose serious works. Everyone knew what Los Angeles was then; S. J. Perelman described the city in the 1930s as "a dreary industrial town controlled by hoodlums of enormous wealth."

Sound movies had begun to emerge in 1927 with Jolson's *The Jazz Singer*. In 1929 and again in 1930, Hollywood came out with at least seventy-five musicals. But overnight the bloom was off. In 1931, fewer than ten musicals appeared. The Gershwins' timing was exactly right. They came away with a great deal of money for what turned out to be very little work. Arriving in mid-November, they moved into a lavish, Spanish-style house that had belonged to Greta Garbo and still contained her furnishings. In a letter to Goldberg, Gershwin quipped that sleeping in her bed did not contribute to peaceful nights for him.

Most of the music for *Delicious* was composed before he left New York, but an extended sequence was composed by Gershwin while he was the guest of Aileen Pringle, a silent movie actress, in Santa Monica. This music was designed to accompany a sequence in which Janet Gaynor runs wildly through the streets of New York. Over the score there are street noises that include everything from the shouts of passersby to the hammering of rivets. In the script his piece was called "Manhattan Rhapsody." In the production list the title was "Rhapsody in Rivets." Gershwin finished his work by the end of January. Later he gave Pringle an inscribed photograph. It read: "For Pringie—this easterner will always look West with swell thoughts of you. George. February 22, 1931." Next to his signature, Gershwin drew the musical notation for the letter G. To this he added some notes from the score he had composed for the movie.

Gershwin enjoyed himself in Hollywood. He played golf, visited friends, went to a party given by producer Joseph Schenck in Agua Caliente, Mexico, where he saw a performance by Edward Cansino and his daughter, who later became Rita Hayworth. Gershwin also attended a performance of *An American in Paris* conducted by Artur Rodzinski with the Los Angeles Philharmonic. Unlike most of his European colleagues, Rodzinski believed in showing off American talent.

Gershwin also revived his friendship with George Pallay, a cousin of Lou Paley. In 1991 Laura Pallay, then ninety-five years old, talked of her memories of the friendship between her brother George and Gershwin. The Abramsons (the Pallay family name before it was changed) had lived first in Harlem and later at 113th Street and Lexington Avenue. Laura Pallay recalls Gershwin coming to their house after he was famous and playing for them on their old upright piano. Laura says George "was really crazy about our mother, Rose, who was a modern woman but pickled herring and had a Yiddish accent." A good reason, then, to visit the Pallay family, for this Rose evoked his own mother with her name, her pickled herring, and Yiddish accent. Aunt Kate Wolpin says that her sister, Rose Gershwin, always claimed that she was her son's inspiration, and there may be truth in that.

Pallay, who had been married twice, was living alone in California. He and Gershwin and their dates spent time together in

Palm Springs. After the Gershwin brothers returned to New York, Pallay sent Ira an item from *Time* magazine about a song, "Month of Maybe," that Ira had written in collaboration with Harry Warren and Billy Rose. It was presented in *Crazy Quilt*, a Billy Rose review.

In his reply to Pallay, Ira informed him that the gross earnings for *Crazy Quilt* that week were $20,692.50, that his share of the royalty on that one song was $9.20, that he and Leonore lived very frugally, which meant that, on this particular week, they managed to get by on $6.90, leaving them with $2.30. This last amount, Ira explained, they added to the $42.50 they had with the First National Bank. Ira wrote that this money was a "sacred fund" set up for "Junior's education," and cited several institutions of higher learning he hoped their not-yet-conceived son would attend.

Ira's letter goes on to record that the week had, in fact, been especially good because in addition to the money he received from the song, he gambled $.75 a hole on a golf game and "actually *won* six holes." This meant, Ira noted, that he and Leonore could treat themselves to dinner at Nicolas' Lobster Palace where they had "everything from bread and butter to coffee."

People often describe Ira as a pixie. This is the word actually used by friends. What the letter to Pallay reveals is a man virtually pathological when it came to money. (His friends, incidentally, all remark on how stingy he was.) Ira seems, in this letter, not to have counted the $30,000 he received for his work on *Delicious* as income. It probably went immediately into savings. In fact, Judy Gershwin says that when the Crash came, George had no money invested, that it was Ira who lost savings. By this time George was investing what he had in paintings. The letter also suggests that Ira wanted to have a child and that, in 1931, he had fantasies of educating him at Oxford, Yale, or Cornell. Kate Wolpin confirms this. She says Lee could not become pregnant and went to Berlin before World War II to consult a doctor there to help her conceive. But to no avail. Like her sister, Emily, she remained childless.

Ira's attitude toward money and the couple's inability to have a child may explain why he allowed his brother's son, Alan, to grow up in near poverty. There is absolutely no evidence that the other Gershwin children, Arthur or Frankie, knew about Alan's existence until he asserted his claim in an article that appeared in 1959 in *Confidential* magazine, a forerunner of today's supermarket sleaze weeklies. In a conversation with *Confidential*, Alan said that the Schneiders had no children of their own. This leaves the identities of the three other children in the Schneider household open to question.

On October 28, 1929, Koussevitzky sent Gershwin a letter he typed himself. It was full of typographical errors and contained a misspelling of a name: "I have seen Mr. Doukelsky [Vernon Duke] who has told me of your wish that I should give performances to some of your compositions. I will gladly do it, but, first of all, may I ask you to compose a piece special for the Boston Orchestra? Next season is the 50th anniversary of the Boston Symphony Orchestra and we would very much appreciate it if you would write a piece for the occasion. I would be pleased to hear from you soon and to know if it suits you." No fee was mentioned, but that probably didn't bother Gershwin. His acceptance of less than $1,000 for an opera that would take him two years to compose testifies to the high value he placed on the opportunity to compose art music.

Yet what he gave Koussevitzky for this important occasion was a piece recycled from a Hollywood score. Gershwin went to work extending the sequence he wrote to accompany Janet Gaynor running through city streets and spent much effort on its orchestration. In May he wrote Pallay he had finished fifty-five pages and expected to be through within a week. "I have an idea," he added, "it is going to sound very good, as I made quite a rich orchestration." On June 11 he wrote again to Pallay: "About the new Rhapsody's title, the reason I have soured on 'Rivets' is that it gives the listener a mental picture before the piece starts that I don't believe the piece carries out. The title may be all right for the picture—where four or five minutes of the concentrated rhythm parts would be used, but—for concert purposes—I think the abstract title 'Second Rhapsody' (while, perhaps, not a very exciting title) would be less confusing." On June 26 Gershwin had at his disposal a studio at NBC and hired fifty-five musicians to read through the score. A recording was made of this reading. Gershwin's interpretation of his work is brisk, angular, characteristically unsentimental, and marked by idiosyncratic accentuations.

To Rosamond Walling he wrote: "It sounded better than I thought it would." To Isaac Goldberg: "My orchestration of the new *Rhapsody* was gratifying. In many respects, such as orchestration and form, it is the best thing I've written."

The critical attacks on his absence of technique and for not doing all his own orchestration had moved him to concentrate heavily on refining those skills. Koussevitzky conducted the work, called *Second Rhapsody*, in Boston's Symphony Hall on January 29, 1932. Just the fact that its composer called the work what he did suggests that nobody knew better than he did that it derived from his first rhapsody and that what was new was an orchestration that the most sophisticated musicians and composers could admire.

He was asserting that he no longer needed a Ferde Grofé to orchestrate rhapsodies for him. The piece did manifest a big advance in his skills. It reveals the influence of Poulenc, one of Les Six, as well as an absorption of Stravinskian rhythms. With this work he was saying to Copland and all the other serious composers—many of whom had also been commissioned by Koussevitzky to write scores for the Boston orchestra's anniversary year—that he was one of them.

Michael Tilson Thomas recorded the *Second Rhapsody* in 1985. In his notes he says he believes the work is stunning in its complex craftsmanship. But for many listeners the melodic inspiration is not there. The sophisticated smooth edges do not compensate for the absence of the melodic and rhythmic inspiration that characterized his first three concert works. The earlier pieces are not only seductive on first hearing; we know they have had more than half a century to prove a staying power usually associated with the "classics." Gershwin is not unique in producing his most popular works when he was young. For many listeners, nothing Stravinsky composed after 1913 can compete with *Firebird*, *Petrouchka*, and *The Rite of Spring*.

In 1990, the widow of Vladimir Selinsky, one of the violinists in the *Girl Crazy* orchestra, repeated a story she had heard from her husband: One day, during rehearsals, it was felt that some music was needed to accompany Willie Howard and another actor as they moved furniture across the stage. According to Selinsky, Gershwin, sitting there in the theater, came up within minutes with "Biding My Time."

Dick Hyman, jazz pianist, composer and conductor, agrees that there is no stagnation in the songwriting. He says, "I keep being amazed at *Strike Up the Band* and the new *Girl Crazy* recording. I am constantly astonished by Gershwin's invention. He knew the rules of the game and then stretched those rules through incredible melodic and rhythmic means."

If, in the 1930s, Gershwin sought physical abuse, it doesn't seem to have satisfied him, because he also managed to gather around him people distinguished for their aggression and hostility. One was Oscar Levant. In a memoir, William Targ, who published two of Levant's books, writes that in a long and active life he had never met anyone as cruel as Levant.

According to Levant's own reminiscences, he first encountered the composer when Gershwin was accompanying the singer Nora Bayes in some material from *Ladies First*. Levant was twelve, and Gershwin was nineteen. In *A Smattering of Ignorance* Levant writes, "I had never heard such fresh, brisk, unstudied, completely free and inventive playing—all within a consistent frame that set off her singing perfectly." After this Levant writes, "Thus were established the two characteristics I have nurtured ever since as the dominating influences of my life—jealousy and revenge." Because Levant's self-denigrating remarks were delivered as a sardonic locution, they sound as though he was kidding. He was not.

Levant says his next contact with Gershwin was when the composer was at work on the Concerto in F in his 110th Street apartment. Someone had arranged an introduction. Levant writes that when he arrived, the composer was at work on the first movement with Bill Daly at his side. With this remark Levant fed into the rumors that the work was more a collaborative effort than Gershwin ever acknowledged it to be. This sentence probably antagonized Ira, who was very defensive about such charges. In *Memoirs of an Amnesiac* Levant writes, "Lawrence Stewart and Edward Jablonski wrote a book called *The Gershwin Years* [1958]. This biography was so controlled that they read me out of it. I was the Trotsky of the Gershwin menage." In describing the meeting on 110th Street, Levant writes, "I was bristling with inarticulateness and stammered some graceless remark. George mistook my confusion and admiration for disapproval, which in turn made him involuntarily hostile. In addition to the work itself, his swift and mettlesome piano playing had so stimulated and excited me that the old dormant envy was reborn."

Al Hirschfeld remembers that in the 1920s, at a place called the Club Duvé on Waverly Place and Sixth Avenue, one flight above Dave's Delicatessen, "there was a young kid playing piano. It was Levant. I used to go there all the time and then told Howard Dietz and George. We all went over to listen to him. George was impressed right away and thought Oscar was the best interpreter of his music he had heard." Hirschfeld believes this was the first time Levant and Gershwin had met. It is possible the composer had forgotten the earlier meeting, when Levant walked in on him and Daly working on the concerto.

It seems that in the 1920s Gershwin was self-protective enough not to go out of his way to welcome an abusive man into his life. For it is obvious that Levant had been doing what he could to get close to him. In his first book Levant writes that through the 1920s, whenever he heard a new song by Gershwin, he would think to himself: "Are our relations to remain forever on the Tchaikovsky–Frau von Meck plane," a plane that kept idolizer and composer apart.

In 1931 Leonore Gershwin brought that barrier down. Levant had written a musical called *Ripples* with Albert Sirmay, who happened to be Gershwin's own music editor. It was playing at a theater close to the Selwyn, which housed the Gershwins' *Strike Up the Band.* Levant wrote:

> As quickly as the score of *Ripples* palled on my audience, it palled on me more. Hypnotically, I would find myself at the rear of the Selwyn, resentfully transported by the fresh rhythms and humors of the Gershwin lyrics and music.
>
> Ironically it was just as I had my first musical show produced that George emerged with a wholly new concept of musical comedy writing. Up until this time his librettos had not encouraged any departure from the cliché of boy-meets-girl songs. For the first time he was provided by George S. Kaufman and Morrie Ryskind with a book whose wry, satiric wit illuminated a new facet of Gershwin's talent.
>
> While in the spell of this discovery one afternoon, I was tapped on the shoulder by a wraith-like figure asking, "How is the show doing?"
>
> This unmalicious intended query returned me to the banality of my own enterprise. At the conclusion of the act, I, in turn, invited the shadowy inquirer to partake of my Jello-like score, having discovered that she was Leonore Gershwin, Ira's wife, whom I had met once before.
>
> After she had seen a few numbers of *Ripples*, she developed in me a scorn for my own music almost equal to hers. . . . Like a missionary after office hours she led me back, symbolically, to the Selwyn, where I remained in spirit for the next nine or ten years.
>
> She suggested that perhaps I would like to spend the evening with George and Ira, and I escorted her back to the apartment house on Riverside Drive. . . . From the first day's supper I worked up to having four and five meals a day with the Gershwins, eating my way through the composition of the music and lyrics for *Delicious* and *Girl Crazy*.

Levant stayed close to Gershwin until Gershwin died, but there is nothing to suggest that Gershwin's feeling for Levant was as strong as it was toward Daly or Pallay. Kay Swift says that if Levant had left, she does not believe anyone would have called him back. But Levant's cruelty was not all that he offered Gershwin. For one thing he played Gershwin's music to the exclusion of anyone else's. For another, he was genuinely funny. Biographers owe him a debt of gratitude, too, for in one of his books, he writes that Gershwin treasured the piano score of Berg's *Wozzeck* and was deeply impressed by the Berg opera when he traveled to Philadelphia for its first American performance, which was conducted by Stokowski.

Levant also does a service when he lists Gershwin's favorite recordings: Stravinsky's *Symphony of Psalms*, Shostakovich's Symphony no. 1, Milhaud's violin concerto, Berg's *Lyric Suite*, Schoenberg's complete string quartets recorded by the Kolisch group, Honegger's Les aventures du Roi Pausole, and Duke Ellington's recordings of his own "Creole Love Song," "Swanee Rhapsody," and "Daybreak Express." Levant also notes what Gershwin studied in score: Stravinsky's *Les noces*, Prokofiev's Piano Concerto no. 3, Debussy's piano preludes, and various orchestral works by Ravel. Gershwin's Concerto in F predated Ravel's piano concerto. The influence, then, is from Gershwin to Ravel, not the other way around.

The apartment to which Levant escorted Leonore was situated at 33 Riverside Drive at Seventy-fifth Street. George and the Ira Gershwins both moved into their apartments in the building in June 1929. Both apartments had terraces. George's Penthouse C had a breathtaking view of the Hudson River and the Palisades. Ira's 17-F faced east toward the buildings and traffic of West End Avenue and Broadway.

Rose and Morris Gershwin spent winters in Florida and summers in upstate New York. The family sold the house on 103d Street on September 23, 1931. During the time George was on Riverside and Seventy-fifth, Margaret Manners moved from the

Mayflower Hotel on Central Park West and Sixty-first Street to 164 West Seventy-fourth Street, almost around the corner from George. This suggests she tried to keep him close to her, at least geographically. She would frequently pick up their son at her sister's Brooklyn apartment and bring him to see his father.

According to Paul Mueller, Gershwin's valet,

> I saw Alan's mother come to the apartment, always with the little boy. Naturally she and Gershwin closed the door and talked and what they said I did not hear. But there was never any question in my mind that he was Gershwin's child.
>
> But there was something more that happened that made me have a big dislike for the man. There was a girl who seemed to me about seventeen or eighteen years old. She used to come to the apartment the back way, up the back elevator. She was so persistent. She was crazy in love with him.
>
> She would come—it was several times—and go into his bedroom. Whatever happened there I do not know. But what disturbed me most was that this girl got so crazy when he didn't want to see her anymore. She would stay at the front door downstairs waiting for him to come home. When it was clear to her he didn't want anything more of her she went back to Broadway and what she did there gave her syphilis. Then she came back again and finally jumped out of the window.
>
> Gershwin was always surrounded by chorus girls. He used to pat their behinds. I remember one incident a few years later, when we were in Charleston, South Carolina. He was invited to a party. We went and he did the same thing there. He did to a Charleston woman what he was always doing to the chorus girls on Broadway. But they didn't object to it and she did. She just turned around and walked out of the room.

When asked how Gershwin reacted to this rebuff, Mueller said that his employer never showed any emotion during the eight years he worked for him. In 1931, George's letters to George Pallay confirm what Mueller observed: that Gershwin was a womanizer who seemed incapable of reacting in what Mueller considered an appropriate way even when an emotional crisis occurred. In one of the letters Gershwin wrote about the death of the young girl to whom Mueller referred: "I don't know whether you've read in the papers the very sad item concerning our little friend Grace Brown. A few days ago she jumped out of the window of . . . Riverside Drive after a misunderstanding with her mother. I was terribly shocked to hear it. Poor kid! I wonder why she did it."

While George and Ira were in Hollywood working on the film score for *Delicious*, they wrote "The Illegitimate Daughter" for *Of Thee I Sing*. It was the first song they composed for that political musical.

The libretto for the show was by Kaufman and Ryskind. It parodies politics and love. When a group of politicians huddle in a hotel room looking for a campaign theme, a chambermaid tells them that, as far as she is concerned, next to money, love is the most important thing in life.

They devise a plan. Announcing that the winner of a beauty contest—who turns out to be Diana Devereux—will have as a prize a marriage to the next president of the United States, the story begins to unfold. The candidate subverts his colleagues' plans when he falls in love with Mary Turner, his secretary, whose greatest asset is the quality of the corn muffins she bakes. The conflict comes when the winner of the contest is discovered to be the illegitimate daughter of the illegitimate son of the illegitimate nephew of Napoleon, in other words an illegitimate child with an impressive lineage.

One would think that this was so central to the plot that it was Kaufman's or Ryskind's idea to make the winner illegitimate. But that turns out not to be so. It was Ira Gershwin's. Here he is on the subject in *Lyrics on Several Occasions:*

> *Genesis of the Illegitimacy*. When we went to California for the film *Delicious* we had already had several discussions with Kaufman and Ryskind on *Of Thee I Sing*, which they were developing. Just before we made the trip they were able to give us a fourteen page outline of the libretto. In Hollywood

> between hours on the film we found time to do some work on the operetta and returned to New York with at least two notions in good shape. One was the anthemy campaign title song (later we changed it somewhat); the other was "The Illegitimate Daughter," as is.
>
> Excerpt from page 11 of the scenario: Throttlebottom also brings out the fact that there is a new angle to the Joan Devereux matter [Kaufman and Ryskind later changed her name to Diana.] It turns out that she had a French father, so the French government is up in arms about the slight that has been inflicted on her.
>
> Joan had to be born in the United States, otherwise couldn't have entered the contest for Mrs. First Lady. Obviously, though, it was far more important to musicalize a French father for her. Should he be a baker in Lyons, or the prefect of police in Dijon, or what? More and more I kept thinking that his political or economic or social importance had to be important, else why France's fuss? Not wishing to use the names of any contemporary personages, I went historical. And, illegitimacy being not too socially disadvantageous among many broadminded Europeans, I scribbled the possible genealogy for her on the margin of page 11: She was an illegitimate daughter of an ill. nephew of Louis-Philippe (or Napoleon) so you can't inflict this indignity.

In an August 1991 letter, Nancy Bloomer Deussen, Julia Van Norman's daughter, repeated her belief that she is George Gershwin's child. In 1931, when she was born, Gershwin stopped all communication with Julia. When he resumed the connection, more than a year later, it was only because Horace Van Norman had written to him, begging him to come back into Julia's life, explaining that his wife seemed to be dying of despair. Van Norman, according to his own account, promised that any reinvolvement with Julia would never result in embarrassment for Gershwin. Whether or not Nancy is George's child is not the point; Gershwin may have considered it at least a possibility.

Only weeks after Nancy's birth Ira wrote "The Illegitimate Daughter." It followed his pattern of taking something deadly serious in his brother's life and deflecting it with wit and irreverence.

Another example of Ira's affinity for parodying something of importance to someone other than himself was his tacking onto the last line of "America," a song that in the United States almost has the status of a national anthem, the word "baby," so that it went ". . . of thee I sing, baby." Kaufman objected to this, insisting that the word "baby" not appear anywhere in the title song. They compromised; the lyric kept the word, but it was dropped from the title. The show opened December 26, 1931, and ran 441 performances. Kaufman directed. Charles Previn, who had conducted *La La Lucille*, Gershwin's first show, was in the pit. The cast included Victor Moore, William Gaxton, Lois Moran, George Murphy, and Grace Brinkley.

This was an entirely new experience for the Gershwins: coming out with a winner—without Aarons and Freedley, Bill Daly, Gertrude Lawrence or the Astaires. During the 1931–32 season, other shows on Broadway included Eugene O'Neill's *Mourning Becomes Electra*, Philip Barry's *The Animal Kingdom*, Maxwell Anderson's *Night over Taos*, S. N. Behrman's *Brief Moment*, Robert Sherwood's *Reunion in Vienna*, and Elmer Rice's *Counselor at Law*. Despite this impressive competition, anthologists Burns Mantle and John Gassner wrote: ". . . not one of these American dramas was as devastatingly complete a revelation of the American scene as *Of Thee I Sing*."

Gershwin invited friends to the rehearsals. Although this came on the heels of Grace Brown's death, the act of writing a fresh Broadway show and showing it off at the piano when he went to parties seemed to put things in perspective for him. Later, on a radio show, Gershwin said *Of Thee I Sing* "was one of those rare shows in which everything clicked just right. After the opening there was little or no 'fixing' to do. . . . it is one show that I am more proud of than any I have written."

Kaufman, a cynical man, tended to ridicule George—and almost everybody else. Angry at his inviting people to attend working rehearsals, he said one day, "This show is going to be a flop." Aghast, Gershwin asked why. "Because the balcony was only half-filled today." Again when hearing that Gershwin played some of the material at a party, he quipped, "If you play that score one more time before we open, people are going to think we are doing a revival." But when he and his two colleagues—Ryskind and Ira—won the Pulitzer Prize for the show, the first musical to be so honored, the prize committee excluded George, stating that it did not believe music should be included in the award. Many years later, Ira told historian Robert Kimball that the exclusion angered George, but he said little about it.

Gershwin's letters to Pallay, when he was transforming the sequence from *Delicious* into his *Second Rhapsody*, conveyed his pleasure from composing. But the composer became depressed after the January 1932 performance conducted by Koussevitzky, particularly after Downes's review in the *Times* in which he wrote that "the 'Second Rhapsody' is imitative in many ways of 'The Rhapsody in Blue,' " cited those instances, and made the claim that the work was "too long for its material." Mueller, who served him breakfast as he was reading the notices, remarked that "he was not at all pleased and felt that they were not quite right."

Harold Arlen has been quoted as saying that once, while he and Gershwin were taking a walk, Gershwin stopped and "kept complaining, 'What do they want me to do? What are they criticizing me for?' " Arlen dated this conversation sometime in the early 1930s.

The critics, the academics, and the European conductors continued to treat Gershwin with something bordering on contempt. Early in 1932 Gershwin came face to face with Toscanini, probably the most feared and respected of all the foreign conductors of the time. The occasion was an evening when the Chotzinoffs tried to do Gershwin a favor. They invited Toscanini to dinner and asked Gershwin to join them afterward. They hoped that the meeting would result in Toscanini's decision to commission or program a Gershwin work.

Gershwin did not come alone; he probably was too frightened. Instead he appeared with an entourage including Oscar Levant. If Toscanini was offended at this breach of etiquette, he retaliated effectively by telling the composer he had never heard a performance of any of his works. Gershwin and Levant sat down and played two piano arrangements of both rhapsodies.

But to no avail. Toscanini never programmed a single Gershwin work during the composer's lifetime, and the next American piece he conducted was one by Gershwin's childhood acquaintance Abram Chasins. Gershwin attended that concert with Levant and sat directly behind Chasins.

In mid-February Gershwin went to Cuba with several male friends for a holiday. They spent their days golfing and at the racetrack. At night they went to clubs with women. One of the group was Bennett Cerf, the publisher; both he and George were interested in the same woman.

Gershwin seemed never to pursue any woman who was not being courted by another man. Still, during this period, the connection with Kay Swift was as intense as at any time since they had met. Emil Mosbacher, another friend who joined them for a few days in Cuba, apparently knew Gershwin well. The composer used to visit him at his Westchester estate where George, according to his host's recollections, would compose in his "teahouse" seven hours each day. "Kay would often come up to visit him when he was working," Mosbacher has said. "George had such great admiration for her, and they both talked to me about marriage—separately, mind you—and I had one answer to both of them. I said I wasn't going to open my mouth. I wasn't that crazy. From George I'd get it every day. He was nuts about her. . . . She used to work day and night to help George with his orchestrations." This remark adds Swift to the list of those people—Will Vodery, Edward Kilenyi, and Bill Daly—who helped Gershwin with his orchestrations. This was a sensitive area for him.

In 1932 Kay was still living with her husband and three children, but George was not suggesting that she leave them. In place of a serious proposal of marriage, he dedicated his 1932 *Songbook* to her. Published by Simon & Schuster, the volume included the sheet music arrangements of Gershwin's favorites among his songs and followed them with his own transcriptions, which he had honed by playing them wherever he found a piano. The songs were "Swanee," "Nobody But You," "I'll Build a Stairway to Paradise," "Do It Again," "Fascinating Rhythm," "Lady, Be Good," "Somebody Loves Me," "Sweet and Low Down," "That Certain Feeling," "The Man I Love," "Clap Yo' Hands," "Do, Do, Do," "My One and Only," " 'S Wonderful," "Strike Up the Band," "I Got Rhythm," and "Who Cares?" The last, from *Of Thee I Sing*, was one of the few songs from the show that could live out of its context.

The *Songbook* also included the first publication of "Mischa, Yascha, Toscha, Sascha," a spoof on the Russian violinists populating the concert scene in New York. The brothers had composed it in their younger days to entertain friends at parties. The dedication to Kay said nothing about his feelings or his debt to her.

In an introduction to the *Songbook*, Gershwin wrote that radio and records had so shortened the life of a song that he agreed to Simon & Schuster's request for this book in the hope that the publication of the songs might be a "means of prolonging their life." Gershwin credits some predecessors, including Luckey Roberts, for his own piano style. He also offers some tips to pianists approaching this music: ". . . our popular music asks for staccato effects, for an almost stenciled style. The rhythms of American popular music are more or less brittle; they should be made to snap and crackle. The more sharply the music is played, the more effective it sounds. . . .

"Most pianists with classical training fail lamentably in the playing of our ragtime or jazz because they use the pedaling of Chopin when interpreting the blues of Handy. The romantic touch is very good in a sentimental ballad, but in a tune of strict tempo it is somewhat out of place."

Initially Goldberg had ghostwritten an introduction for him. But Gershwin turned it down and wrote his own, explaining that the style did not sound like his.

Two weeks after the book's publication, Morris Gershwin died. After the sale of the house, he and Rose had been living in a suite at the Broadmoor Hotel on upper Broadway. Rose had always let Morris know that she did not like short, squat men like him. On his deathbed he told his wife he knew she would marry again and that her next husband would be a tall man.

Mueller says he saw no evidence of Gershwin suffering over his father's death. This does not mean he did not. Rather it suggests that Gershwin put all of his "feelings"—whether romantic love, sexual passion, or despair—into music, not words.

Kaufman and Ryskind disliked Gershwin for the same reasons John O'Hara did: he pushed himself relentlessly into the spotlight and acted cocky. On the opening night of their show, after the applause had died down, Gershwin walked to center stage and addressed the audience. He described in detail the incident in his teens when he botched the job as accompanist to a comedian at the Fox Theater on Fourteenth Street. Gershwin ended the story saying he had walked out without collecting his day's pay. "I got that," he went on, "about twelve years later. The Fox Company sent me to write the music for a picture and it was agreed that I was to receive a hundred thousand dollars. When it came time for signing the contract, I changed the figure to read $100,003.13 and when eyebrows were raised I told the story. 'You see, I've got an eighth of a week's salary coming on the basis of twenty-five a week,' I remarked, and the revised figure was solemnly agreed to."

The speech could not have delighted Ira, who had received $30,000 of the $100,000. It could not have pleased Kaufman or Ryskind to see the composer of their show behave as though he were its only author and talk of its success as it related only to himself. It surely offended the Pulitzer committee, who found comedians, vaudeville, and hundred-thousand-dollar fees alien to their notion of art. Unfailingly insensitive to the feelings of others, Gershwin knew what mattered most to him, that *Of Thee*

I Sing was a show capable of playing to capacity houses for the first twenty-eight weeks of its run and grossing, in the end, more than $1,400,000.

But along with this kind of arrogance came the most overwhelming self-doubt, and that doubt escalated to pain when Gershwin confronted the problems of composing the larger concert forms. Whatever anguish he himself felt was compounded by Downes's enumeration of defects in the *Second Rhapsody* in his review in the New York *Times*.

Gershwin did not respond by tackling yet another concert work. Instead he pulled together his favorite songs and wrote etudelike transcriptions of them for his *Songbook*. But once he had finished, he decided to rectify his lack of a formal music education. He got in touch with Joseph Schillinger, the composer and theorist who had been recommended to him by a number of musicians over the years. This time it was not Glazunov or Henry Cowell who was the go-between. It was Joseph Achron, a composer and violinist, who brought Gershwin to the mathematically oriented Russian immigrant teacher.

The meeting probably came about through Jascha Heifetz, who commissioned Achron to write a violin concerto for him in 1932. Heifetz, Achron and Gershwin were often together at the Chotzinoffs'. Schillinger presented Gershwin with two irresistible gifts. One was a system based on mathematical formulas that showed a composer how to unify a long work through a melody rather than through those forms that depend on harmony. Like Schoenberg, Schillinger emphasized a horizontal melodic approach, not a vertical harmonic one. This was the arena in which Gershwin's critics had persuaded him he needed the most help.

The other gift was Schillinger's personality, for he was a condescending bully who degraded Gershwin to his face, the kind of personality to whom Gershwin now was increasingly drawn. In 1989 Frances Schillinger, his widow, said, "Schillinger thought *Porgy and Bess* was the best he could get out of Gershwin and he certainly didn't think much of that." She said that Gershwin took three lessons a week, each lasting an hour and a half, and that they began in the spring of 1932 and lasted until the summer of 1936. When asked which composers her husband held in respect, she replied without hesitation: Wallingford Riegger, Charles Ives, Henry Cowell, and Aaron Copland, Americans who were experimental in their ways but not beloved by a large public as Gershwin had been since his twenties. Frances Schillinger added that her husband "thought a great deal of Schoenberg and when Schoenberg met Schillinger in New York, Schoenberg told him that everyone in California who had ever studied with him spoke very highly of him."

Schillinger's techniques proved very useful to songwriters, arrangers, and orchestrators. Glenn Miller and Benny Goodman were both Schillinger students. Miller's "Moonlight Serenade" was originally a Schillinger exercise. In a preface to *Kaleidoscope*, a book Schillinger published in 1940, he wrote, "When the late George Gershwin . . . met me for the first time, he was at a dead end of creative musical experience. He felt his resources, not his abilities, were completely exhausted. He was ready to leave for Paris where he contemplated studying with one of the leading composers. A mutual friend, Joseph Achron, who believed that study with me would save Gershwin both from a trip and a disappointment, recommended me as teacher to George.

"When we met, Gershwin said, 'Here is my problem. I have written about seven hundred songs. I can't write anything new anymore. I am repeating myself. Can you help me?' I replied in the affirmative and, a day later, Gershwin became a sort of 'Alice in Wonderland.' Later on he became acquainted with some of the materials in this book by playing them thru [*sic*]. 'You don't have to compose any more—it's all here,' he remarked."

The Gershwin Archive at the Library of Congress contains three notebooks Gershwin kept during his studies with Schillinger. They contain diagrams, graphs, and sketches that should put to rest the myth that he was not a composer but a tunesmith. In Volume I, several exercises are carried out in syncopated rhythms for he was then at work on the *Cuban Overture*. In this work, which he initially called *Rumba*, Gershwin demonstrates to the listener that a musical intellect is at work.

He starts off with a lot of busy stuff, a sixteenth-note figure accompanied by its mirror image, something he had never done before and probably learned from Schillinger. Along with that, the piece displays two innovative ideas that may have had nothing to do with his teacher. Whereas the conventional musical phrase is generally contained within a framework of four bars, Gershwin writes five-bar phrases, one after the other.

He places his rhythm section in front, directly facing the conductor, rather than in back with the percussion instruments. On the title page of his manuscript, he drew pictures of these instruments—Cuban sticks, bongo drums, a gourd and maracas —and identified them showing where each was to be situated. Also on the title page Gershwin wrote: "Composed July 1932, Orchestration begun August 1st. First performance Philharmonic Orchestra, Lewisohn Stadium, August 16, 1932."

The conductor presiding over the evening was Albert Coates, a Briton giving the world premiere of an American work based on Latin rhythms. Gershwin later described the event as "the most exciting night I ever had." It was the first all-Gershwin concert at Lewisohn Stadium and the eighteen thousand seats were sold out. The press claimed thousands more were turned away.

The concert included the overture from *Of Thee I Sing*, conducted by Daly; the Concerto in F with Daly conducting and Levant at the piano; "Wintergreen for President" from *Of Thee I Sing*, with Daly conducting; the *Second Rhapsody* with Coates conducting and Gershwin at the piano; the world premiere of *Rumba*, with Coates conducting (after Gershwin had coached Coates rigorously during rehearsals); and a medley of songs arranged by Daly—"Fascinating Rhythm" "The Man I Love," "Liza," and "I Got Rhythm"—with Daly conducting. In his program notes Gershwin says *Rumba* had been inspired by a recent trip to Havana and that he tried to combine Cuban rhythms with original thematic material. The result, he said, was "a symphonic overture which embodies the essence of Cuban dance."

Gershwin had just begun working with Schillinger and probably did believe then that this system, which was a numerical one, would be the answer to whatever problems he had. Although he stayed with Schillinger for years, it is unlikely that he believed this for very long. One can see Schillinger's tricks and devices in the Broadway shows Gershwin did immediately after that—*Pardon My English* at the end of 1932 and *Let 'Em Eat Cake* in the fall of 1933. They are also evident in Gershwin's *I Got Rhythm Variations*, an orchestral treatment of one of his favorite songs, composed in 1934.

But there is evidence that he never rated the Schillinger system as highly as some associates have claimed. For one thing he must have realized that, without knowing it, he had always written in a linear way, that his musical thinking had always been rich in what is called "stepwise motion." There was more emphasis on this after the spring of 1932 but nothing so substantive that it could be called a revolution in style. For another, Zena Hanenfeldt, Gershwin's secretary in 1936 and 1937, said in 1990 that one of her main duties was "doing the Schillinger homework each night; Mr. Gershwin found it boring." Finally Gershwin began to add to his music library scores that would inevitably bring him more artistic and intellectual nourishment than could be gained through Schillinger. Bach's *The Art of Fugue* and scores by Beethoven, Berg, and Schoenberg were now on his shelves and informed whatever he composed.

Probably more indicative than anything else that Gershwin knew the difference between a set of devices and the real thing was his seeking out Schoenberg as soon as the Viennese composer arrived in the United States in the fall of 1933—more than a year after Gershwin had begun to work with Schillinger. Schoenberg had been forced to leave his post at the Prussian Academy of Arts in Berlin because he was a Jew. At first he settled in New York at the Ansonia Hotel. Paul Mueller says he sometimes drove Gershwin the few blocks from the Riverside Drive apartment at Seventy-fifth Street to the hotel on Broadway and Seventy-fourth. Mueller would then wait several hours in the car for his employer to emerge.

This helps explain why Gershwin was the only American

composer to contribute to a scholarship fund for Schoenberg students at the Malkin Conservatory in Boston. Schoenberg had moved there after a few months when he found New York too damp for his health. The other contributors to the fund were the Steinway and Knabe piano companies and the widow of A. Lincoln Filene, the owner of a Boston department store. It also helps explain why, when Gershwin moved to Beverly Hills in 1936, Schoenberg, who had by then settled there, lost no time in making arrangements with Gershwin to use his tennis courts each week. By this time the two composers knew each other well.

It is hard to pinpoint, however, just who the European composer was to whom Schillinger referred when he said Gershwin had intended to go abroad to study with someone in Paris. It is possible it was Vincent d'Indy. In a letter to Gershwin dated March 10, 1928, before he went to Europe for the last time, Charles Loeffler, a French composer who taught Kay Swift, wrote him the following: "Have a good time in France and do a lot of writing. If you could get M. Vincent d'Indy to study for a while, principally Orchestration, and take in some ideas on Tonality and free form, you would fare well and someday thank me for having spoken to you of him. He is a Grand old gentleman. His orchestration is marvelous in sound and uncannily thoughtful and clever. He has the genius for teaching."

It is hard to know if Gershwin dismissed the suggestion to study with d'Indy in 1928 because he was too busy or because he knew that he needed no assistance in "Tonality and free form." The chances are that what Schillinger gave him was not only the notion that he was being a good, disciplined boy by studying what seemed like an offshoot of counterpoint, but a Teutonic man, not a "Grand old gentleman," who would beat him up figuratively.

Certainly, when it came to teachers, Gershwin needed an autocrat, a tyrant whom nobody could push around. Both Schillinger and Schoenberg filled that bill. So did Henry Botkin, a man Gershwin invariably introduced as "my cousin, Botkin, the painter." He was a cousin, he came from Boston, and he was a serious professional artist who made his home in Europe during the 1930s. According to Carl Ashby, a painter who was Botkin's close friend, "Botkin was a Napoleon type. He was small, with a shriveled hand, a little guy who always got things done."

Botkin was crucial to Gershwin's development as a painter and his success as a collector. Gershwin always credited him for both. Ira may have stimulated his brother's interest in painting not only by starting to do it himself but also by giving him a set of watercolors. But Botkin helped Gershwin develop technique and told him what to look for in art. Gershwin learned fast. Here are some excerpts from a letter he wrote to Botkin after receiving the first paintings his cousin sent him from Europe:

> The pictures are as you said they would be, much more beautiful than the photographs could possibly show—and from now on, I appoint you my official framer of pictures, because I think the frames are beauties.
>
> I believe that each picture is a fine example of the artist. The two favorites of most of the people who have seen them so far seem to be the Modigliani and the Rouault.
>
> The Rouault is a gorgeous painting, although it is a little darker in tone than I thought it would be. The Rouault gives me great pleasure as a painting and I hope you will find more of his work to send to me.
>
> "The Suburbs" of Utrillo is painted with a much more vigorous brush than some of the ones I have seen in America. It is a very luminous picture. It seems to throw out its own light. I am crazy about it, and it fits perfectly in my living room.
>
> The Derain is a masterpiece of simple color and the Pascin, while the least exciting of the five, has a strange quality that seems to grow on me. Before the pictures arrived I sent you a cable which, unfortunately, did not reach you as you had already left for Nice. I wanted you to find out how much I would have to pay for the Renoir picture of two women in the doorway. In the cable I believe I made an offer of $1,500 plus the Pascin as a trade-in.

Ashby says Botkin told him that Rouault remained Gershwin's favorite painter and that his goal was to emulate him.

"Rouault was a Catholic," Ashby says, "and did watercolors of prostitutes. There was a great deal of projection of feeling in Rouault's work and that is what I sensed from Henry that Gershwin wanted to see in his own work."

After George died, Bennett Cerf, in a July 17, 1943, article in the *Saturday Review of Literature*, described this event: "At a memorable dinner one evening Gershwin said, 'A man told me today that I never need write another note; I could make a fortune with my palette and brush.' 'Isn't it amazing,' said one awed lady, 'that one man should possess a genius for two of the arts.' 'Oh, I don't know,' said George modestly. 'Look at Leonardo da Vinci.' "

This narcissism also led him to produce self-portraits. One of them, in top hat and tails reflected in mirrors, seems to be saying that he was well aware of his egocentricity. (Ira showed that he also knew, because he produced his own parody self-portrait showing himself as a short, squat man in his underwear.) George also had the facility to capture the essence of others: He did portraits of his mother, father, paternal grandfather, Ira, Arthur and Leonore (Frankie was in Rochester by that time) and of Mueller, Loeffler, Lewisohn, Daly, several Paleys, Kay Swift, and many more. Ronell says she turned down his request for her to pose nude for him.

His greatest works, portraits in oil, came at the very end of his life and were of the men whom he held most in awe: Jerome Kern and Arnold Schoenberg (based on an Edward Weston photograph). Gershwin also sat for other artists. Once, when sitting for Diego Rivera, he got bored and asked if he could paint the painter. He did. Probably the most striking portrait ever done of Gershwin was a sculpture by Isamu Noguchi in 1929. The elegant dark bronze head with its smooth languorous features evokes not only Gershwin's self but the essence of his music as well. Ann Ronell remembers accompanying Gershwin to a Noguchi sitting and afterward walking down Fifty-seventh Street with him wearing an elegant fur-trimmed coat. She says that everybody they passed doffed their hats to them.

While Gershwin appears to have been comfortable using

words like "beautiful" and "gorgeous" when he talked about painting, when it came to music, increasingly he tried to impress the critics with the display of his intellect. He persisted in writing Italian directions in his scores—even in as American a work as *An American in Paris*—and his program notes took on a self-consciously technical tone. Here is an excerpt from the notes he wrote for the *Cuban Overture:*

> The first part (Moderato e Molto Ritmato) is preceded by a (forte) introduction featuring some of the thematic material. Then comes a three-part contrapuntal episode leading to a second theme. The first part finishes with a recurrence of the first theme combined with fragments of the second.
>
> A solo clarinet cadenza leads to a middle part, which is in a plaintive mood. It is a gradually developing canon in a polytonal manner. This part concludes with a climax based on an ostinato of the theme in the canon, after which a sudden change in tempo brings us back to the rumba dance rhythms.
>
> The finale is a development of the preceding material in a stretto-like manner. This leads us back again to the main theme.
>
> The conclusion of the work is a Coda featuring the Cuban instruments of percussion.

Most critics continued to treat whatever Gershwin now did in the concert field with contempt. The all-Gershwin Lewisohn Stadium concert was reviewed in the New York *Times* not by Olin Downes but by the fledgling critic Howard Taubman, who wrote: "The Rhumba, despite the addition of maracas, gourd, bonga and other Cuban instruments, was merely old Gershwin in recognizable form." Taubman went on to attack the concert because it was, according to his own view, devoted "to Broadway, popularity, the Great God publicity." Taubman summed up the event this way: "Mr. Gershwin did his cause more harm than good in allowing so revealing a program to be presented. For if he had any pretensions to being considered a truly gifted composer, the almost unvarying sameness and formlessness of this body of music did not help him."

Julia Van Norman's love for Gershwin had turned into an obsession by this time. Her letters to him became uninhibited, unleashing suppressed feelings into a torrent of tender and passionate love. This is an excerpt from a six-page handwritten letter, dated May 14, 1933:

> In your "Cuban Rhapsody" you have attained a breadth of conception and a reach of vision that seems as yet impossible to any of these others. The work is beautiful and tremendous, and left me in a trancelike state, after I had heard it performed under the rise and fall of your baton. I had the curious notion that I wanted to cry, as I always do when I come in contact with something superlatively beautiful. I meant to tell you this. I was so oppressed, however, by the knowledge that your breakfast was waiting for you yesterday morning that I was unable to say just what I wanted to say. I feel that the composition did not receive the praise it merited, at the time, although it is the finest thing you have written, my dear. It was so poignantly beautiful to me that I seem inarticulate when I try to tell you just how I feel about it.
>
> So many of these composers seem vague and uncertain of their destination. Your music is so definite and sure of its purpose, as you are, George. You do not move in the grey confusion of a fog, but you see clearly some lovely light that is, as yet, only a blurred outline to so many of the others.
>
> I feel, and know that you possess a priceless gift, and when I speak as I do of conserving your energy, it is only that I feel your work is going to be of vital importance, and that its achievement will bring you swift and certain happiness. Fulfillment of yourself is bound to bring contentment, and the great body of your work is not yet written. And so, loving you so greatly, and believing in the significance of your music, I want you to be free to write it. Sometimes, too many well-meaning people, yapping at one's heels like so many friendly terriers, are sure disaster for an artist. And too much success can be a handicap. So you must conserve your valuable, virile body and your keen mind, for the task that lies before you. For the thing is of great import—I know that. And because my love for you is not petty, but profound and deep and sure,

I dare to tell you this. My creed begins, "I believe in George. . . ."

In 1990 Horace Van Norman said, "One day Julia asked George if he loved her. He said no. She cried herself to sleep. . . . Still I think George was dependent on her. She gave him something that was very important to him, something he did not want to give up. The only people who knew about the connection between Julia and George were Paul Mueller and Kay Swift. What my wife wanted more than anything else was to be free to marry George. But George told her to cool it. I remember Kay Swift once asked me if Julia was prettier than she was. Kay was not so pretty, but she was a witty, intelligent woman. Even after my letter asking George to resume contact with Julia, he would write discreet, formal letters to her while she felt there were no limits on hers. There were phone calls; she did most of the calling. And she would write eight or ten page letters. She also began writing poetry then. 'Sonnets to a Dark-Haired Man' was a takeoff on Shakespeare's 'Sonnets to a Dark-Haired [*sic*] Lady.'

"She placed some of them in a poetry journal and George had a great admiration for her work. He encouraged her in every way and she looked forward to being accepted by the establishment."

Gershwin not only encouraged Julia; he made an effort to help Horace Van Norman when he tried his hand at writing songs. Although Van Norman says that despite their "dirt-poor" condition Gershwin never sent them gifts or money or even tickets to his Broadway shows, Gershwin did listen to the songs Van Norman wrote. Van Norman says, "My first attempt to play for him was a disaster. It seemed to him to be an outright theft of Bill Daly's work. George said I should never play them for anyone. I set about writing more tunes, determined to have him like them. About a year and a half later I went up to him with Julia and he sent us to Dreyfus. Dreyfus told me to give up any hope, that I had absolutely no talent. George told me Dreyfus was always hard, that I should not be too depressed about this and keep on trying."

Gershwin's connection to the Van Normans continued throughout the last ten years of his life. In one of her letters to him, Julia Van Norman describes her pain at his telling her he was afraid that she would "mess up" his life. As afraid as he said he was, he still continued to return some of her calls, see her from time to time, and write one letter in reply to every half dozen of hers.

Beginning in 1932, Gershwin received overwhelmingly bad reviews of his concert works as well as his shows. Rarely did the reviewer distinguish between the book, lyrics, and score when panning *Pardon My English* of 1932 or *Let 'Em Eat Cake* a year later. And Gershwin was doing his most craftsmanlike composition at that time.

Because these shows failed, Ira Gershwin made the decision not to allow the songs to be performed. He believed it was bad business to remind the public that the Gershwin brothers had ever been engaged in any production that was not a hit. Aarons and Freedley gave the Gershwins the book for *Pardon My English* in the fall of 1932. It spoofed psychiatry. The story centered on an otherwise decent man who, when he was hit on the head, became a kleptomaniac. As with his other shows, *Pardon My English* dealt with things going on around him at the time. Gershwin often told people he had been kicked in the head by a horse and that this was the cause of his increasing headaches. Julia Van Norman refers to this story in one of her letters.

Kay Swift and her husband, James Paul Warburg, had begun psychoanalysis with Gregory Zilboorg. Although half a century later Swift disclaimed any pain caused by Gershwin's many liaisons, it is hard to believe his persistent refusal to make a commitment to her did not cause her anguish. As for her husband, no amount of social sophistication could have protected him from being deeply wounded by the attachment she had for

Gershwin. A song the couple wrote together tells of a woman's fear that the man she loves will walk away from marriage saying "Can't We Be Friends?"

Yet even in this troubling situation, Ira jokes, just as he did with his "illegitimate" child song. He wrote "Freud and Jung and Adler," a parody song about psychoanalysis, when the Warburgs were in treatment. If you ever have the notion, it goes, that Mrs. Grundy's "Always keeping her eye on you on Sundays/And you suddenly find you're standing in your undies," then you must certainly see the most famous "sex psychos, we."

In November 1933, on a radio show hosted by Rudy Vallee, Gershwin told the radio audience that *Pardon My English* was in rehearsals and that he was then completing the score. Many people moved in and out of this show. Among the writers were Herbert Fields, Morrie Ryskind, and Jack McGowan. Among the directors were Georgie Hale, George S. Kaufman, Ernst Lubitsch, and Worthington Miner. Not one of these people was able to rescue the show. Gershwin, who usually conducted the orchestra on opening night, had assessed the situation well enough to stay out of the pit that evening.

Horace Van Norman says that George told his wife that the show was "backed by gangsters and goons who told him what he had to write." The musical closed in less than five weeks. Still the Gershwin brothers did their work well. They wrote twenty-one songs. Fifteen were used. Seven were published. The more memorable ones were "My Cousin in Milwaukee"—which Anna Sosenko, who built Hildegarde's career, says was written about her client—and "Isn't It a Pity?" There also was "The Lorelei," which includes the expression of a wish "to bite my initials on a sailor's neck."

The lyrics recall those of "Treat Me Rough," written for *Girl Crazy* just two years before. In a 1989 conversation, Robert Israel, a composer who heads a company called Score that provides music for television and film, said that when he was 13, and intent on going into music, his father sent him to a psychiatrist to make him change his mind. Israel went to a white limestone building on Fifth Avenue and took a private elevator up to the fifth floor where he was greeted by Dr. Bernard Hoffman. Hoffman told him that a woman patient had opened her blouse and revealed to him a back filled with bruises and scratches. She said, "This is what Gershwin did to me."

The moral of the doctor's tale was that if as great a musician as Gershwin could have done something like that, music was a field that should be off limits to a wholesome boy.

Composer David Diamond, who won the Elfreda Whiteman scholarship medal in 1935, received it in a ceremony attended by Gershwin, who, Diamond says, asked him only one question: "How'd you learn to orchestrate like that, kid?" Diamond claims he got to know Gershwin slightly and Levant well and that Gershwin had a number of books in his library by Richard von Krafft-Ebing, the German psychiatrist who specialized in deviant sexual behavior. According to Diamond, Levant told him that Gershwin was interested in sexual perversion.

Pardon My English proved a disaster for everyone involved. Pursued by creditors, Vinton Freedley was forced to leave the country. Alex Aarons never recovered; this was his last Broadway show. In addition to the failure of *Pardon My English*, Gershwin had to cope with "The Gershwin Myth," the magazine piece by Langley that claimed that a good part of Gershwin's composition and orchestration was not executed by the composer himself. Ira reported that George was so incensed he considered taking legal action. But he did not. Daly may well have been a sort of "secret sharer," one who helped Gershwin without ever getting public credit.

In 1932 the cruel treatment of Gershwin seems to have become relentless. It was probably provoked by the packed stadium concert which no critic seemed able to tolerate. Here, for example, is Oscar Levant, Gershwin's idolizing friend who had appeared as a soloist at that event. He reported this story in *The Memoirs of an Amnesiac:*

> In 1932 I was with George and Ira Gershwin and Sam Harris, the producer of *Of Thee I Sing*, on the 20th Century Limited en

route to Chicago where they were opening a second road company of that hit. In George's presence I asked Sam, "Who's your favorite songwriter?"

"George M. Cohan," he replied.

I'd forgotten that Cohan and Harris had been partners.

"Who's your second favorite songwriter?" I pressed on.

"Irving Berlin," he replied.

I'd forgotten that Harris and Berlin had been partners in *The Music Box Revue* and the Music Box Theater.

I gave up, helplessly embarrassed.

Harris's responses were odd considering that Gershwin was the songwriter of the hit show that Harris was producing at the time. But it is difficult to understand Levant's questions and to believe his claim that he was "helplessly embarrassed." William Targ, Levant's editor, writes in *Indecent Pleasures*, his own memoir: "There have been several difficult authors in my life; one of them could have easily doubled for the Marquis de Sade. But the meanest of all was the late Oscar Levant. . . . While editing his last two books, *The Memoirs of an Amnesiac* and *The Unimportance of Being Oscar*, I endured mental cruelty and obscene vituperation beyond belief."

Clearly Oscar Levant was a sadist. Levant says that he repeatedly delivered scathing remarks to Gershwin but that his attitude toward the composer was one of "pure idolatry."

Gershwin continued to push ahead, trying to make a kind of art he had never made before and reveling in the luxuries his earnings could buy. Either he was oblivious to the envy that contributed to the harsh treatment he received or he was actually telling everyone that he wanted them to "treat me rough."

After *Pardon My English* closed, Gershwin moved out of his Riverside Drive apartment and into a lavish fourteen-room duplex at 132 East Seventy-second Street. No longer was his decor modern. This, his last home in New York, conveyed a sense of tradition and elegance. Gershwin's collection of art as well as his own paintings hung on the walls of every room, on the stairwell and in the hallways.

A Picasso, *The Absinthe Drinker*, and a portrait Gershwin had done of his paternal grandfather hung in the large living room, which was flooded with sunlight in the afternoon. The rug was taupe, the walls gray, the draperies wine, a window seat green. There were large comfortable couches on either side of the fireplace and chairs distributed throughout the space. Two concert grands stood on one side of the room. There were rooms for everything: one for his memorabilia, a gymnasium where he worked with his personal trainer, a formal dining room, an English den, and a reception space. In his music studio he had a third piano and a desk he had designed himself, tilted at an angle he found most comfortable, with sliding shelves and racks and a pencil sharpener that disappeared when not in use.

Levant complained that with all this space, there was not even one guest room for him. Obviously Gershwin did not want overnight guests; he had planned the apartment to suit his own pleasures and needs. Henry Cowell, who came there to teach him from time to time, probably found the place astonishingly lavish, as would Cowell's colleagues. The conspicuous consumption it reflected in depression times could not have endeared Gershwin to the concert music community.

Frankie Godowsky remembers bringing a Rochester woman to the apartment. Frankie cringed when she recounted how, with the woman preceding Gershwin up the interior stairs to look at the rest of his art collection, Gershwin placed his hands on her lower back. Gershwin did not make a distinction by this time in his life between Broadway chorus girls, a Charleston matron, and a friend of his sister's. He found women attractive and apparently made no effort to keep his hands off them.

The new apartment gave him much more privacy than he had had with Ira and Leonore in the adjoining apartment at 33 Riverside Drive. When he moved to East Seventy-second Street, they followed him, but only as far as a building directly across the street. Now the brothers could only wave to one another. In fact, Hanenfeldt, George's secretary, reports that she never saw Ira during her working day. She says that once, after starting her morning's work, she did see Kay Swift walk out of George's bedroom.

. . .

Sam Harris, pleased with the success of *Of Thee I Sing*, brought in George S. Kaufman, the Gershwins, and Ryskind to make *Let 'Em Eat Cake*, the third of the trilogy that began with *Strike Up the Band*. He managed to do this despite friction between Ryskind and Ira over lyric credits, the same problem Dietz had had with Ira five years before. The show opened in the fall of 1933.

By that time Gershwin had been writing to Dubose Heyward, discussing transforming *Porgy* into an opera. But he kept saying he did not yet feel prepared for such a challenge. He prepared himself with *Let 'Em Eat Cake*. The Kaufman-Ryskind libretto provided an appropriate framework for Gershwin to experiment with ideas and techniques. In 1933, in a letter to Pallay, he wrote that he was glad the summer was over because it had been "tough." As for *Let 'Em Eat Cake*, he said there was "a lot of good stuff in the show . . . but it seems to me it still lacks a little love interest. If the show is funny enough people won't mind and Boston will tell us everything. After all, this is an entirely new kind of show and it is very hard predicting what the audience's reaction will be."

The audience's reaction was negative. Imagine the political and economic climate: Roosevelt had entered the White House in March, six months before, and Hitler had become chancellor of Germany at the same time. His rising dictatorship with its integral anti-Semitism was palpable even in the United States. It was in this context that Kaufman and Ryskind came up with a book in which John P. Wintergreen, president of the United States in *Of Thee I Sing*, is now out of office. Unemployed like everyone else, he starts to manufacture Maryblue shirts. The Mary comes from his wife's name; the blue shirts are a takeoff on Hitler's brown shirts. Then, with his burgeoning army of blue-shirted men, Wintergreen stages a coup and takes over the U. S. government.

Gershwin wrote a rich score with more dissonances and a thicker texture than anything he had previously done for Broadway. The most obvious piece of counterpoint appears in "Mine," the only love song in the show, which he wrote first as a Schillinger exercise. Wintergreen sings of his love for Mary while, in a countermelody, his followers inform the audience that he is telling the truth:

> The way they're making love you'd swear
> They're not a married pair.

Let 'Em Eat Cake was a cynical show, not only about American politics but also about love. It reflected Gershwin's own view, expressed to his aunt almost ten years before, that romance and marriage are irreconcilable. In an interview after the opening, Gershwin said he had written "most of the music for this show contrapuntally, and it is this very insistence on the sharpness of a form that gives my music the acid touch that it has." Gilbert Seldes, the author of an essay published in the program book of the original Whiteman *Rhapsody* concert, said something similar: "Gershwin's work gets more complicated and interesting and brittle and unmelodious every year. . . . so he composes to be heard, not to be sung."

In 1924, with *Rhapsody in Blue*, Gershwin put American music on the world map. Just about the time American music had found its own voice, Schoenberg and Stravinsky, those two formidable Europeans, came to the United States and changed the course of music here. With the weight of their reputations, the very real strength of their scores, and hundreds of years of European tradition behind them, they and their European followers took over the development of the American concert music world.

Even Gershwin, a supreme melodist, a sophisticated harmonist, and a musician whose rhythmic motives skipped across barlines from the earliest days of his career, knew he had begun to repeat himself. Welcoming extramusical formulas, Gershwin hoped they would provide him with the means to find the structure he knew he needed for the large works to come.

ON November 25, 1933, Gershwin wrote to Dubose Heyward accepting an invitation to come to Charleston, South Carolina, to talk about their proposed work. He said he would come for a few days with his friend, Emil Mosbacher, and that he hoped to get some sense of the town. Gershwin did no composing in Charleston, but later, when he and Mosbacher were spending three weeks at Mosbacher's Palm Beach estate, he wrote the *I Got Rhythm Variations*, a new work for orchestra.

It was to receive its world premiere on a tour that Gershwin was financing himself to celebrate the tenth anniversary of *Rhapsody in Blue*. Despite the gains he had made in compositional technique and orchestration, Gershwin was still held in contempt by serious American composers. In 1923 Copland, Virgil Thomson, Roger Sessions, and others founded the League of Composers, which emphasized intellect over emotion in accordance with the European aesthetic of the time. A year later Gershwin composed *Rhapsody in Blue*, a work that went against everything these serious composers believed in. In *Modern Music*, a journal published from 1924 to 1945, which consistently reflected the league's position on all matters musical, Gershwin's name rarely appeared, and when it did, it was in a pejorative context. In fact, in 1983, when a collection of essays from that journal was published, Minna Lederman, its editor, commented that her omission of Gershwin in the journal made her prouder than anything else about the magazine. "He was so popular," she said, "that it was ridiculous." As much as Gershwin was intimidated by European composers and the American critics who held them in awe, he wanted American audiences to know that their own music—jazz—could serve as the basis for legitimate concert works.

The idea for the anniversary tour came from Harry Askins, a Tin Pan Alley associate. Gershwin made Askins his tour manager, and Askins devised a grueling itinerary. The composer and thirty musicians traveled to twenty-eight cities giving twenty-eight concerts in twenty-eight days. The only relief was that the program was the same every night: The Concerto in F, Gershwin songs with Gershwin at the piano, tenor James Melton singing "Home on the Range" and one or two other standards of the day, followed by *Rhapsody in Blue*. After the intermission: *An American in Paris*, Melton singing Negro spirituals, the *I Got Rhythm Variations*, "Wintergreen for President" in its orchestral arrangement by Daly, and Daly's arrangement of a medley of Gershwin songs with Gershwin at the piano. Melton was on the program to give Gershwin a rest and, at the same time, provide listeners with familiar songs.

For the *I Got Rhythm Variations*, Gershwin used what he had learned from Schillinger. He turned his 1930 tune inside out, looked at it from various angles, then made it contrapuntal, dissonant, and complex. The form of the work was simple: an introduction, the statement of the theme, six variations, and a coda. In the last chord of the composition, Gershwin injected the pitch G. Maurice Peress, who recorded the work in 1991, notes that the G is out of the context of the harmony but can be explained either as a continuation of the song's melodic line or as the composer's secret signature. That practice echoes many classical composers including J. S. Bach.

Even in this situation, with new devices and techniques on his mind, Gershwin was preoccupied with his effort to convince the world he was orchestrating the piece himself. When he returned from Palm Beach, all he told the reporters who met him was that he had then orchestrated fifty-three pages and had twenty-five more to go, which was why he had to end his remarks.

Leo Reisman, the leader of what Jerome Kern called "the string quartet of dance orchestras," assembled the musicians for Gershwin's tour. Because Reisman broke his hip before they left, Charles Previn, recently in the pit for *Of Thee I Sing*, conducted all twenty-eight performances. The concerts began on January 14 in Boston. The ensemble was smaller than the orchestras that had played the Gershwin pieces at Lewisohn Stadium and the Metropolitan Opera House. The result was a cleaner and more elegant texture. The touring ensemble consisted of one flute, one oboe doubling on English horn, one bassoon, four saxophones doubling on other reed instruments, three horns, three B-flat trumpets, two trombones, percussion, and strings. Musicians included violinist John Corigliano, later concert master of the New York Philharmonic, Harry Glickman, later concert master of the Brooklyn Philharmonic, and Harry Fuchs, principal cellist of the Cleveland Orchestra under George Szell.

Mitch Miller, then twenty-three, was the oboist and remembered the tour well. In 1988, he said,

> Gershwin came from the pop song world. He was not a happy man. His serious works had been clobbered by the critics. The purpose of the tour was to see that he was taken seriously by the people. Why else would he embark on such a project? It could not have made a nickel for him. In some places we were playing in high school auditoriums. Even with the houses sold out, he could not possibly have come out even.
>
> Gershwin was always sweet. He never raised his voice. He did not have a commanding personality. He was the consummate craftsman. Gershwin had a poker face. It was impossible to judge his reactions. He never looked exultant or distressed.
>
> We traveled like a circus train. The musicians slept in the train, only occasionally in a hotel. Admission to the concerts was three and four dollars. Audiences were always good. Receptions followed the concerts, and Gershwin sat at the piano

and played beautifully. He did not fraternize with the musicians.

I remember when we pulled into Detroit. I followed him down the steps of the train. He looked back at us and said, "I smell burning garbage." I remember thinking that that was funny because neither I nor anybody else smelled it.

Nobody else smelled burning garbage because Gershwin's olfactory sensation came from a slow-growing tumor on the right temporal lobe of his brain.

In the spring of 1934, according to Julia Van Norman's letters to him, Gershwin was suffering from depression, anxiety, and personality problems. His telling reporters that he had to go home to start orchestrating right away seems almost childlike. Not only was he facing trouble in the serious music domain where his competitors were Schoenberg and Stravinsky among others, but now Cole Porter was in New York and beginning to dominate Broadway. Gershwin's longtime producer Vinton Freedley and his star Ethel Merman were both working with Porter in *Anything Goes*.

Gershwin's stomach trouble grew worse. Virtually every Van Norman letter refers to it. Friends report an enema bag constantly nearby. Still nobody took his complaints seriously, and Leonore, his sister-in-law, attributed them to his relentless quest to call attention to himself. Although she did not say this in front of Gershwin while he was still in apparently good health, she did speak that way when he was out of range.

Kay Swift pushed Gershwin to see Gregory Zilboorg, the renowned psychoanalyst who was treating her and her husband. She may have felt that Zilboorg would try to steer her longtime lover into a commitment to her. Why Gershwin accepted her suggestion is another matter. Frankie Godowsky says, "George went to Zilboorg because he wanted to improve himself. He felt inadequate because of his lack of an education." But Isamu Noguchi, the sculptor who had done a head of Gershwin and was a friend of Zilboorg's, said that Gershwin had sought out Zilboorg because of the reputation he had in the field of "suicidal mania."

Noguchi added that Zilboorg said that Gershwin's thoughts were very much on the son he hardly saw.

Gershwin did want to improve himself, and Zilboorg was a brilliant man. Also Gershwin seems to have felt something inexplicable going on inside him and he wanted to gain some control over it. More important than the reason Gershwin sought treatment is that in selecting Zilboorg he added yet another person to the malevolent circle surrounding him. Now, in addition to Leonore, Levant, and Schillinger, there was Zilboorg, an overbearing analyst who went out of his way to cut Gershwin down. Jablonski quotes Swift as saying her sending George to Zilboorg had been a "mistake . . . , that Zilboorg often exhibited envious hostility toward his successful, celebrated patient," and, to her dismay, the analyst frequently discussed Gershwin's sessions with her.

It may have been to her "dismay" years later, but at the time, Swift must have been grateful to learn whatever she could of the reasons Gershwin put off marrying her. Zilboorg's talking to her about Gershwin was not out of character for him. In 1989, a distinguished New York physician, who insisted on anonymity, talked of his experience with Zilboorg, who he believed was responsible for his wife's suicide. "My wife," he said, was "part of a powerful Canadian family and Zilboorg restricted his practice to those in the power structure. He was brilliant, dangerous in both simple and complex ways, vicious and exploitative. He did whatever was necessary to create a relationship with his patients which invariably did him some good, financially or otherwise. He went to Europe a couple of months every year and his patients always paid his way. Marshall Field, the financier, took him to Europe annually. It was Zilboorg's itinerary and Field's funding."

This physician once went to Zilboorg's apartment for a consultation. "He greeted me," he went on, "inviting me into his office where he was dictating to three secretaries in three different languages. He brought me in there to show off. He was brilliant but strangely insecure. He had to tell you about his power, to demonstrate it, and he always discussed his relationships with his patients and his patients' lives with whoever would listen."

One might think a doctor whose specialty lay outside the field of psychiatry and whose wife committed suicide after treatment by Zilboorg would present a biased view. But the essence of what he says was confirmed in 1990 by Dr. Paul Brauer, a psychoanalyst who studied with Zilboorg. "Zilboorg was a very difficult man," Brauer said. "He was considered by the professional community to have had psychopathic qualities. He took advantage of his patients, socialized with them more than other analysts thought an analyst should, and did not hesitate, for example, to give patients his advice. He was a flamboyant character. At the time he was first practicing, analysis was hampered by a certain rigidity; there were things considered to be sins. Zilboorg didn't see things that way. While it is true he was very brilliant, his colleagues found much of what he did abhorrent. In the 1950s, the New York Psychoanalytic Institute defrocked him."

The New York Psychoanalytic Institute has always been the most Freudian and arguably the most prestigious of the psychoanalytic institutes in the United States. It took away Zilboorg's right to practice under its aegis. Brauer adds that a decade or so before, "the atmosphere was that Zilboorg had missed the diagnosis on Gershwin." Physicians other than Brauer—neurologists, cardiologists, internists—have come forth to confirm what Brauer says: that when they were in medical school, rumors were rampant that Zilboorg had misdiagnosed Gershwin. The point of the stories was that an overemphasis on the patient's psychodynamics at the expense of his physical being could lead to the patient's death.

What we have better understood since then is the notion that there is no boundary between psyche and body. If this is correct, then Gershwin's extreme narcissism, severely wounded by the turn of events, may have transformed itself into aggression against himself. If that hypothesis has any validity, then conceivably to help himself on this self-destructive path, he sought out sadists. Even his choice of an analyst led to his tragic end.

Gershwin visited Zilboorg five days a week at thirty-five dollars an hour from the spring of 1934 through the late fall of 1935, when he and his analyst took a trip to Mexico.

Zilboorg impressed Gershwin with his erudition and achievements. He was multilingual, wrote copiously in his own field, studied photography with Joseph Fassbender, repeatedly claimed that he outperformed his teacher and that he designed furniture better than Le Corbusier. (Later he told people *The Little Foxes* was "a good play Lillian and I wrote." Hellman was a Zilboorg patient.)

Gershwin's attachment can also be explained by the fact that patient and analyst had common roots in Russia. Zilboorg served as secretary to the minister of labor in the Kerensky cabinet until the Bolshevik Revolution forced him out. Zilboorg was not merely Russian. He was also a Jew and in those anti-Semitic times, that was a bond not to be dismissed. Few Jews talked openly about anti-Semitism then. But anti-Semitism touched Gershwin at every turn. Paul Mueller remembers trying to check into a hotel in Toronto while they were on the tour. The concierge said that Mueller would be welcome but not Gershwin.

The Gershwin brothers would not have written "Freud and Jung and Adler" after George had begun his own analysis. He would not have gone along with Ira ridiculing the three at that time. Similarly, they might not have written "Mischa, Jascha, Toscha, Sascha," in the 1930s. They wrote it in 1921 with no vehicle in mind—just another song to be sung at parties. The figures it mocked were Russian Jews: Mischa Elman from Talnoe, Jascha Heifetz from Vilna, Toscha Seidel from Odessa, and Sascha Jacobson from nearby Finland. The verse Ira wrote tells of these men who "began to play the fiddle in Darkest Russia," and the chorus goes on to proclaim that, where money is concerned, Russian names are better than Jewish names:

Names like Sammy, Max or Moe
Never bring in the heavy dough

Many public figures, as early as the 1920s, discussing the character of American music, found its "Jewish element" disgusting. In *Yankee Blues: Musical Culture and Yankee Identity*, Macdonald Smith Moore writes: "Henry Ford's organ, *The Dearborn Independent*, took note of the organized eagerness of the Jew to make an alliance with the Negro. In the United States, 'picturesque, romantic, clean' popular songs had been replaced by 'the African period, being the entrance of the jungle motif . . . which swiftly degenerated into a rather more bestial type than the beasts themselves arrive at.' Jews took over and directed the spread of this 'monkey talk,' jungle squeals, grunts and squeaks and gasps suggestive of 'cave love' to the general public. The Jews provided just the right 'touch of cleverness to camouflage the moral filth.' *The Dearborn Independent* served as a touchstone of extreme anti-Semitic opinion during the 1920s. Its analysis of the Jewish relationship to jazz differs in its viciousness, but not in character, from the spectrum of opinions expressed elsewhere."

Here is more from the *Dearborn Independent:* "Many people have wondered whence came the waves upon waves of musical slush that invade decent homes and set the young people of this generation imitating the drivel of morons. Popular music is a Jewish monopoly. Jazz is a Jewish creation. The mush, slush, the sly suggestion, the abandoned sensuousness of sliding notes are of Jewish origin. . . .

"The song pluggers of theater, vaudeville and radio are the paid agents of the Yiddish song agencies. Money and not merit dominates the spread of this moron music which is styled Jewish, jazz and swing. Non-Jewish music is stigmatized as highbrow."

Gershwin probably took such attitudes personally. Coming on top of assaults on him by the critics, the academics, and his psychoanalyst, they succeeded in dismantling his defenses, and he became vulnerable to serious illness.

In an essay, "Serious George," published in the winter 1990 issue of *Boston College Magazine*, William H. Youngren writes that such academic composers as Daniel Gregory Mason at Columbia University and Edward Burlingham Hill at Harvard had planned the development of American music in a quite different way when Gershwin startled the world with *Rhapsody in Blue* in 1924. They thought "America would find its authentic musical voice in the work of composers like themselves, men who came of Anglo-Saxon stock, had attended Ivy League colleges and had gone on to conservatory training under European masters. To them Gershwin's successful bid for recognition as a composer of extended concert works was a serious affront.

"Mason wrote of the 'insidiousness of the Jewish menace to our artistic integrity,' and deplored the fact that 'our whole contemporary attitude toward instrumental music, especially in New York, is dominated by Jewish tastes and standards, with their Oriental extravagance, their sensuous brilliancy and intellectual facility and superficiality, their general tendency to exaggeration . . .' There had to be some way of proving," Youngren writes, "that a Jewish song plugger from the Lower East Side who had come up through the Tin Pan Alley ranks, apparently with little or no formal training, was a fraud."

How did Gershwin react to all of this? We do not know. As Mitch Miller says, he maintained a poker face and did not reveal his feelings to the musicians, with whom, in fact, he did not fraternize. And he was as uncommunicative with his friends. Mabel Schirmer says Gershwin never talked about such things, or, for that matter, about people—not about Kay or Emily or Ira or Leonore. However silent he may have remained about anti-Semitism in music, Gershwin almost certainly knew that Felix Mendelssohn, grandson of Moses, as well as Gustav Mahler and Schoenberg all converted from Judaism in order to have careers in music.

The 1920s was, in fact, the first decade in the history of Western music that Jews (excluding these converts) were even allowed to try to enter the exalted field of concert repertoire. Seen in that context, it may be that Gershwin, Copland, and, in the 1930s, David Diamond were grateful that they managed as well as they did. Illuminated in this way, the situation was one in which Copland, also a New York Jew, albeit one who studied in France, went out of his way to separate himself from a Tin Pan Alley–trained Jew.

To describe all of this is not to suggest Jews had more difficulty than blacks in moving in a musical world. In Washington, D. C., blacks could perform in public but were not permitted to sit in the audience until 1939. As late as 1945, Marian Anderson sat on a bench outside an all-white restaurant in Virginia eating a sandwich, while waiters served German prisoners of war inside.

Franklin Roosevelt did a little to combat the atmosphere. He invited Gershwin to the White House in December 1935 and Marian Anderson the following year.

Although they were dissimilar in temperament, religion, style, and class, Dubose Heyward and Gershwin had followed some of the same paths early in their lives. They grew up poor, dropped out of high school, had big ambitions to make money and art.

But Heyward's adolescence differed from Gershwin's in one important way: he contracted polio and lost the use of both arms. Treatments in Philadelphia subsidized by a wealthy aunt helped him regain some strength, but he always had trouble with his right hand. A slow, meticulous writer like Ira, he was obliged to write even more slowly because of the effects of polio. Therefore, he chose each word of his prose with the same effort toward economy as he chose each word of his poems. Heyward was first and foremost a poet.

On the basis of his poetry, he was admitted to the MacDowell Colony in Peterborough, New Hampshire, for the summer of 1922. There Heyward met Dorothy Kuhns, a playwright. He was thirty-seven, she thirty-two. They married during the summer of 1923, when Gershwin was working in London on *The Rainbow Revue*.

Of these three young artists, Dorothy Heyward was probably riding highest at the time. Her play, *Nancy Ann*, won the 1923 Harvard Prize for Drama, which guaranteed the work a production on Broadway. Her high spirits were short-lived, however, because the reviews were harsh. The play closed quickly, and she became depressed. Heyward appears to have been solicitous of his wife, and to lift her spirits he insisted that they go to his cottage in the Smoky Mountains and take a rest from civilization.

Under these circumstances, Heyward began his first novel. Its central character was a disabled Negro who moved around in a cart drawn by an old goat. An item that had appeared in the *Charleston News and Courier* in March 1924, was his source. It read: "Sammy Smalls, who is a cripple and is familiar to King Street, with his goat and cart, was held for the June term of Court of Sessions on an aggravated assault charge. It is alleged that on Saturday night he attempted to shoot Maggie Barnes at number four Romney Street. His shots went wide of the mark. Smalls was up on a similar charge some months ago and was given a suspended sentence. Smalls had attempted to escape in his wagon and was run down and captured by the police patrol."

According to Hollis Alpert's *The Life and Times of Porgy and Bess*, the story moved Heyward to remark to his sister: "Just think of that old wreck having enough manhood to do a thing like that." When he read the item in the spring of 1924, Heyward was working in the insurance business and writing poetry and short stories on the side. But now he decided to devote himself to a full-length book about the Gullah Negroes; he had always lived close to them and knew their music and their ways.

He probably chose Sammy Smalls as his protagonist because, like Sammy, he was a cripple intent on proving what he could do in the world. While Heyward was writing, Dorothy was reading. She read a large number of mystery novels, and, in between, her husband's pages as he completed them. Even before he finished his first draft, she began adapting it into a play. Heyward is reported to have paid little attention to her effort. According to Alpert, he did not believe that Broadway would go in for "serious treatment of Negro people. A comic song-and-dance revue like *Shuffle Along*, yes, but there was simply no audience for plays about black life portrayed by black actors."

It is important to view the transition of the novel *Porgy*, in 1925, to the play *Porgy*, in 1927, to the opera *Porgy and Bess* in 1935 with this in mind, for the fact is that the very language in the opera that has occasioned outrage came straight from the novel. Here, to cite just one example, is Heyward's Bess talking to Maria: "I ain't been expectin' no fabors off none ob you folks. How come yuh tuh care ef I lib er die attuh dat row I mek." The humanity with which Heyward invested his characters took precedence over everything else in 1925.

After Heyward finished his first draft, he sent it to John Bennett, another insurance agent in Charleston, who also wrote in his spare time. Bennett responded positively, saying Heyward had taken a simple Negro beggar and transformed him into a heroic man. At the next meeting of the Poetry Society of South Carolina, Bennett invited John Farrar, the speaker, to look at Heyward's new work. Farrar was the editor of *The Bookman*, a literary journal as well as an acquiring editor for the George H. Doran Company. He accepted Heyward's book for publication. Three sections ran in *The Bookman*, a fourth in *The Forum*, another literary journal. Farrar handled a prepublication publicity campaign and by the fall of 1925, when *Porgy* appeared in its entirety, Heyward had become a literary celebrity, widely regarded as an authority on the South, on southern literature and the southern Negro.

Despite the use of dialect and a depiction of lives governed by superstition, brutality, gambling, and drugs, the Gullah Negro was believed to have emerged as a compassionate figure and Porgy, the protagonist, as a tragic hero. Surely there were blacks at the time who may have felt offended by Porgy. But the poem with which Heyward preceded his novel set the tone for his treatment and the general response among blacks was favorable:

Porgy, Maria and Bess,
Robbins, and Peter, and Crown;
Life was a three-stringed harp
Brought from the woods to town.

Marvelous tunes you rang
From passion, and death, and birth,

You who had laughed and wept
On the warm, brown lap of the earth.

Now in your untried hands
An instrument, terrible, new,
Is thrust by a master who frowns,
Demanding strange songs of you.

God of the White and Black,
Grant us great hearts on the way
That we may understand
Until you have learned to play.

In 1925 the New York *Herald-Tribune* coined the expression "the Harlem Renaissance," to refer to the vitality that could be found in the life that centered in and around 135th Street and Lenox Avenue. In this socially aware context, the Theater Guild, which had been founded in 1919 and was run by a six-member board headed by playwright-critic Teresa Helburn, accepted *Porgy* for production. Before the show went into rehearsal in September 1927 as the opening work of the Guild's season, with Rouben Mamoulian as director, the Heywards and Gershwin met for the first time. The Heywards had gone to Atlantic City for a holiday; Gershwin was in Philadelphia working on *Strike Up the Band.* He made the short trip to the New Jersey resort town to talk about his wish to transform the work into an opera.

Later Heyward said he was most impressed by Gershwin's faculty of "seeing himself impersonally and realistically." Gershwin assessed himself accurately enough to know he was not yet knowledgeable enough to embark on his ambitious plan. He also was exceptionally busy at the time. With one successful show after another, his desk was jammed with unfinished work. When *Porgy* appeared as a play, both Heywards were credited as the playwrights. Brooks Atkinson gave a muted review. He described it as an "exposition of group psychology with its weird melody singing over the body of a murdered crapshooter, its breathtaking screams at a vulture hovering near, its incantations, its comic interludes and its heavy mass rhythms."

Even without a composer, the play had a great deal of music in it. Atkinson continued, "One may fairly wish that the performance revealed a finer sense of rhythmic movement, with better modulated transitions between the active and passive scenes, or that the waits between the scenes were less disenchanting." Other reviewers were more enthusiastic and the show was a box-office success. Gershwin did not attend the opening on October 10, because he was out of town for tryouts for *Funny Face*. But he attended a later performance with Kay Swift, who recalled that he responded enthusiastically.

There is no ambiguity here; from the time in 1926 when he first read the book, he had committed himself to making it the subject of his most ambitious enterprise. If he did agree with Atkinson's reservations, he probably believed he could deal with them. What he could not rectify was the inevitable loss of detail that comes from the transfer of a novel into a stage work. Atkinson, in his review, also dealt with this matter: "In the novel," he wrote, "Heyward could define the change in Porgy's life after Bess had come to him with a simple description of facts: 'The change in Porgy, which Peter had been the first to notice, was now apparent to all who knew him. The defensive barrier of reserve that he had built about his life was down. The long hours when he used to sit fixed and tense, with the look of introspection upon his face, were gone. Even the most skeptical of women were beginning to admit that Bess was making him a good mate. Not that they mingled freely with other residents of the court. On the contrary, they seemed sufficient unto themselves in the midst of the intensely gregarious life that was going on around them. Porgy's earnings were adequate to their modest needs, and Bess was always up and out with the first of the women, and among them all there was none who could bargain more shrewdly with the fishermen and hucksters who sold their wares on the wharf.' "

The Theater Guild program printed the words of all the spirituals used in the show. Their titles follow: "I Can't Stan Still," "Bess' Lullaby," "Deat' Ain't Yuh Gots No Shame," "Dere's Somebody Knockin' at de Do," "Lonesome Grabe-yard," "We Will All Pray Togedduh on Dat Day," and "De Primus Land." A note in the program includes this paragraph: "The dialect employed by the Negroes of the South Carolina Low Country is known as 'Gullah.' It is so obscure, and contains so many words of African origin, that, in order to render the dialogue comprehensible it has been translated into a conventional negro dialect, retaining only certain characteristic grammatical eccentricities. The word 'Buckra' means a white man, and 'Shouting' means the bodily rhythms that accompany the music."

Years later Dorothy Heyward spoke about the use of the word "nigger": "I had used it in writing the play when one Negro was speaking to another, just as Dubose did in the novel. We heard it in Charleston fifty times a day." Although some cast members apparently expressed their objections to this, the Heywards refused to delete it from the play. Not only, as Mrs. Heyward pointed out, was the word in common usage among the blacks at the time; it also appeared frequently in *Show Boat*, which had its world premiere the same year, and it appeared in the title of *Nigger Heaven*, Van Vechten's successful novel.

Virtually the only quote available from an African-American about the play *Porgy* comes from James Weldon Johnson, a leader of the Harlem Renaissance and an executive of the National Association for the Advancement of Colored People. Johnson not only praised the use of more than sixty black performers as well as the quality of those performers' work; he also had good things to say about the show: "In *Porgy*," he wrote, "the Negro removed all doubts as to his ability to do acting that requires thoughtful interpretation and intelligent skill."

The play itself, Johnson maintained, "loomed high above every Negro drama that has ever been produced."

Six years after this production, in 1933, Gershwin telephoned Heyward to say he was clearing his desk to begin *Porgy*. Soon afterward, Heyward began sending him sections of the libretto.

On February 26, 1934, just after he returned from the tour, Gershwin wrote to Heyward, "I received your Second Act's script and think it is fine. I really think you are doing a magnificent job with the new libretto and I hope I can match it musically.

"I have begun composing music for the First Act and I am starting with the songs and spirituals first. I am hoping you will find some time to come up North and live at my apartment—if it is convenient for you—so we can work together on some of the spirituals for Scene 2, Act 1. Perhaps when the weather grows a little warmer you will find the time to do this. I cannot leave New York to go south as I am tied up with the radio until June 1st; then I shall have a two months vacation—which time I shall devote entirely to the opera. Of course I would prefer you to come North to stay with me long before June 1st and we could do a lot together.

"I saw *Four Saints in Three Acts*, an opera by Gertrude Stein and Virgil Thomson, with a colored cast. The libretto was entirely in Stein's manner, which means that it has the effect of a 5-year-old child prattling on. Musically, it sounded early 19th century, which was a happy inspiration and made the libretto bearable—in fact, quite entertaining. There may be one or two in the cast that would be useful to us. Hoping you and your wife and child are 100% well and looking forward to seeing you soon, I am, As ever, George G."

The letter reveals that, despite Levant's complaint that there was no guest room, Gershwin could accommodate a guest if he chose to, and that Gershwin had taken a radio job. Although, in a 1934 press interview, he refers to the show as "four broadcasts within seven days," *Music by Gershwin* appears to have settled down to two fifteen-minute segments each week. Broadcast by CBS, it later became a half-hour show aired once a week.

His comments on *Four Saints in Three Acts* also indicate that he attended at least some of the music events attended by New York's musical avant-garde. In 1931 Gershwin had gone to Philadelphia for the first American performance of *Wozzeck*, conducted by Stokowski. No letters have turned up that disclose his reaction to the Berg score, but there is ample evidence in *Porgy and Bess* that *Wozzeck* impressed him.

Clearly *Four Saints in Three Acts*, the most famous of Thomson's works, did not. Thomson was two years older than Gershwin and had all the credentials Gershwin lacked: a Harvard education; piano lessons with Heinrich Gebhard, Boston's most celebrated teacher; and years of study with Boulanger. With *Four Saints* Thomson became the first white composer to use an all black cast for an opera. Gershwin used Edward Matthews, who had performed in *Four Saints*, as Jake the fisherman in *Porgy*, for which Thomson never forgave him.

In March 1934 Gershwin held a press conference in which he praised the development of radio broadcasting. "The concert tour," he said, "if it taught me nothing else, proved conclusively that radio has raised the tastes of the average man and woman and has educated them to a real appreciation and enjoyment of the best that music has to offer. . . . It has not only raised the standards of tastes, but has made the average listener music-conscious."

Gershwin also said that however exhausting his twenty-eight city tour had been, it could not compare to the exhaustion he felt from the relentless schedule of the radio shows. The reporter wrote that Gershwin "admitted that four broadcasts within seven days offered a far more baffling problem than his whirlwind tour. The activity during those twenty-eight days was more physical than mental, for while we covered 12,000 miles in less than a month, our program was unchanged in the various cities in which we played. But four broadcasts in a week is something else; it means you've got to take your coat off and keep up a pretty steady pace; it means preparing an entirely different program for each broadcast. At that rate it doesn't take long to exhaust even an extensive repertoire."

Dubose Heyward wrote an article in the October 1935 issue of *Stage* magazine in which he described the nature of his collaboration with Gershwin at the time *Porgy and Bess* received its first New York performance:

> . . . then in October [1933], exactly two years ago, our impatience got the better of what may prove to be our better judgment, and the actual adventure of composing began.
>
> It is the fashion in America to lament the prostitution of art by the big magazine, the radio, the moving pictures. With this I have little patience. Properly utilized, the radio and the pictures may be to the present-day writer what his prince was to Villon, the King of Bavaria was to Wagner.
>
> At no other time has it been possible for a writer to earn by hiring himself out as a skilled technician for, say, two months, sufficient income to sustain him for a year. And yet the moving pictures have made it possible. I decided that the silver screen should be my Maecenas, and George elected to serve the radio.
>
> During my first year I wrote the screen version of *The Emperor Jones*. For this I may have lost the friendship of Eugene O'Neill. I haven't dared to look him up since. And to finance my second year I made a pilgrimage to Hollywood to tinker at Pearl Buck's *Good Earth*. My selection for this assignment presented a perfect example of motion picture logic. When I arrived on the lot and asked why I had been offered the job, it was made perfectly plain to me. Negroes were not a Caucasian people. Neither were Chinamen. I wrote understandingly of Negroes. It was obvious then that I would understand the Chinese. . . .
>
> At the outset we were faced by a difficult problem. I was firm in my refusal to leave the South and live in New York. Gershwin was bound for the duration of his contract to the microphone at Radio City. The matter of effecting a happy union between words and music across a thousand miles of Atlantic seaboard baffled us for a moment. The solution came quite naturally when we associated Ira Gershwin with us. Presently we evolved a system which, between my visits North, or George's dash to Charleston, I could send scenes and lyrics. Then the brothers Gershwin, after their extraordinary fashion, would get at the piano, pound, wrangle, swear, burst into weird snatches of song, and eventually emerge with a polished lyric. Then too, Ira's gift for the more sophisticated

lyric was exactly suited to the task of writing the songs for Sporting Life, the Harlem gambler who had drifted into Catfish Row.

I imagine that in after years when George looks back upon this time, he will feel that the summer of 1934 furnished him with one of the most satisfying as well as exciting experiences of his career. Under the baking suns of July and August we established ourselves on Folly Island, a small barrier island ten miles from Charleston. James Island with its large population of Gullah Negroes lay adjacent, and furnished us with a laboratory in which to test our theories, as well as an inexhaustible source of folk material. But the most interesting discovery to me, as we sat listening to their spirituals, or watched a group shuffling before a cabin or country store, was that to George it was more like a homecoming than an exploration. The quality in him which had produced the *Rhapsody in Blue* in the most sophisticated city in America, found its counterpart in the impulse behind the music and bodily rhythms of the simple Negro peasant of the South.

The Gullah Negro prides himself on what he calls "shouting." This is a complicated rhythmic pattern beaten out by feet and hands as an accompaniment to the spirituals, and is indubitably an African survival. I shall never forget the night when at a Negro meeting on a remote sea-island, George started "shouting" with them. And eventually to their huge delight stole the show from their champion "shouter." I think that he is probably the only white man in America who could have done it.

Another night as we were about to enter a dilapidated cabin that had been taken as a meeting house by a group of Negro Holy Rollers, George caught my arm and held me. The sound that had arrested him was one to which, through long familiarity, I attached no special importance. But now, listening to it with him, and noticing his excitement, I began to catch its extraordinary quality. It consisted of perhaps a dozen voices raised in loud rhythmic prayer. The odd thing about it was that while each had started at a different time, upon a different theme, they formed a clearly defined rhythmic pattern, and that this, with the actual words lost, and the inevitable pounding of the rhythm, produced an effect almost terrifying in its primitive intensity. Inspired by the extraordinary effect, George wrote six simultaneous prayers producing a terrifying primitive invocation to God in the face of the hurricane.

We had hoped, and it was logical, that the Theater Guild would produce the opera. An excursion into that field of the theater was a new idea to the directors. But then they had gambled once on *Porgy* and won. There was a sort of indulgent affection for the cripple and his goat on Fifty-second Street. Most certainly they did not want anybody else to do it, and so contracts were signed.

Having committed themselves, the Guild proceeded to deprive us of all alibis in the event of failure by giving us a free hand in the casting and a star producing staff. . . .

We were in rather a dither about the name. The composer and author both felt that the opera should be called simply *Porgy*. But there was a feeling in the publicity department that this would lead to a confusion in that amorphous region known as the public mind, and that *Porgy* in lights might be construed as a revival of the original play, rather than as the Gershwin opus. There had of course been *Pelleas and Melisande*, *Samson and Delilah*, *Tristan and Isolde*.

"And so," said Heyward, with the humility characteristic of those who draw their sustenance from the theater, "why not *Porgy and Bess?*"

To which Gershwin replied with the detachment to which I have referred and which could not possibly be mistaken for conceit, "Of course, it's right in the operatic tradition."

Two years! It doesn't seem that long. There has been so much to do. The published version of the piano and vocal score, fresh from the press, runs to five hundred and sixty pages. And when that was finished, George tackled the orchestration single-handed. The resulting manuscript is impressive. It contains seven hundred pages of closely written music, and it is the fruit of nine months of unremitting labor.

For my own part, I had a play which needed to be cut forty percent for the libretto, yet nothing of dramatic value could be sacrificed. The dialogue had to follow that of the drama, but it had to be arranged to form a new pattern, to escape monotony

> and adapt itself to the music. And then there were the spirituals, and the lyrics on which Ira and I worked.
>
> In the theater every production is a gamble. In some, naturally, the odds are greater than in the others. *Porgy and Bess* has, I believe, a fair chance of scoring. But whether it does or not, we who have written and composed the opera cannot lose. We have spent two years doing exactly what we wanted to. It has been a very special sort of adventure. That, at any rate, is in the bag.

In addition to everything Dubose Heyward recounts, in 1991 Paul Mueller said that he and George traveled by car to the Deep South: "Mr. Gershwin wanted to understand the relationships among the Negroes, how they lived and how they perceived themselves."

Heyward's article covers the highlights of the two-year period preceding the opening. But it does not answer the question of why a work, said to have been planned for the Met, came to be presented by the Theater Guild. Gershwin had said to Heyward in 1933 that Otto Kahn had offered him $5,000 to bring *Porgy* to the Met, but that may not have been true. After all, in 1929 Kahn had offered only $1,000 for a Gershwin *Dybbuk*. Heyward says that Gershwin preferred a Theater Guild production to one by the Met because the Guild was more likely than the Met to use an all-black cast, because the Guild's seats would be less expensive than the Met's, and because the Guild offered a longer run of the work than the Metropolitan Opera's repertory system. According to Ira, Kahn had told George that only two performances would be done during the opera's first season.

But all these considerations became academic when Otto Kahn died on March 29, 1934. It was highly unlikely that the Met without Kahn would consider mounting an opera about blacks. Not a single black was singing there at the time. Marian Anderson was at the peak of her career (Toscanini had said a voice like hers appears only once in a century). Yet even she had not sung at the Met. It is surprising that Kahn was willing to risk his position there to pressure the company to do *Porgy and Bess*. His own tastes mirrored the company's conservative bent.

When his son Roger set out to form a dance band—which he eventually did—Otto fought him bitterly. If the father reacted so negatively to his son's move into popular music, why would he support the commission of an opera that would inevitably contain echoes of Broadway?

The chances are that he did not, for no letters about *Porgy and Bess* between Gershwin and the Met have come to light. That it ended up with the Theater Guild must initially have disappointed Gershwin, who had been telling all his friends and associates that his opera would "resemble a combination of the drama and romance of *Carmen* with the beauty of *Die Meistersinger*." When his work opened in New York, after many rehearsals in Boston and a week of performances there, it had been stripped of many of its operatic properties and of its designation as an opera. Board members of the Theater Guild were afraid the word would frighten off audiences. The final decision to call *Porgy and Bess* a folk opera was a compromise.

Heyward, in his article, did not describe how George brought Ira into what had been planned as a two-man collaboration. Ira's involvement made a great deal of sense. On the one hand, as Heyward writes, he could create exactly the right lyrics for the sophisticated Sporting Life, something Heyward thought he himself could not do. When the songs were copyrighted, Heyward received full authorship for "Summertime," "My Man's Gone Now," and "A Woman Is a Sometime Thing." Ira received full authorship for "It Ain't Necessarily So," and "There's a Boat Dat's Leavin' Soon for New York." Heyward and Ira shared credit for "I Got Plenty o' Nuttin' " and "Bess, You Is My Woman Now."

It is understandable that in his narrative, Heyward would not have delved into the nuances of feeling between the blacks and whites created by the work. In 1990, Eva Jessye, director of the chorus, said that Gershwin used the word "nigger" during rehearsals.

Todd Duncan, who became famous for the role of Porgy, has told many interviewers that after his first audition, when Gershwin called him to come in a second time, "I just wasn't very interested. I thought of Gershwin as being Tin Pan Alley and beneath me." Duncan, then thirty-two, was teaching music at Howard University and had sung in a black performance of *Cavalleria rusticana* at the Mecca Temple on West Fifty-fifth Street in Manhattan. Olin Downes heard him there and recommended him to Gershwin.

Gershwin had originally wanted Paul Robeson for the role. But he was unavailable, so Gershwin auditioned more than a hundred men before selecting Duncan. At first Duncan dismissed Gershwin, but he is very moving when he describes how he grew to love Gershwin and his songs.

The soprano who sang the role of Clara in the opening production of *Porgy and Bess* was Abbie Mitchell. In a way, that is ironic since she was the wife of Will Marion Cook, who set out to be the first black composer of a black opera almost forty years earlier. Over those years Abbie Mitchell had sung the female lead in many of Cook's musicals. Then, after decades of hard work as well as a marital separation, Cook watched Mitchell make her name in an opera about blacks by a white man.

More to the point, the music itself had its roots in the black world. Gershwin himself acknowledged this when he inscribed to W. C. Handy a first edition copy of *Rhapsody in Blue*. His comment that Handy's blues were the "forefathers" of *Rhapsody* applied to *Porgy and Bess* as well. Consider, after all, the melodic link between Gershwin's "Summertime" and Handy's "St. Louis Blues."

Gershwin's music did not come only from the blacks he heard in his younger days in Harlem. He also went to the Yiddish Theater, mostly for the musical comedies. These productions included songs from Russia and Romania and Hasidic melodies from Poland and Transylvania, which inevitably brought a feeling of melancholy homesickness for places from which many in the audience had emigrated.

In an article that appeared in a 1936 issue of *B'nai B'rith Magazine*, Goldberg, Gershwin's biographer, wrote that he always regretted that Gershwin had not finished setting *The Dybbuk*, because he heard him play snatches of the music he had composed for that score. Goldberg added that "it would be, from an artistic as well as psychological standpoint, a pity if Gershwin, during his experiments with Negro-American and native American material, did not find a libretto of Jewish atmosphere for the exercise of his expanding gifts." Goldberg then makes the point that there "is a strong affinity between Hasidic melodies and certain types of Negro song.

"Listen to a tune like George's 'My One and Only,' or some of the strains in *Funny Face*," he observes, "and you can turn them into Jewish melodies by a subtle emphasis in the singing. The 'blue' notes of a typical black melody have their counterparts in certain chromatics of the scale . . . so commonly found in Hasidic tunes. Is it an exaggeration to say that the Jew in Gershwin—I mean the unselfconscious Jew—helped to make him our foremost writer of American-Negroid music?"

What Goldberg admires—the striking similarity in the music of the Jews and blacks—is treated with scorn by anti-Semitic composers of the time. Constant Lambert, a British composer, in *Music Ho! A Study of Music in Decline*, published by Faber & Faber in 1934, echoed the *Dearborn Independent* when he wrote,

> The importance of the Jewish element in jazz cannot be too strongly emphasized, and the fact that at least ninety percent of jazz tunes are written by Jews undoubtedly goes far to account for the curiously sagging quality—so typical of Jewish art—the almost masochistic melancholy of the average foxtrot. This masochistic element is becoming more and more a part of general consciousness, but it has its stronghold in the Jewish temperament.
>
> There is an obvious link between the exiled and persecuted Jews and the exiled and persecuted Negroes, which the Jews, with their admirable capacity for drinking the beer of those who have knocked down their skittles, have not been slow to turn to their advantage. But although the Jews have stolen the Negroes' thunder, although Al Jolson's nauseating blubbering masquerades as savage lamenting, although Tin Pan Alley has become a commercialized Wailing Wall, the only jazz music of technical importance is that small section of it that is genuinely

> negroid. The "hot" Negro records still have a genuine and not merely galvanic energy, while the blues have a certain austerity that places them far above the sweet nothings of George Gershwin.

Gershwin was working on *Porgy and Bess* when *Music Ho!* was published. In his writings Levant discusses Lambert's anti-Semitic tract, and if Levant was aware of it, Gershwin surely was too. But there is no evidence that he reacted to it.

Lambert's reference to Jolson has nothing to do with *Porgy*, but, coincidentally, Jolson was involved with the project. Some reviews of the play in 1927 noted Gershwin's plan to turn it into an opera. But before that Jolson adapted the play for radio. More publicity about Gershwin's intentions followed. Jolson offered $30,000 for the film rights to do *Porgy* in blackface. Heyward accepted the offer, but the movie was never made.

Then Jolson asked Heyward for a deal in which he could do a blackface *Porgy* for a Kern-Hammerstein musical. Heyward wrote about it to Gershwin. A man less secure in his musicianship than Gershwin might not have responded this way: "I think it is very interesting," he replied, "that Jolson would like to play the role of Porgy, but I really don't know how he would be in it. . . . It might mean more to you financially if he could do it —provided that the rest of the production is well done. The sort of thing I have in mind is a much more serious thing than Jolson can ever do. If you can see your way to making some ready money from Jolson's version, I don't know that it would hurt a later version done by an all-colored cast." Gershwin added that what he had in mind was "more a labor of love than anything else." But Kern and Hammerstein both got busy with other shows and this project disappeared.

Jolson's persistent and continued interest in doing *Porgy* could have been precipitated by his concern that once blacks began to appear in shows created and produced by whites, Jolson's role as the most successful blackface in show business would be finished. He must have sensed this when he ordered George White to kill Gershwin's *Blue Monday Blues* back in the 1922 *Scandals*. And he probably felt increasingly threatened by Lew Leslie's *Blackbirds of 1927*, a huge Broadway success with a score by Jimmy McHugh and lyrics by Dorothy Fields. When Jolson felt challenged he became extremely self-protective. In 1991, Joey Adams, the veteran comedian, characterized Jolson as "the biggest son of a bitch I have ever known. One night I asked him if I could appear on stage with him at the Winter Garden with my impersonation of him. I was getting $80 a week doing that at Leon and Eddie's. He not only refused what I asked him; after listening to me do it, he offered me $100 a week never to do it again."

However disappointed Gershwin may have been at not having his work performed at the Metropolitan Opera, things turned out better the way they occurred. The Theater Guild gave him far more power than any opera house would have; opera houses were used to producing operas by dead composers, who can't make trouble.

Gershwin auditioned and chose Todd Duncan for Porgy, Ann Brown for Bess, Ruby Elzy for Serena and John W. Bubbles for Sporting Life. Gershwin believed that Astaire had modeled his own dancing on Bubbles from the start of his career, and Gershwin, whose admiration for Astaire dated from his Remick days, paid attention to Astaire's judgments. Bubbles was undisciplined, but Gershwin never regretted his choice. Difficult in rehearsal, he dazzled in performance.

Gershwin was also accorded the right to choose the production ensemble. He selected Alexander Smallens, the conductor of *Four Saints in Three Acts*, as his music director. After the opening of the Thomson-Stein work, Gershwin went backstage and told Smallens he was writing an opera and would like him to hear it. Smallens accepted the invitation, heard it and agreed to conduct it. It would have been more considerate for Gershwin to have waited until the next day and not intrude on Thomson's show. But again, Gershwin displayed his characteristic lack of sensitivity.

Soon afterward, at a Town Hall reception for Stravinsky, Gershwin asked Alexander Steinert, a coach for the Russian Opera Company, if he would coach the singers for his opera. Again the answer was yes. Gershwin overrode Heyward's negative vote against Mamoulian and sided with the Theater Guild in selecting him over everyone else. Apparently Heyward believed Mamoulian's hyperkinetic direction of the play reduced the power of his poetry.

Mamoulian has eloquently described what it was like for him to watch the Gershwin brothers go through the score for him. "It was touching to see how Ira, while singing, would become so overwhelmed with admiration for his brother that he would look from him to me with half-open eyes and pantomime with a soft gesture of his hand, as if saying, 'He did it. Isn't it wonderful? Isn't *he* wonderful?' " Throughout the years when Rose looked coldly on George's work and Morris said he *had* to like it, Ira's absolute belief in his brother's genius must have provided a significant counterbalance to their hostility. (To say Rose criticized George is not to imply she withheld help when she could give it. Kay Swift says Mrs. Gershwin "hated" the costumes chosen for *Porgy and Bess*, that she thought they looked as if they'd come from Saks Fifth Avenue. According to Swift, Rose went to the Lower East Side and outfitted most of the cast herself.)

The Gershwins invested their own money in the production. The Theater Guild estimated that its costs would run as high as $100,000, a great deal of money at the time, even for a major production like this. George and Ira invested 15 percent of the required capital, and George convinced Heyward to buy in for another 5 percent.

In July 1935, two months before the Boston tryout, Gershwin persuaded William S. Paley, head of the Columbia Broadcasting System, to underwrite the cost of an orchestra of forty-three musicians and also make available a company recording studio. Gershwin may have succeeded in getting all of this without giving up a share of the profits because Paley felt he owed Gershwin something for the use—without Gershwin's knowledge—of his *Rhapsody in Blue* as the theme of *The Old Gold Program*, CBS's first important radio show. The show starred Paul Whiteman and his orchestra. Paley paid the band $30,000 a week and Whiteman another $5,000. Whatever the reason, when *Porgy and Bess* had its first rehearsal with an orchestra, Gershwin conducted and CBS engineers recorded some of these sessions.

The performance recorded in these sessions began with Jasbo Brown on the piano. (That was cut before the opera reached New York.) Then Edward Matthews sang "A Woman Is a Sometime Thing," Ruby Elzy sang "My Man's Gone Now," Abbie Mitchell sang "Summertime" and Duncan and Brown sang "Bess, You Is My Woman Now." In the finale, with everyone singing full voice over the richly textured orchestra, Gershwin's voice is heard singing along. When he played piano or conducted, he did not inhibit himself from singing.

When Duncan, whom Gershwin chose to play Porgy, described his second visit to the composer's East Seventy-second Street apartment, he said he had thought he would sing three or four songs for the guests. Instead he spent an hour singing perhaps thirty pieces—operatic arias, lieder, and spirituals. Then Gershwin led him upstairs to his studio and he and Ira—with Gershwin at the piano—sang through the then incomplete *Porgy and Bess* score.

Duncan said that when they began, he was appalled "by their awful voices" but soon the beauty overwhelmed him: "I was in heaven," Duncan recalled. "Those beautiful melodies in this new idiom—it was something I had never heard before."

Porgy and Bess did not receive its first production in an opera house, but its various components were in the hands of sophisticated artists with experience in opera and ballet. Mamoulian, who had directed the play and then gone to Hollywood to make movies, not only had had experience in opera; he was also a knowledgeable musician. With the score always open in front of him, Mamoulian directed the movements of the performers to accord with the rhythm of the score. Serge Soudeikine, the set designer for the work, had not only been married to Vera Stravinsky before she divorced him to live with the composer but he also worked regularly for Diaghilev, the ballet impresario.

Duncan spoke of Gershwin's "beautiful melodies," but it was the counterpoint of many passages that was the source of the composer's own pride. Morton Gould, the first rehearsal pianist for *Porgy and Bess*, remembers Gershwin—at their first meeting—at the piano playing through the thickly contrapuntal material in an effort to impress whoever might be listening. Gould says that when they began to rehearse, he was stunned by beautiful songs, songs that had become so easy for Gershwin to make that he ignored them in favor of his new and complex orchestral texture.

In a September 21, 1990, letter, composer Elie Siegmeister wrote, "I took another look at the fugue in the murder scene of *Porgy and Bess* and found it to be a very respectable, traditional fugue—with jazz subject and countersubject—fully developed and quite an achievement for one whom Virgil Thomson, Copland and many others looked down the ends of their respective noses at. I can think of no other full-fledged fugues in opera except the one in *Falstaff*—and Gershwin's is, I think, far more dramatic."

Levant, who also studied with Schillinger, attributed the new texture to what Gershwin learned from their teacher. "There always seemed to me in *Porgy and Bess* a considerable evidence of his studies with Schillinger—not, of course, in the melodic writing or the songs, but in the working out of the rhythmic patterns, the planning of such episodes as the fugal background for the crap-game scene and in some of the choral passages. Schillinger's theories of cyclical harmonic progressions, with an intricate leading of the bass notes, his scheme of rhythmic permutations, extended George's resources considerably." Gershwin gave credit to Schillinger for those expanded resources when he spoke to other composers. Charles Previn went to Schillinger on Gershwin's recommendation. And Paul Whiteman, in an interview published in the Los Angeles *Times* in June 1942, said Gershwin had told him "of his delight in the 'master patterns' and the new release he felt in orchestrating *Porgy and Bess* by Schillinger's mathematical variations."

Gershwin's use of several voices in the crapshooters' finale at the end of the first scene, the exquisite blending of the voices in "Gone, Gone, Gone," and the technique behind those orchestral passages with xylophones intended to evoke African strains apparently benefitted from the Schillinger studies. Yet Nicolas Slonimsky says, "George told me that the only aspect of *Porgy and Bess* that he ever got out of Schillinger was the treatment of the theme before the opening of the second act."

Gershwin believed that this score was richer than anything he had composed before. Surely one of his purposes was to impress those composers to whom Siegmeister refers. One was Roger Sessions, a formidable figure in the composing establishment. Sessions was probably the first major American composer to use Schoenberg's twelve-tone system as an integral part of his own work. Gershwin was exceptionally eager to meet Sessions.

When he arrived at Gershwin's East Seventy-second Street apartment, Gershwin is reported to have greeted him with his thick manuscript for *Porgy and Bess.* "Do you think this is long enough to be an opera?" he asked Sessions. Milton Babbitt tells the story to show that Gershwin was so ingenuous that he thought that he could impress the avant-garde just by showing a handwritten score of more than seven hundred pages. One wonders if Gershwin pointed out to Sessions any part of the score that used the twelve-tone idea. The fugue Siegmeister mentions is perhaps the most complete expression of that, although those who consider themselves twelve-tone composers would not include such sporadic use of the method as a bona fide application of it. Even they, however, would probably concede the presence of a dense, chromatic, atonal idiom in parts of this score. When Porgy returns from jail in Act III, to cite one such example, and hands out presents to his friends on Catfish Row, he does so to the accompaniment of a musical texture highly reminiscent of Berg.

Near the end of Sporting Life's music, which contains within it "There's a Boat Dat's Leavin' Soon for New York," Gershwin uses a D-major chord over an A-flat-major chord, in other words, a simultaneous presentation of two different key centers. It echoes Stravinsky's use of F-sharp major over C major in the closing measures of *Petrouchka*, which Diaghilev pressed him to remove in favor of the traditional single tonality. Stravinsky refused Diaghilev and the device grew to be famous as "the Petrouchka chord." In using something similar in *Porgy and Bess*, Gershwin shows his respect for Stravinsky, as he showed his respect for Schoenberg in an orchestral fabric that was new for him.

In a letter from California a year after the opera's premiere, Gershwin wrote Schillinger, "I've been considering doing some studying either with Schoenberg or Toch. I haven't gotten down to make the decision yet, but it might be a good idea for me to keep working." Schillinger replied by suggesting he study with both. This has been widely interpreted as a snide answer to a stupid question, because Schoenberg and Toch were so removed from each other in style and substance that one could never consider them as interchangeable. This was a time when composers lined up in one of a few camps, zealously rejecting everything outside of theirs. But Gershwin seems to have believed that whatever was being done in music that could be useful to him was something he ought to know about.

Gershwin may not have understood the musical politics of the time, but he understood music. He knew it intuitively. And he delighted in finding the theories and techniques that confirmed what he knew. In the fall 1987 issue of the *Journal of the American Musicological Society*, Charles Hamm says that it is a widely circulated "myth" that Gershwin would have preferred his opera to be performed in its entirety, as it is being done today, rather than with the extensive cuts that were made before it opened in New York October 10, 1935.

What Hamm does not take into consideration is Gershwin's temperament and personality. Gershwin wanted, above all, to avoid confrontation. Therefore, he allowed himself to be pushed into making changes that he probably wouldn't have made on his own.

The CBS-financed rehearsal in July was followed by a more formal rehearsal that took the form of a concert performance at Carnegie Hall. *Porgy and Bess* was performed then in its entirety for a small, invited audience. Even before it opened at the Colonial Theater in Boston, significant cuts were made during rehearsals. Then, after the first public performance, many more deletions were made, though the first-night audience in Boston applauded for fifteen minutes, and the reviews were favorable. The Colonial Theater had to turn down thousands of requests for tickets because the run was limited to a week. Among those who attended that first night were the presidents of Harvard, Radcliffe, Wellesley and MIT along with Koussevitzky.

The New York premiere, the formal world premiere, brought forth celebrities from every field. Novelists Fannie Hurst, Edna Ferber, and J. B. Priestley; playwrights Ben Hecht, Elmer Rice, and Robert E. Sherwood; opera stars Kirsten Flagstad and Lily Pons; actors Leslie Howard, Joan Crawford, Katharine Hepburn, and Norma Shearer; and concert stars Fritz Kreisler and Jascha Heifetz. Both theater and music critics reviewed the show, among them Brooks Atkinson, Alexander Woollcott, John Mason Brown, Samuel Chotzinoff, and Virgil Thomson, who wrote frequently for *Modern Music*.

George and Ira sat in a back row with Kay Swift. She had spent many hours helping George notate the score. (By this time Kay was divorced from Warburg and had custody of their three children.)

Swift also spent time organizing a lavish postopening party at the penthouse apartment of publisher Condé Nast on Madison Avenue. With Jules Glaenzer, Marshall Field, Averell Harriman and William Paley paying for the party, she hired Enrique Madriguera's Latin band. That offended Paul Whiteman, who gathered together his twelve men and pushed onto the bandstand. But as soon as the cast members arrived, Gershwin sat down at the piano and played through the score once again with the singers.

What the first-night audience saw was a stage filled with remarkable black singers who had been rehearsed by sophisticated coaches and directors. What they heard, however, was considerably less than what Gershwin had composed. After the Boston opening, he, Mamoulian, Steinert, and Swift walked in the Boston Common, arguing over cuts. According to Steinert: "Very few composers would have stood by and witnessed with comparative calm the dismemberment of their brainchild until it had been reduced by nearly a quarter." Mitch Miller was in the pit for *Porgy and Bess*. "When the cuts were made," he says, "the musicians all agreed they had taken the balls out of the show."

The opening of the work with Jasbo Brown alone at the piano was cut. In a November 12, 1933, letter, Heyward proposed to Gershwin the opening scene should merge with the overture: "It would be very effective to have the lights go out during the overture, so that the curtain rises in darkness, then the first scene will begin . . . as the music takes up the theme of the dance hall piano." The libretto opens with Jasbo Brown, playing piano, on stage.

Heyward later said he chose the name because "according to tradition, jazz has taken its name from Jasbo Brown, an itinerant Negro player along the Mississippi, and later, in Chicago cabarets." Gershwin agreed with Heyward and wrote 133 bars of music for Jasbo Brown to play on stage with the black singers and the orchestra finally joining him. A little of this can be heard in the recording made in the CBS studio. All of it can be seen in the score in the Gershwin Archives at the Library of Congress.

By the time the opera arrived in New York, the scene was gone altogether and after only twenty bars of Jasbo's music played by a piano in the pit, the orchestra introduces "Summertime."

The very scene Heyward described in his article—the one inspired by what he and Gershwin heard as they stood outside a black church—came out entirely. Gershwin had tried to recreate what he heard by opening Act II Scene 4 with six prayers, each clearly notated with its own melody and text—freely sung over a consistent bass line. Gershwin wrote: "Ad libitum." The impression is one of three women and three men, each singing over the group's humming during the prayer.

Here Gershwin anticipated by almost twenty years the idea behind the "chance" music of composer John Cage. The decision was made to do away with this, probably because the result did not sound neat. Gershwin's use of this idea, long before it was called aleatoric, calls to mind a remark he made after starting to work with Schillinger. He said that he was pleased to find that what he had been performing as parlor games at the piano had genuine theoretical premises. But Gershwin must have been pained by what he allowed to be cut. The cuts included many complex orchestral passages, the ones he had shown off to Morton Gould and others, as well as reprises of many songs.

The cuts sometimes hurt the development of the music and the harmonic structure on which it was based. Among them were most of the trio sung by Serena, Maria, and Porgy and virtually all the music that accompanied Porgy's belief near the end that Bess was dead. There were major deletions in the opening crap game, in the climactic passages of the fight when Porgy actually kills Crown, in the music with which Bess seeks shelter after Crown's death, and in the "Buzzard Song." Not only was the recitative—music designed to imitate speech—leading up to the song taken out; the whole song disappeared. Thirty years later Wilfrid Mellers, a British musicologist, wrote in *Music in a New Found Land:* It is "the turning point of the opera. The anguished appogiaturas, the strained gawky leaps and flapping winged chromatics are darker in character than any music we have heard previously, since the anguish is now that of personal experience—of growing up—and is not, like the dirge, a communal lamentation. The appearance of the buzzard marks Porgy's realization of the significance of his love; and although conflict is manifest in the rondo structure, the song turns into a victory for love/life over death."

Two days before the New York opening, at a birthday party held on the stage of the Alvin Theater for Mamoulian, Gershwin handed the director a roll of pages from his score tied with a red ribbon and said, "This is my thank you for making me take out all that stuff." Gershwin may have been making an ironic gesture in thanking Mamoulian for the cuts he must have viewed with at least mixed emotions. Nobody likes cuts, no matter how much they may improve the dynamic structure of a work. And in this case, it is not clear that this editing accomplished anything but to shorten the running time of the show.

After the Condé Nast party, the reviews made it clear that Gershwin had made a mistake in going along with Mamoulian. Most reviewers criticized the work as being "Broadway." In the New York *Times*, Olin Downes wrote that Gershwin "has not completely formed his style as an operatic composer. The style is at one moment of opera and another of operetta or sheer Broadway entertainment." But the strongest negative reaction came from Virgil Thomson, still generally considered one of America's best critics.

"One can see, through *Porgy*," Thomson wrote in *Modern Music*, "that Gershwin has not and never did have any power of sustained musical development. . . . The material is straight from the melting pot. At best it is a piquant but highly unsavory stirring-up together of Israel, Africa and the Gaelic Isles. . . . His lack of understanding of all the major problems of form, of continuity, and of serious or direct musical expression is not surprising in view of the impurity of his musical sources and his frank acceptance of the same. Such frankness is admirable. At twenty-five it was also charming. *Gaminerie* of any kind at 35 is more difficult to stomach. So that quite often *Porgy and Bess*, instead of being pretty, is a little hoydenish. . . . It is clear, by now, that Gershwin hasn't learned the business of being a serious composer, which one has always gathered to be the business he wanted to learn. . . . His efforts at recitative are as ineffective as anything I've heard. . . . I do not like fake folklore, nor fidgety accompaniments, nor bittersweet harmony, nor six-part choruses, nor gefilte fish orchestration."

These remarks—including the smarmy anti-Semitism—concerned technique. When Thomson addressed musical substance, he found "nothing of much interest, little exercises in the jazz-modernistic style, quite cute for the most part, but leading nowhere. The scoring is heavy, over-rich and vulgar. It is nervous, too, like the whole musical texture. . . . *Green Pastures*, the last act of *Run, Little Chillun*, *Four Saints in Three Acts* are all little eminences on the flat horizon of American opera. . . . Two of these are straight folklore. The third is straight opera. *Porgy and Bess* is the least interesting of the four, because it is not straight anything. It is crooked folklore and halfway opera, a strong but crippled work."

Thomson doesn't hesitate to mention his own opera *Four Saints* without saying it is his, and even accords it the distinction of being the only real opera in the list.

Vladimir Selinsky, a violinist who played in the pit of *Girl Crazy* in 1930 and later in Gershwin's radio shows, told his wife that soon after the opening, Gershwin told the musicians he was "upset" by the reviews, most particularly by Thomson's essay. He tried to answer the attacks and wrote a defensive article that appeared on October 20, 1935, in the New York *Times:*

> It is true that I have written songs for *Porgy and Bess*. I am not ashamed of writing songs at any time so long as they are good songs. In *Porgy and Bess* I realized I was writing an opera for the theater, and without songs it could neither be of the theater nor entertaining, from my viewpoint.
>
> But songs are entirely within the operatic tradition. Many of the most successful operas of the past have had songs. Nearly all of Verdi's operas contain what are known as "song hits." *Carmen* is almost a collection of song hits. . . .
>
> Of course the songs in *Porgy and Bess* are only a part of the whole. The recitative I have tried to make as close to the Negro inflection in speech as possible and I believe my songwriting apprenticeship has served invaluably in this respect, because the song writers of America have the best conception of how to set words so that the music gives added expression to the words.
>
> I have used sustained symphonic music to unify entire scenes, and I prepared myself for that task by further study in counterpoint and modern harmony.

An unidentified man brought Alan to *Porgy and Bess* early in its run. Alan remembers that the house was crowded, and men wore tuxedos. Father and son dined afterward in a quiet restaurant. Then George went off to a party, and Alan was delivered back to the Schneiders in Brooklyn.

In *Our Two Lives*, Halina Rodzinski, widow of conductor Artur Rodzinski, writes about a time Gershwin traveled to Cleveland to attend a performance her husband conducted of Shostakovich's *Lady Macbeth of Mzensk*, a League of Composers' production. She notes that Gershwin attended a second time when Rodzinski repeated it at the Metropolitan Opera House in New York. During the Rodzinskis' Manhattan visit, Kay Halle, a friend of Gershwin's, brought them to the composer's apartment. Halina Rodzinski describes his life style as "elegant" while characterizing Gershwin himself as "natural, unaffected, and utterly unspoiled." After lunch the composer brought his guests into his studio and showed Rodzinski his score for *Porgy and Bess*.

Halina Rodzinski writes that her husband said, "Give it to me for a Cleveland premiere. We'll create a sensation every bit as great as *Lady Macbeth* did."

Gershwin, she goes on, "doubted whether those who had commissioned it would relinquish the score for a purely operatic premiere. 'I'll try my best,' he promised. Unfortunately Gershwin's best was not enough with the business men who had invested in a Broadway hit, and so *Porgy and Bess* entered the annals of American musical theater as a musical comedy. But when we sailed for Europe, there was still hope that *Porgy* might crown Cleveland's coming season."

It never did. A publisher's note that accompanies the full score in the Beinecke Library at Yale University leaves no doubt as to how the composer himself viewed his work: "This is the Original Unabridged Version of *Porgy and Bess*. Due to time limitations in the theatre, the actual playing version has several deletions."

. . .

In December 1991, Gunther Schuller, a composer, conductor, and author who has worked in the worlds of concert music and jazz, called *Porgy and Bess* "a work of genius. It has great songs. It has the construction of opera. I love the dramatic, transitional music, the music we are hearing today now that all the cuts have been restored. And the work is so gorgeously orchestrated. . . ." With these remarks Schuller distances himself from virtually everything Thomson wrote about the work. And although he probably distances himself as well from many of the criticisms voiced by blacks, he approaches them with understanding: "Of course the blacks lashed out at Gershwin," Schuller explains. "Joplin and those before and after him had tried to write their own operas. Theirs was a proud history. And, as so often with black music, they got ripped off. Whatever difficulties *Porgy and Bess* faced, it was far more successful than anything any of them had ever done.

"Nor was it the first time the blacks had been ripped off in music or—for that matter—the last time. It happened with the minstrel, ragtime, jazz and later with rhythm and blues. The blacks have always invented the music. The whites take it over. Then the blacks invent something new."

The sense of rage black musicians felt at the situation Schuller describes must have been the primary reason they attacked Gershwin and not Heyward, who, after all, was the one who created the characters and re-created the dialect. Duke Ellington, who, in 1931, wrote a six-minute concert work of his own called *Creole Rhapsody* (Schuller writes that it borrowed a great deal from Gershwin) attacked his white colleague in 1935 in an article in *New Theater* magazine. Ellington wrote that *Porgy and Bess* did not use the Negro idiom. "It was taken from some of the best and a few of the worst. Mr. Gershwin didn't discriminate—he borrowed from everyone from Liszt to Dickie Wells' kazoo band. . . . The times are here to debunk Gershwin's lampblack negroisms." He concluded that "no Negro could possibly be fooled by *Porgy and Bess*."

Ellington may have been reacting in part out of envy: in 1930, he had begun composing an opera called *Boola*, which he said would chart the history of the black peoples from Egypt to Harlem. He never finished it.

Ralph Matthews, music critic for the *Afro-American*, also wrote harshly about the work. He claimed it was neither opera, musical comedy, nor drama with music and that, most certainly it was not Negro. Matthews dismissed it as a "musical hybrid" and went on to say "there are none of the deep sonorous incantations so frequently identified with racial offerings. There is none of the jubilee spirit of *Run, Little Chillun*, and none of the deep soul stirring songs of *The Green Pastures*. The singing, even down to the choral and ensemble numbers, had a conservatory twang."

Hall Johnson, another African-American musician and conductor, said he had attended four performances of *Porgy and Bess* and that what saved it was the "intelligent pliability of the large Negro cast assembled to project it while obviously working under strict direction. . . . They still are able, however, to infuse enough of their own natural racial qualities into the proceedings to invest them with a convincing semblance of plausibility. This is true even in the musical and dramatic moments most alien to the real Negro genre. If these singing actors had been as inexperienced as the composer, *Porgy and Bess* might have turned out to be as stiff and artificial in performance as it is on paper. Fortunately for all concerned, this is not the case." In this instance, when a black writer finds the work admirable in any way, it is despite, not because of Gershwin.

Later J. Rosamond Johnson, James Weldon Johnson's brother, a composer who served as assistant conductor of the chorus, wrote that, at the end, when Gershwin stood on stage surrounded by colleagues and friends, Johnson told the composer: "You're the Abraham Lincoln of Negro music." Gershwin not only thanked him at the time, he sought him out the next day to thank him again. The Johnson brothers were among the few who went on record at that time applauding Gershwin for *Porgy and Bess*.

Friends were not much help. In *Memoirs of an Amnesiac*, Levant wrote: "At the first performance of *Porgy and Bess*, I naturally squirmed a little; I had been a Schoenberg pupil, and there were so many song hits with Broadway endings. I turned to critic John V.A. Weaver, who was sitting next to me, and said, 'It's a right step in the wrong direction.' I have felt enormous remorse for that remark, as I have for many of my other soundings and phrases about my best friend's work. It was harsh, but I reconsidered and I now think it is a glorious paean to American Jewish music."

Levant's reconsideration is hardly a major compliment, and even that took decades for him to articulate, long after his "best friend" died. But his writings are always provocative and his description of the bows taken at the first performance is worthy of repeating here: "George was never nervous whenever he had to appear professionally and his stage deportment was always impeccable. He had an innate aristocracy; there was no excess in him and no redundancy of movement. I'll never forget his bow the opening night of *Porgy and Bess*. It was a beautiful one. And it should have been the last bow of the evening, but Mamoulian took that." This gives eloquent testimony to the fact that Mamoulian considered himself the person most central to the work being presented to the New York public that night, and that he was an egocentric, controlling man.

Some weeks after the opening, Ann Ronell visited New York from California, where she was living with her husband. Gershwin took her to a performance. In 1990 she recalled how she spoke admiringly of the work, pointing out details that had impressed her. She was unable to cheer Gershwin. She says he spoke sadly about the reviews. She recalled that the feeling that afternoon as they walked up Fifty-fifth Street to her hotel was very different from the one she had experienced a few years before when she and Gershwin had left Noguchi's studio and promenaded proudly on Fifty-seventh Street. Ronell says Gershwin refused to accompany her upstairs to her suite where old friends were waiting to greet her. They were his friends, too, but he did not want to face them after the humiliating insults that had appeared in print.

. . .

A month into the run, Gershwin and Zilboorg went to Mexico. Edward Warburg, James's cousin and a Zilboorg patient, joined them. Swift says Warburg told her Zilboorg did everything possible to increase Gershwin's misery. He maneuvered them into spending time with people who spoke no English—Zilboorg spoke fluent Spanish. She spoke of one particular party at which the guests included Carlos Chávez, the composer, Noguchi, and the Mexican artists Diego Rivera and Miguel Covarrubias. The discussion turned political. Zilboorg harassed Gershwin verbally and, to make matters worse, he was carrying a loaded gun. Despite Zilboorg's hostile treatment of Gershwin, Edward Warburg remained a patient of Zilboorg's for a period of twenty-six years, a fact that he revealed to Katharine Weber, a relative.

The Mexican experience did not provide Gershwin with indigenous music that inspired him—as he had hoped it would—nor did the vacation give him an emotional lift. When his ship docked in December 1935, some musicians in the pit orchestra met him and played strains of *Porgy and Bess*. Mitch Miller remembers it as a sad reunion. The house was then sparsely filled. After the New York reviews appeared, interest and enthusiasm waned. The opera ran 124 performances, to which the Theater Guild had been committed. It lost $70,000. Neither the Gershwins nor Heyward recouped anything at all from their investments, even though the Guild lowered ticket prices to stimulate sales.

Marcel Strauss, grandson of Johann Strauss, Jr., was in the audience at the last performance. In the 1970s, he told Alan Gershwin that his father was in the back of the house, tears streaming down his cheeks. There is no other occasion where anyone ever reported that Gershwin cried.

But the composer had a memento from the opening night: a silver tray signed by 143 people listed as "friends and admirers." Close friends included Bill Daly, whose last professional connection to him was *Let 'Em Eat Cake*, and Henry Botkin, his cousin and art expert. Other names on the tray included Cole Porter,

Jerome Kern, Jimmy Durante, Ethel Merman, Irving Caesar, Lynne Fontanne and Fanny Brice, all from Broadway. Koussevitzky was the only important conductor and Heifetz one of the few concert performers.

It was a different audience from the one that had crowded Aeolian Hall eleven years before to hear Gershwin. That group included Stravinsky, Stokowski, Rachmaninoff, Kreisler, Galli-Curci, and Alma Gluck. In 1924 European and American musicians wondered if the ingredients that made up jazz could infuse art in such a way that something would emerge that had been unimaginable to them.

By 1935 the suspense was over. Many composers had experimented in this way, but serious music, in the main, went on unaffected by popular genres.

Those who claim Gershwin remained untouched by people's response to his work are wrong. He not only consulted Bill Daly on whether a passage was better this way or that, he asked the same questions of Irene Gallagher, secretary to Max Dreyfus, at the beginning of his career, and of Zena Hanenfeldt, his own personal secretary, at the end. He even asked Alan, his young son, to cite his preferences as they sat at the piano, creating sixteen-bar pieces.

In *The Musical Life*, a memoir by Irving Kolodin, the music critic for the *Saturday Review of Literature*, Kolodin writes of a visit he paid Gershwin at the composer's East Seventy-second Street apartment. Levant had arranged the introduction. Kolodin says he asked Gershwin if he had ever considered reworking *Rhapsody in Blue*. Gershwin replied that he had, but "people seemed to like it the way it was, so I left it that way."

Kolodin continues: "Having people 'like' what he did was a necessary part of Gershwin's functioning, even more than with most creative artists. Aside from the question of royalties, and how long a show ran, and earning power generally, he needed a quick affirmative reaction from his listeners, no matter how few or many there were." Kolodin paraphrases part of their conversation to reveal how important public opinion was to Gershwin: " 'Oscar tells me you were at the Venice Festival in 1932 when my Concerto in F was played.' 'That's true,' I said. 'Fritz Reiner conducted and Harry Kaufman was the soloist.' 'Tell us about it,' prompted Gershwin. 'I never had a chance to hear about it from anybody who was there.' 'Well,' I said, 'Reiner had a lot of trouble with the Scala orchestra, which was playing the festival, especially with the trumpet-in-the-hat effect in the slow movement. But you know Fritz. By the time of the concert he had a really fine performance. It went so well Kaufman had to repeat the finale.'

" 'Think of it,' said Gershwin. 'They had to repeat the finale. The only other time that ever happened was when Von Bulow played the Tchaikovsky *Concerto* for the first time in Boston in 1875, and he had to repeat the finale.' "

Kolodin says he was "astounded" by this "bit of esoteric information." He later looked it up and found Gershwin was right.

Ann Ronell recalls how she tried to lift Gershwin's spirits after the reviews of *Porgy and Bess* by telling him that "when *Carmen* opened, it got only bad reviews. And look what happened to *Carmen*." Ronell says Gershwin had not known about the initial harsh reaction to *Carmen* and that her story did indeed cheer him up. Ronell did not tell him how soon after *Carmen*'s premiere Bizet died—at the age of thirty-six.

AS much as Gershwin loved New York, the city no longer seemed friendly to him. Almost as soon as he got back from Mexico, he went to Boston to spend New Year's Eve. With his mother and Ira and Leonore present, he hosted a New Year's Eve party there. Ira had to be in Boston for tryouts for the *Ziegfeld Follies of 1936*, which had a score by Vernon Duke and himself. When George began to immerse himself in *Porgy and Bess*, Ira, to keep money coming in, increased his collaboration with others. In August 1934, *Life Begins at 8:40* with music by Harold Arlen and words by Yip Harburg and Ira, opened at the Winter Garden and ran 237 performances. The *Ziegfeld Follies of 1936* ran about as long. Fanny Brice, Josephine Baker, Eve Arden, Bob Hope, and Gertrude Niesen were in the cast, and George Balanchine staged the ballets.

Gershwin was pleased to be in Boston for at least one reason: *Porgy and Bess* had triumphed there. Both the public and critics raved, and Koussevitzky hailed it as "a great advance in American opera." Moses Smith, the critic of the *Evening Transcript*, wrote what Gershwin most needed to hear, that he had "traveled a long way from Tin Pan Alley" and now had "to be accepted as a serious composer."

Levant was not the only one to speak out against the work at its New York premiere. According to David Diamond, who later wrote incidental music to a Theater Guild production of Shakespeare's *The Tempest*, Cheryl Crawford, then an assistant stage designer for *Porgy and Bess*, made her opinions well known. After the curtain fell, she vehemently told those around her that the Guild should never have done the work, that *Porgy* had been a wonderful play, and that nobody should have allowed Gershwin to turn it into an opera. Diamond says Gershwin stood there looking like he had been run over by a truck.

By the mid-1930s, the New York theater scene was populated with people strongly left wing; many were members of the Communist party. They belonged not only to the Theater Guild but to such organizations as the Group Theater, then headed by Harold Clurman, Copland's first cousin. Gershwin was not at ease with these people. At his East Side duplex, with his valet dressed in a white jacket and his lavish entertaining, he was sneered at by political radicals. And that was not hard for them to do at that time. People in the arts in the 1930s behaved the way people in the arts do today. He started looking toward Hollywood. Berlin and Kern had already moved to the West Coast.

By February of 1936, he let his agent, Arthur Lyons, know that he wanted to sign a movie contract. Lyons did not get one overnight. While he waited, Gershwin did whatever he could to promote his opera. When it closed at the Alvin Theater the weekly income was $15,000. Smallens and the cast were getting $4,100. This meant the Theater Guild, the Gershwins and Heyward had to divide what remained. The arrangement was such that even if the orchestra had been reduced in size, the Guild would have had to pay all the musicians. So the Guild closed the show and took it on a five-city tour, starting in Philadelphia in late January 1936.

To generate publicity in Philadelphia, Gershwin appeared as the piano soloist in a performance of the Concerto in F, with Smallens conducting. He also played a suite he had arranged from the opera, retitled *Catfish Row*. In this work, he restored much of what had been cut.

Gershwin did not continue on with the tour. After the Philadelphia concert and the tour's opening performance, he came back to New York for the Broadway opening of the *Ziegfeld Follies*. Work on the show had so exhausted Ira that he went with Leonore and director Vincente Minnelli on a trip to Trinidad. George was not with them; he could never have tolerated such a slow pace. Diamond says George, in the years he knew him, was "very hyper—like he was shot up on benzedrine." Ten years before, Stravinsky had characterized him as "nervously energetic." Leonore used to say about Ira, who generally did his writing lying down: "If only he had a little of George's energy."

At home with virtually nothing to do, George wrote a song for the stage show Kay Swift was producing at Radio City Music Hall. He wrote it with Albert Stillman, who was staff lyricist at the theater, where Kay was staff composer. Gershwin and Stillman had collaborated on some songs to be performed by Buck and Bubbles, the team that had played in *Porgy and Bess*. One song was called "The King of Swing."

A great deal else was going on in the musical life across the United States while Gershwin was immersed in his major work. Probably the most striking success was Cole Porter's *Anything Goes*, 1934's biggest hit. It opened at the Alvin Theater, the theater identified with so many Gershwin triumphs, was produced by Vinton Freedley, Gershwin's longtime producer, and starred Ethel Merman.

While Gershwin was working on his opera, Porter and Moss Hart did *Jubilee* in 1935, Richard Rodgers and Lorenz Hart opened *On Your Toes* in 1936. That year a second movie based on *Show Boat* (the first had appeared in 1929) was released. The new version—with Paul Robeson, Helen Morgan, Hattie McDaniel, and Irene Dunne—was a success.

Because Gershwin was no longer perceived as the indefatigable winner he had been, negotiations with Hollywood did not go well. George had told Lyons to ask for $100,000 and a percentage of the profits. The first reply came in June from RKO, an offer of only $60,000 for twenty weeks of work for an Astaire-Rogers movie with a working title of *Watch Your Step*. After several exchanges of telegrams, the Gershwins agreed to $55,000 for sixteen weeks of work on the movie, to be released as *Shall We Dance?* The contract carried with it an option for the next RKO musical, this time at a fee for $70,000 for sixteen weeks' work. This movie turned out to be *A Damsel in Distress*, with Astaire and Joan Fontaine.

By the end of June 1936, Samuel Goldwyn let Lyons know he was eager to have the Gershwins write the score for his next musical. They still were not thinking of a permanent move. Zena Hanenfeldt says Gershwin kept the apartment intact when he left New York; the furnishings and paintings remained where they were. Before they left for Los Angeles, George had three more concerts booked, one at the Ravinia Festival in Chicago and two Lewisohn Stadium all-Gershwin evenings on July 9 and 10.

The stadium concerts were important to Gershwin. Memories of the sold-out houses of the year before were still in his head. The program this year seemed irresistible: Gershwin conducting *An American in Paris;* Smallens conducting *Rhapsody in Blue* and the Concerto in F with Gershwin at the piano; Todd Duncan, Ann Brown, Ruby Elzy, and the Eva Jessye Choir doing songs from *Porgy and Bess.* Still, while the previous year, 17,000 people attended each of the concerts, only 7,000 came on July 9. The New York *Times* reported that "it was George Gershwin night at Lewisohn Stadium, and there were empty seats in the amphitheatre." The *Times* went on to attribute the meager audience to a record-breaking heat spell.

Levant writes that later, backstage, Gershwin asked Minnie Guggenheimer about the crowd. Although she put the best smile on her face and described it as grand, he reminded her of the crush for seats that had attended the events only a year before. Levant says Gershwin brightened slightly when someone reminded him about the heat.

Though only two major symphony conductors, Reiner and Koussevitzky, had led performances of Gershwin, many others conducted Gershwin whenever they could. In 1933, the conductor Henry Levine presented *Rhapsody in Blue* and sent Gershwin corrections in the piano score. (Gershwin sent him a note of thanks for the "new corrections in the Rhapsody pianoforte.") On June 14, 1934, William Daly conducted the Chicago Symphony Orchestra in a typical all-Gershwin program that included the *Rhapsody*, the concerto and *An American in Paris*.

Music publishers rent the players' parts to orchestras. But each player makes his own corrections to the point where scores often become unreadable. This happened most particularly to *Rhapsody in Blue*. On January 8, 1978, Frank Campbell-Watson, onetime editor-in-chief of Music Publishers Corporation, wrote to Professor William Youngren of Boston College in reply to a request for information about the way Gershwin wanted his *Rhapsody* performed: "A few years later [Campbell-Watson joined the firm in 1933], Warner's managed to secure from Dreyfus the Gershwin catalog (excepting *Porgy and Bess*). This entire catalog of Gershwin naturally fell into my lap, together with voluminous correspondence from symphony conductors and others here and abroad regarding the impossible condition of the rental scores and parts. They were unreadable, full of musical as well as copying and extraction errors and replete with all manner of ideas for improvement. This was all new to me, so after making a complete survey of the catastrophe, I called George, renewed our early friendship and told him what I had found and that if something was not done quickly, at no small expense, public performances of his work would be a thing of the past.

"All of this took place three weeks (!) before George made his last trip to the coast. I don't think anyone realized what a desperately sick man he was and how difficult it would be to discuss the details involved. . . . Realizing that I had learned his scores, he begged me to do the whole revision and editing. He just wasn't up to it either to help or to judge the changes I had recommended."

This meeting took place in July 1936. Diamond says that Gershwin was sick at least four months before that: "I stopped to say good-bye to George in March 1936 before leaving to study in Fontainebleau. He complained about severe headaches to me." Mitch Miller, in describing Gershwin's looking at the musicians behind him and asking if they smelled burning garbage as he did, puts the tumor back to February 1934. Some neurologists claim the potential for such a tumor resides in the person from the time of birth and that it is the breakdown of the immune system that allows it to flourish.

Few medical authorities would disagree that unremitting stress can contribute to that immune-system breakdown. Gershwin's career began to plunge in 1932. The first of these times of great stress probably occurred when, after composing the score for *Of Thee I Sing*, the judges excepted him from the Pulitzer Prize.

From this time on, George experienced nothing but failure as a composer, though the evenings at Lewisohn Stadium surely pleased him. But that was about all. During that period his creative work met with severe criticism: *Second Rhapsody*, January 29, 1932; *Cuban Overture*, August 16, 1932; *Pardon My English*, January 30, 1933; *Let 'Em Eat Cake*, October 21, 1933; *Variations on I Got Rhythm*, January 14, 1934. About this time Gershwin painted the self-portrait in watercolor that he gave to Mueller. Then, of course, came the reception to *Porgy and Bess*, October 10, 1935.

In a tape Irene Gallagher, Dreyfus's longtime associate, made in 1972, she says flatly that "George was sick all his life." She refers to a growth on his neck and connects it with the tumor that finally killed him. But the growth appears to have been a kind of fatty cyst called a nonmalignant lipoma. Alan Gershwin has a lipoma in the same spot. Still Gallagher may have been right when she dates Gershwin's illness back many years. The symptoms of stomach distress that began in 1922, could, according to Dr. Ruth Richards, a psychiatrist at the Harvard Medical School and Massachusetts General Hospital, have been connected to the diseased right temporal lobe of his later years.

In the program notes for *The Gershwin Collection*, a recording by Dave Grusin and other musicians, Michael Feinstein, the singer and pianist who worked as Ira Gershwin's archivist from

1977 until Ira's death in 1983, wrote, "Ira never got over his brother's death and always felt guilty about it."

Like just about everyone else around Gershwin, most particularly Leonore, Ira dismissed George's complaints as symptoms of a neurosis. They took their cues from Zilboorg, who pronounced the difficulties as psychological, and they accepted this diagnosis because they wanted to believe that this once towering figure had been reduced to childlike behavior because things were no longer going well in his career.

Shortly before Gershwin died, Irving Berlin told the press that "there is nothing wrong with Gershwin that a song hit wouldn't cure." This was particularly ironic because the new songs were among his best. Those written for Broadway did not succeed because the shows for which they were composed failed, so the songs were not played after the shows folded. As for the songs composed for movies, Hollywood's treatment usually buried the music.

Zilboorg proved no help to Gershwin, although Gershwin still telephoned him from time to time. That he was no help is not surprising. Katharine Weber says her grandmother, Kay Swift, told her that during the last eight months of her year-and-a-half-long treatment with Zilboorg, he engaged in sexual intercourse with her. Weber emphasizes this was not a romantic liaison; the sex took place during the sessions at the patient's expense. Weber quotes Swift: "He was the only man with whom I ever had a sexual relationship to whom I was not physically attracted." To the end of his life, Zilboorg maintained Gershwin could not have had a brain tumor in 1934 and 1935 without his knowing it. But that is precisely what happened: Gershwin had a tumor growing on the right temporal lobe of his brain and Zilboorg did not know it.

However sick Gershwin was, he continued his relations with women. While helping Swift in her job at Radio City, and keeping Julia Van Norman content, he also began to court Kitty Carlisle. Carlisle, who later married director and playwright Moss Hart, said in 1990 that she and Gershwin spent much of their time at clubs in Harlem. This was the twilight of the era of the great night spots around Lenox and Seventh avenues between 130th and 135th streets. The Cotton Club, the Savoy Ballroom, the Ubangi Club, Small's Paradise, the Club Hot-Cha and a few others featured black entertainers. Some evenings, however, Gershwin and Carlisle stayed home. She remembers that "the floor was strewn with papers and he tried to explain to me how he had worked out these passages in the 12-tone system." Gershwin's few lessons with Schoenberg at the Ansonia Hotel had had a profound effect. Unlike most of Gershwin's friends, Carlisle did not find him an egotist. Perhaps that is because she knew him at this last, disappointing stage of his life. "George was *not* confident," she says. "What I remember most were his complaints about his tummy."

Gershwin escorted Carlisle to *Porgy and Bess.* She says they sat in a box, stage left. Gershwin also gave two seats to the Van Normans. As late in his short life as this, Gershwin continued to propose to women. In 1989 Julia Van Norman said he talked about marriage to her.

About that time, Gershwin proposed to British actress Elizabeth Allen in a letter that was made public in 1991. Carlisle says Gershwin also proposed to her, but "it was not a formal proposal. I was then staying at the White Horse Inn. I sent him a telegram saying no. I didn't give the real reason—that I needed to sweep someone off his feet. What I said was that my career had just begun to take off and I believed that what he needed was a real wife who could devote herself entirely to him. George liked his social friends. He felt I would make a very understanding wife and he knew I admired him. But the real problem was I felt no need from him." And so Carlisle repeats what Rosamond Walling said many years before: both women felt he did not respond to anything particular about them but was in search of a good-looking, intelligent, gracious woman who would supervise an elegant life for him.

Nowhere is there evidence to be found that Gershwin ever said "I love you" to anyone. When he gave a photograph to Ronell and inscribed it with "love," he made a point of telling her how exceptional that was, that he rarely went beyond the word "affectionately." This is ironic. Ned Rorem, one of our finest composers of art songs, puts Gershwin's songs in a class with Schumann's. In an essay on Gershwin that appeared in his book *Settling the Score*, Rorem writes that the songs are "virtually always about love—lost, found, longed for, disposed of—never about death. Death will come only with *Porgy and Bess.*" Death does come with *Porgy and Bess.* "Oh, he's gone, gone, gone, gone, gone, gone, gone," sung after Crown kills Robbins in the crap game in Act I, and the funeral scene, are among the most moving parts of the opera. Gershwin put everything he could into *Porgy and Bess*, and he dedicated it "To My Parents." Gershwin loved his parents, all the more so because their love for him was always in question.

When Gershwin first decided to set *Porgy*, he probably identified with the protagonist, an innocent man confronting a corrupting world. But by the time he started to work on the piece, he seems to have identified with Bess, a person incapable of fidelity to anyone. Hanenfeldt says Gershwin told her Swift wanted to marry him, but that he could not do that because he was not "worthy" of her. After Bess remains in Kittiwah and allows herself to be seduced by Crown and returns to Catfish Row, where Porgy nurses her back to health, she sings the very same words: "I wants to stay here, but I ain't worthy,/You is too decent to understan'."

On August 10, in a parade of taxicabs, the Gershwins and friends went to Newark Airport to see George, Ira, and Leonore off to California. Mabel Schirmer says George asked her to go in the same cab with Swift and him, then put her between them. Obviously he did not want to deal with any intimate discussion from Kay.

Horace Van Norman says Julia was devastated at Gershwin's leaving New York. But, he adds, "She knew it meant he was leaving Kay Swift." As Gershwin flew from Newark, Fanny and Ben Schneider and their nephew Alan took a train to the

Coast and settled in a house in Altadena, California, a suburb of Pasadena, where Alan's care was alternately in their hands and the hands of some of his mother's show-business friends. Paul Mueller set out for the coast in Gershwin's car with Gershwin's dog in the back seat. The trip seemed interminable. In the desert Mueller had to deal with extreme heat and the dog fell ill. It had to be hospitalized there and Mueller continued the trip on his own. The dog arrived after he did.

After Alan settled in Altadena, his visits with his father resumed. Every two weeks, in the dark of night—as had happened in Brooklyn—a car pulled up at the house and a man delivered an envelope filled with crisp new bills. Murray Schneider says he was jealous of Alan because his own parents treated Alan better than they treated him. "Alan," he explained, "was their meal ticket."

Alan had no sense of being privileged. His life seemed dreadful to him. He believed his mother was dead. He saw his father intermittently, and even then Gershwin never spoke intimately to him. Unlike the other children in the Schneider house, he didn't attend school and had no friends. Presumably to prevent him from sharing his secret with others, he had tutors from time to time in New York and California. Alan recalls that Gershwin disappeared from Alan's life several months before he died and that, at the time, he could not understand why the visits had stopped.

A letter Gershwin wrote December 4, 1936, strongly suggests that he did have Alan on his mind. In the spring of 1936, Vincente Minnelli had been present when George and Ira were doing a parody of the Viennese waltz. Almost as soon as the Gershwins arrived in California in August and began looking for a suitable house, they received a telegram from Minnelli. He said they should work on the Strauss takeoff because he wanted to use it for a Broadway revue. They did it in a day and airmailed it to New York. Minnelli used it with success in his show. The song was called "By Strauss."

Four months later, when it was being prepared for publication, George received a letter from the editing department of his publisher. The writer complained that the verse was "unusually long" and "would take up at least three pages. . . . Is there anything you can suggest that would help us to get the number out in the usual amount of pages?" The usual amount of pages was two. The letter Gershwin wrote in reply on December 4 said, "Dear Selma: I am very sorry that the verse 'By Strauss' is so long that it requires perhaps an extra page in the publication copy, but then it's always been my policy to give the public a lot for their money; and I think it would be a good idea to put on the title page—'This song has an extra long verse so you are getting more notes per penny than in any other song this season.' . . . And if the song doesn't sell I would like my grandchildren (if I ever have any) to see the trouble that their grand-daddy took with verses. In other words, dear Selma, I would like the song printed as I wrote it, with no commas left out. Love and kisses, George."

Gershwin was no longer going to allow anyone to cut notes from a score. The *Porgy and Bess* experience had cured him of that. Gershwin's letter also refers to future grandchildren. If he did not have a child in 1936, when he was thirty-seven, he probably would not have written about grandchildren.

In early 1961, Richard Rodgers called Alan Gershwin and told him to watch a television show scheduled to be aired on January 15. It was called *The Gershwin Years.* Rodgers was writer and narrator. Rodgers told Alan to look at it because he had included this letter that Gershwin wrote which referred to his future grandchildren. By that time Alan had one child of his own, a girl, George's granddaughter. The transcript ends with Rodgers saying, "I knew George Gershwin very well, and on Christmas evening 1934, my wife was in bed, being very careful before the birth of our second child. Suddenly George Gershwin arrived at our home. Together, he and I carried my wife downstairs into the living room and put her on a couch. George went to the piano and played and sang the uncompleted score for *Porgy and Bess* for us."

Rodgers paid back a debt he felt he owed Gershwin by recognizing Gershwin's son, even if it was in a private way. Rodgers was one of the very few people who did.

On more than one occasion, Alan Gershwin has gone to a lawyer to determine his rights as George Gershwin's son. The first time came soon after the end of World War II. Alan had served on Iwo Jima and Okinawa. He called Ira, and Ira told him he could come to the house in Beverly Hills and stay there awhile. Ira said he could do this on the condition that he never appear when someone else was there. When a visitor, whom Alan thinks was George Pallay, arrived, Alan was sent upstairs. Then disobeying Ira's order, he descended the staircase. The visitor, struck by his striking resemblance to George, dropped his glass of whiskey. Enraged, Ira and Lee sent Alan away.

When he returned to New York, Alan says, he told Ben Schneider what had happened. According to Alan, Ben contacted Ira through intermediaries. Eventually Ben received a payment of $300,000 in cash from Ira, most of which was divided among the Schneiders and their emissaries. Alan says he spent his share quickly and foolishly.

In the 1960s, increasingly troubled by the Gershwin family's repudiation of him as an "impostor," and without any money of his own, Alan consulted Martin Leeds, a lawyer. Alan told Leeds he wanted to write a book about the tortuous aspects of his life. Leeds sent him to Bennett Cerf at Random House. Alan gave Cerf his title: *The Man Who Stole My Life.* Cerf laughed, Alan said, and told him Ira was such a good friend that he could not possibly become involved in the project. According to Alan, Cerf suggested that Alan transform his story into a work of fiction.

Several times since then, Alan tried to interest lawyers in his case. But each time a Gershwin lawyer would deny Alan's claim. Ira triumphed easily. The lawyers approached by Alan accepted Ira's denials partly, it would seem, because of Ira's money and power and partly because Alan, before the work on this book was done, had never been capable of putting the pieces of his story together: that he and Albert Schneider are the same person and that George Gershwin is his father.

In the 1960s, Ira fell down a flight of stairs soon after hearing from one of the lawyers Alan had contacted. Levant telephoned Alan and accused him of upsetting Ira so much that Ira had begun to cause injury to himself. Levant ordered Alan to desist.

In 1972 Irene Gallagher, George's secretary, talked about the Ira Gershwins on tape. She said, "Ira was not a hard man but he was married to a very hard woman. I have stories about Lee that nobody would believe. Lee was the boss. She was the *complete* boss.

"Lee's family had a summer place in New Jersey, a restaurant in Manhattan called Three Steps Down, and a lot of property in Greenwich Village. The Strunskys," she went on, "were rich in real estate and money but Lee wanted the prestige that the Gershwin name would bring." In *No Cover Charge*, published in 1956, Robert Sylvester wrote about the Strunskys: "In these early days, the Village had its own William Zeckendorf—or rather, a whole family of same. These were the Strunskys. They were the Village landlords de luxe. Even veteran Village operators today have trouble sorting out and identifying the various Strunskys. . . . The Strunskys not only owned and rented buildings but took occasional flights at running nightclubs themselves. In one, a cellar called Three Steps Down on West Eighth Street, it was no uncommon thing to wander in and find a pianist named George Gershwin playing for his brother and in-laws."

Gallagher went on: "George Pallay told me that Gershwin was so miserable at the end of his life, living with Ira and Lee, that he spent time living with him. Pallay said he was the most comfort that George had at the time. I did not believe what Pallay said, because Ira would not have tolerated George living with somebody else."

She went no further speculating why Ira, or perhaps Leonore, would not have tolerated such an arrangement, but it would seem to be because they felt it crucial that nobody else influence George or get close to him in any way. This attitude is consistent with everything Ira did about George. Ira behaved toward George's teachers the way he behaved toward other lyricists such as Irving Caesar and Gus Kahn. Schillinger's wife has said that in the late 1930s, when she met Vernon Duke on Fifty-seventh Street, he insisted she go with him to the nearby Russian Tea Room where he told her that Ira was trying to eliminate Schillinger from the Gershwin life story. It is reasonable to expect him to have expended at least the same energy to remove George's son from the story.

More important, it is unlikely that either Leonore or Ira would have permitted any friend of George's to encourage him to make out a will which would continue to provide for his son. As soon as George died, the money stopped coming to the Schneiders. Alan returned to Brooklyn and his unattractive life.

The complicated dynamics among George, Ira, and Leonore presented difficulties when they started to live together under the same roof for the first time in eight years. In California, they rented a single, large, comfortable house. Today it belongs to Rosemary Clooney. In a profile of the singer that appeared in the August 3, 1992, issue of *The New Yorker*, Whitney Balliett described it in detail:

> The house, a big two-story Spanish stucco-and-red tile, is two blocks from Sunset Boulevard and three from the Beverly Hills Hotel. . . . [It] has baronial touches: a giant wooden front door . . . that has a Prohibition-era peep-hole door, a two story entrance hall with a four-abreast staircase, a wrought-iron banister, and a sizeable chandelier; and a huge sunken living room. . . . The back yard of the house is early Beverly Hills de-luxe: there is a guest house on one side and a fifty-foot tiled pool on the other; the pool has its own cabana, and beyond the pool is a tennis court.

Balliett reports there are five bedrooms and adds: "The house has ghosts." He mentions the crooner Russ Columbo, in 1934, accidentally fired an antique dueling pistol and was killed. By the time the Gershwins moved into the house, two years after

Columbo's death, the tumor on George's brain was growing. Still, deciding to cohabit with his brother and sister-in-law seems almost as self-destructive an act as Columbo's playing with a loaded antique pistol.

When asked why George would have consented at this stage of his life to such an arrangement, Frankie replied, "He hated to be alone." Kate Wolpin says that from the start George was critical of Leonore. "He said he could have no respect for someone who did not have children and still did not go to work or have a career." George was not fair. Lee ran the household in California as she had run the previous ones, with great skill. She used what she had learned in the Strunsky restaurants when she and her sister had served as hostesses. Some remember Lee generously. But virtually everyone speaks of her cruelty.

Several friends report that when, at the end of her life, Emily visited her sister Lee in Beverly Hills, Lee did not permit her sister to speak. "She had to shut up," Frankie explains, "because Lee was supporting her." Emily, her older sister, referred to in the Gershwin line "a day in June could take lessons from you," was not only beautiful but unfailingly kind. George wrote Emily warm letters throughout his life. Rose Shaw, publicity director for the *Porgy and Bess* tour of the 1950s, says, "Lee always played the grande dame. Whether we were in Egypt or Yugoslavia, she would say: 'This is so much better than being bored in Hollywood, bored with Bogey and Betty and all the rest.' "

Shaw says she cannot remember Lee ever talking of George and that when she mentioned Ira, she did so without affection. Truman Capote, in his account of this tour, tells the following story: The group went to the Hermitage museum in Leningrad where they were led by the guide to the treasure vault where the czars' jewels were displayed. Capote quotes Lee, " 'I wish I'd *never* come here,' she said, forlornly fingering her diamonds. 'I feel so dissatisfied, I'd like to go home and crack my husband on the head.' Miss Ryan asked her, 'If you could have any of this you wanted, what would you take?' 'All of it, darling,' replied Mrs. Gershwin."

In the spring of 1991, in the white marble mausoleum in

Westchester County where the Gershwins are buried, five of the six places were occupied by the bodies of Morris, Rose, Ira, George, and Arthur. One remained vacant. When asked which Gershwin would occupy the last place, the caretaker replied that it would be Leonore Gershwin. Frankie later explained this saying that although she was the sister and Lee was only a sister-in-law, Leonore had not let her alone until she had given up her place to her.

David Raksin, composer of "Laura," says of Leonore, "She was a very odd lady, prone to thinking everyone had ulterior motives. She was a little paranoid, had very mean streaks. She was a real prize bitch. She objected to the way I said 'beautiful.' She thought it branded me a Philadelphian. She probably was too smart to walk between Ira and George. She invariably condescended to Ira but I never saw her behave that way to George."

Donald Kahn, lyricist Gus Kahn's son, says that "when George was alive, he dominated the scene. But after George died, Lee got strength she never had before." Robbie Cohen, widow of entertainment lawyer Sidney Cohen, who knew Ira and Leonore Gershwin after George's death, says of Leonore, "A lot of people told me Leonore loved George, not Ira. Many men were hanging around the house then. It was the place to go. Everyone felt at home. There was always pinochle and poker. But Leonore was not likeable. She needed to control people. She had to tell them what to buy and what to do. When my daughter died, she tried to take over in that way for me. But as desperately unhappy as I was then, I was not vulnerable to this approach."

In October 1990, novelist, short-story writer, and composer Paul Bowles wrote of a conversation his wife, June, had with Leonore:

> I met Lee and Ira through Oscar Levant, who lived nearby on the same street in Beverly Hills. I'd known Oscar years before, in New York. I was impressed by the feeling of stability Lee suggested. She seemed to know at every minute exactly what

she was thinking and doing. I felt that she did not have a vague bone in her body. She was decisiveness personified. Twice she came to Tangier. She and Jane got on very well together. I remember a bit of conversation between them in the Minzah bar. Jane was, as usual, being amusing and witty about someone who apparently cared a great deal about money. Suddenly Lee sat up straighter, and said with great seriousness: "*We* don't joke about money." Jane couldn't get over it, and discussed it at length later, with me.

When George's tumor began to interfere with his behavior, Leonore had him removed from the house. June Levant says Leonore complained to her about how disgusting George had become, dribbling out of the side of his mouth, and said she could stand it no longer. They arranged to send George to Yip Harburg's much smaller house, for Harburg was going to New York. Ira and Leonore remained in the large house and kept Mueller there to wait on them. A male nurse from Germany was hired to attend George, and Mueller visited every day. So, at the end of his life, George Gershwin was living in unassuming quarters with a servant he didn't know.

In 1955, Vernon Duke's *Passport to Paris* was published. He writes, "There have been so many incorrect and distorted versions of George's last days that I deem it a duty and an honor to give here a short and accurate account of what really happened, for which I'm indebted to Lee Gershwin." There follows the account which, in the main, holds that Gershwin's first symptoms appeared only weeks before he died, at which point every effort was made to get the best medical care. Duke says Dr. Earnest Simmel, a Los Angeles psychoanalyst, suggested George be moved to a quiet house where there would be none of the activity that characterized the one on Roxbury Drive. Duke also claims that the first sign that the disease was organic, not neurotic, occurred on July 9, 1937, two days before Gershwin died.

In later biographies the date was pushed to February of that year, when during a rehearsal, Gershwin almost fell off the podium, and the next evening, at the performance, played wrong notes in the Concerto in F. In a 1987 biography, the onset of the trouble was dated three months earlier, when Gershwin reported to Pallay that, while having his hair cut, he suffered a blackout and smelled burning rubber. Harvey Cushing, a pioneering Boston neurosurgeon, was still giving consultations, but he was not called. Nor did Gershwin himself—when he was still capable of doing it—demand the best professional care. That may be because he persistently denied the virulence of the disease and the possibility of dying, or perhaps, as Noguchi said, he was suicidal. S. N. Behrman writes of his efforts, at the very end, to get the best medical attention for Gershwin. Behrman writes, "While I was trying to get Dr. Abraham Flexner, Moss Hart, who was in analysis, came in. He didn't see why I was making all this fuss. 'I myself,' he said, 'have had suicidal impulses—I have been helped over them.' "

In a 1990 conversation, Kitty Carlisle Hart said Moss later told her he had seen George put his fork in his ear at dinner. It is difficult to understand how people could interpret such a gesture as anything but evidence of a neurologic disease, though Hart was a stage director and playwright, not a neurologist.

Though Frank Campbell-Watson wrote that George was desperately sick in July 1936, Gershwin's early letters from California do not reveal serious problems. A week after the Gershwins arrived in Beverly Hills, George wired Zena Hanenfeldt: "Please send two hundred cigars. . . . Did I leave my tune book on the piano? Find copy of Spanish numbers in studio. Letter following will tell what to do with it. Having fine time." Almost immediately the Gershwins moved into 1019 North Roxbury Drive. On September 9, George asked Hanenfeldt to send him the following paintings from his collection: Picasso: *Absinthe Drinker;* Pascin: *Girl with Cat;* Gauguin: *Self Portrait;* Utrillo: *Fishermen's Houses;* Modigliani: *Portrait of Doctor* and *Woman's Head;* Rousseau: *Ile de la Cité;* Derain: *Road through the Forest;* Thomas Hart Benton: *Burlesque;* Max Jacob: *Religious Festival;* Siquieros: *Landscape;* Chagall: *Rabbi and Slaughter House;* and Gershwin's own portrait of his paternal grandfather. He told Hanenfeldt to get prices by rail and ship, to check the extra-insurance costs, and to send the works through the Budworth Company. There does not seem to be any problem with his thinking in September 1936. That is because the left temporal lobe, the dominant side of Gershwin's brain, remained unaffected by his disease. The next day George sent Hanenfeldt still another letter asking her to ship his painting box with "all the colors and brushes I have." He said he planned to paint while he was in California.

As the response to his music became more problematic, he invested increasing time and energy in painting. He told his secretary that as soon as she had done what he asked, she should put everything left in the apartment in storage. "We are giving a big party Saturday night," Gershwin added, "for Moss Hart's new teeth, he having had all sorts of things done to his teeth with porcelain. We expect 75 people." In October Gershwin wrote Hanenfeldt; "I am still anxiously awaiting the rhythmic and scale book that you have made up. Perhaps you could get Mr. Schillinger to write a little explanation about how to use such material—or maybe you can do it yourself." Hanenfeldt had studied with Leon Theremin, the inventor of the electronic instrument named for him, so she knew something about advanced techniques.

On October 20, George sent money to Kate Wolpin, who had told him she needed it. Gershwin was generous to his family and friends. In *Passport to Paris*, Vernon Duke writes that George lent him money several times and that twice he brought him to Max Dreyfus to try to get him a contract at Harms. George Antheil later wrote that he knew at least four composers—he did not say whom—George was supporting at the time he died. Gershwin wrote to Mabel Schirmer on September 1, three weeks after he arrived in Beverly Hills, and described the California sunshine and noted all the "cronies" he met there—Kern, Berlin, Hart, Levant, Harpo Marx, Yip Harburg among others. He said their house was "really lovely. . . . It is in Beverly Hills and has many charming things about it. It is a nice, spacious, cheery house with a fine workroom. The living room is very large, white walls and a fine Steinway piano. The furnishings aren't all to our taste but then—you can't have everything. . . . Have you seen Kay? I haven't written to her nor have I seen her. I should like to know if you ever see her."

If Kay was not out of George's mind, he still held to the notion he expressed to Sam Behrman that marriage was destructive for a songwriter. That fall Ann Ronell gave a party at her house in the San Fernando Valley and invited friends and such celebrities as John Ford and Gershwin. She says that after introducing Gershwin to her husband, Gershwin led her to a quiet room and asked, "Why did you get married? It will not be good for your career."

Gershwin's letters to Julia Van Norman were different from those he wrote to Emily Paley and Mabel Schirmer, who were family friends. With Julia Van Norman, he was far more candid. In November he wrote her: "Hollywood has grown up since our last visit and has actually got something to offer besides a sun and an ocean and interesting scenery. It's getting some brains. I was delighted to find in many instances a point of view that was progressive and searching in places that formerly thought only of money. They are buying talent now where formerly they bought women and men who could boast Roman noses and bedroom eyes. It is promising. Of course, it still contains yes-men, charlatans, phonies, career-women, show-offs, cheats, stupid executives, neurotics by the yard, and disappointed stars. Somebody said, 'Nobody has any roots in Hollywood' and it is true. And it's sad-making very often. People check in and out like a hotel. Everybody seems to have an angle. It's hard to meet a person who isn't trying to get something from somebody. . . .

"I've been out quite a lot with movie stars, with a leaning towards the foreign ones like Luise Rainer, Simone Simon and others. They are very interesting but a movie star is a movie star. They leave you with a sort of emptiness when you say goodnight."

. . .

On December 4 Bill Daly died. His obituary listed the cause of death as a heart attack. Irene Gallagher had lunched with him that very day and in 1972 she said she believed he killed himself. He was found drowned in his bathtub. No evidence appears in letters of Gershwin's reaction. If, at the least, Gershwin continued to depend on Daly for help in his concert works, Daly's death would have been a crucial professional loss. If he still felt as he did before—Levant had written that Daly was the only man for whom Gershwin felt a special affection—then Gershwin's sense of loss would have been profound.

In the first week of 1937, George wrote to Emily with the effusiveness that always characterized his communications to Leonore's sister:

> I have been wanting to write to you for sometime to tell you how happy your letter made me. What a grand person you are, dear Em. So generous, so understanding, so beautiful. Your yearly letter from Miami has gotten to be a necessity. It nearly always comes when I am a little below par & always does the trick of cheering me in an important way.
>
> I talked about you with another member of the "Emily Paley Society" last night. It was at Eddie Robinson's house. Gladys [Robinson's wife] was the one. She loves you and admires you so between us we had a wonderful time. The whole evening was memorable. Stravinsky was the guest of honor & was charming. He asked if he and Dushkin could play for the group. They played seven or eight pieces superbly.
>
> Stravinsky and mother got on famously. Isn't Hollywood wonderful? Gladys sat me next to the most glamorous & enchanting girl in the west, Paulette Goddard. She really is an exciting creature. Gladys knows my taste better than I thought. The whole evening was grand.

The portrait of Gershwin revealed here is different from the man who compulsively entertained on the piano at New York parties. Here is Gershwin, sitting politely in Edward G. Robinson's house, listening to Stravinsky and Dushkin, not sitting down to play at all. In *A Smattering of Ignorance*, Levant writes about his musical life in which Gershwin was an auditor, not a participant. "He took great interest in the contemporary music that was being played in Los Angeles at the time, where contrary to the usual opinion, the musical atmosphere was a sharp and bracing one. Stravinsky made a guest appearance with the Los Angeles orchestra, conducting his own works; there were the Schoenberg Quartet Concerts; the WPA Schoenberg and Pupils Concerts; the presence of Ernst Toch and Aaron Copland on the coast—all these things interested and stimulated him."

One aspect of Gershwin's temperament that did not change with the California climate or the development of his disease was his relentless pursuit of women. In the fall of 1936 his primary woman was Simone Simon, whom Levant describes as "vixenish, catlike and pretty." Gershwin had met her in Paris in 1928 and helped her immigrate to the United States. In 1931 he escorted her to Stokowski's performance of *Wozzeck* in Philadelphia. In California, Gershwin coached and accompanied her in some Massenet operas. Simon told friends he had told her he would compose a light opera for her, but there is no evidence he meant it. He may have made such a promise in the way he sang the same unpublished song for every woman of the moment, inserting her name in the appropriate place, a device recalled by Kitty Carlisle Hart. Simon gave him a solid gold key to her Beverly Hills house.

Then Gershwin met Goddard. Other guests at the Edward G. Robinson house included Marlene Dietrich, Frank Capra, and Douglas Fairbanks, Jr. But Gershwin did not even mention them in his annual letter to Emily. Goddard's impact on him was stunning. Leonore told Nancy Gershwin that "Goddard's beauty was so great it was almost painful." In addition to attracting him with her beauty, she must have given George the feeling he was in familiar territory, for she possessed an important trait common to the women at home. She shared Rose's and Leonore's obsession with diamonds.

In *Holy Terror*, Bob Colacello's book about Andy Warhol, the author writes about Goddard when she was a member of Warhol's circle: "Paulette was wearing a typical Goddard getup: a svelte white dress . . . and the most remarkable diamond necklace any of us had ever seen. Hanging from a chain of two-karat diamonds were at least a dozen larger diamonds in ascending size from five karats to twenty karats, and each one was a different shape: round, oval, oblong, square, pear, marquise. Andy was transfixed. 'I never saw a necklace like that,' he said. 'Why are they all different shapes and sizes?' 'They're all my old engagement rings,' Paulette explained matter-of-factly. 'I always sent back the setting and kept the rock.' "

Colacello quotes a conversation with Goddard about a couple they knew who had married but were not living together. " 'That's the best kind of marriage to have,' said Paulette. 'I call it a maitre d' marriage. Not too much romance, just someone to take care of all the boring stuff, like dealing with servants, the menus, the reservations. That's what Erich used to do for me. He wrote all morning and in the afternoon he took care of all that.' " Her husband, Erich Maria Remarque, was the German author of the novel *All Quiet on the Western Front*. At the time of the Robinson party, Goddard had been secretly married to Charlie Chaplin for ten months, so a marriage with Gershwin was not much of a possibility. The ideal husband she described to Warhol sounds much like the ideal wife Gershwin described, someone to run a gracious home.

When Merle Armitage was preparing his memorial collection of essays on Gershwin, he asked for an essay from Albert Heink Sendrey, a German composer who settled in Los Angeles. Sendrey started his piece saying that he was in his bathtub one day (he doesn't date the episode but it probably took place in the fall of 1936), reading the *Hollywood Reporter*, when Schoenberg called and told him to be at Gershwin's house in an hour. Sendrey writes that the day was perfect and

> the hour was peace over that creamy-white house on Roxbury Drive. The only sounds were the buzzing of insects over the pool, and the rhythmic patter of balls on the court somewhere

behind. A breath later I beheld a memorable and spectacular sight.

There they were, separated by a mere net, perhaps the two greatest and certainly the most discussed musicians of this decade. On one side the younger one who had succeeded in making a respectable woman out of that little hussy, Jazz. . . . On the other side . . . the older man, agile, small of stature but immense of mind, who is beating new paths for music through the wilderness of the unknown, over which we are as yet unable to follow him. . . .

There they were, those two contrasting giants of modern music, George Gershwin and Arnold Schoenberg, united in one common thought to make a little ball scale the top of a net, as though nothing else mattered. Let short-sighted humanity sneer at dissonance . . . love fifteen . . . let them call the *Rhapsody in Blue* a mere fad . . . fifteen all . . . let them walk out pulling grimaces and holding their ears . . . thirty-fifteen . . . let them say: once Tin Pan Alley, always Tin Pan Alley . . . forty-fifteen . . . so Boris Morros thinks *Verklärte Nacht* would make a swell picture score? . . . forty-thirty . . . let them speak of *Porgy and Bess* as a musical dwarf beside a literary Goliath, if it makes them happy . . . game and set, 6-2.

Hello, Al, glad to see you—do you mind waiting until Mr. Schoenberg has a chance to take his revenge? Thanks, get yourself a drink, they are in the cooler beside the pool, then come over and watch a real match. . . ."

I return, sucking something wet and cold through a straw. Already George has taken another game in storm from the unsuspecting little Meister.

"It ain't fair, George," I protest meekly on Schoenberg's behalf.

But Gershwin is playing an unforgiving game, with relentless hard drives, chasing the little man about the court with well-placed shots. I seem to detect a glint of humor in his eye, and a faint smile playing about his lips. Schoenberg is now doing all he can to return sleek volleys and drives, and I see the reason why. Wonderful showman that he is, George is playing to an audience, if only to a one-man audience, but an audience nevertheless. And he finds in admiration and praise a

> stimulant, whether his music is the object of this admiration, or merely a game he happens to indulge in. Here he is the exact opposite of his elder opponent, who has learned to shut his mind against public opinion, knowing it was not yet ready to comprehend what he is achieving, and also realizing that any laudatory tribute would be outweighed by adverse criticism, often hostile disparagement.

The game goes to George.

Sendrey writes that at this time, Schoenberg remains unperturbed while Gershwin plays with "a rhythmic stride which contains a movement unconscious of itself, a thing of great beauty, nonchalance combined with ease." Another game goes to Gershwin; the score is now three-love. The fourth continues to go in his favor.

Sendrey continues: "The sun burns down on the court, and I suck frantically through my straw. As I reach the bottom, a faint bubbling, gargling noise emerges from my bottle—George, about to serve again, looks over, visibly irritated at this interruption. I smile an apology somewhat stupidly, but already this incident has made its impression on his service, which is erratic and lands in the net. Could it be that George mistook this accidental bubbling for an uncouth sign of disapproval, or sardonic innuendo, commonly termed 'raspberry,' done on purpose?"

The writer goes on to say what Kolodin said about George: that "he needed praise and admiration like a flower needs sunshine and rain—banal image but irrefutable fact—and it is the opinion of some that had his *Rhapsody* not been the unprecedented success it was, he would never again have attempted anything in the realm of serious music, and his *Preludes*, his Concerto in F, his *American in Paris*, and, of course *Porgy and Bess*, would never have been written.

"He had been playing to the grandstand, and he had honored me in letting me be his grandstand audience. Now I had repaid him with what he feared most, for the sake of his inspiration, and yet always pretended to care nothing about: taunting disapprobation, sarcastic criticism. It was to him as though an entire tribune filled with people had voiced their disrespectful opinion—his grandstand collapsed, likewise his game. . . . The score was now thirty-forty, in Mr. Schoenberg's favor."

Sendrey goes on to make an analogy of the way Gershwin makes music and plays tennis. He writes that his composition appears so effortless that it leads one to believe as soon as he reaches some kind of impasse, rather than wrestle with it, he throws it away.

Then he starts on something entirely fresh. "With one last 'don't give a damn' slam he attacked the ball, aiming it right into the net. But in that last stroke he had regained all his poise, all his balance, all his harmonious timing, he was once again the master of counterpoint, rhythm and perfect form. . . .

"And then, without the least trace of rancor toward his strawsucking audience which had spoiled his game, he said just what he would have said when getting up from his piano after having torn up an embryonic idea, some incompleted line of musical expression: 'We'll continue later—now let's have some lunch.' "

Gershwin gave a concert in Seattle on December 15 and followed it with concerts in San Francisco, Berkeley, Detroit, and Los Angeles. During the February 1937 engagements in Los Angeles, Gershwin revealed symptoms of something more than neurotic problems. That was when he fell from the podium during a rehearsal. Mueller caught him before he hit the floor. At the second of the two concerts, he stumbled over a passage in the Concerto in F.

Levant writes that Gershwin angrily told him that he saw Levant's face just as his memory failed. Reviews of the concert followed the now-familiar pattern. Here is Richard Drake Saunders in the *Musical Courier:* "In more ways than one it was a show, rather than a concert. Gershwin has a certain individual flair, and an occasional work of his on a program is all very well, but an entire evening is too much. It is like a meal of chocolate eclairs. . . . It fulfills a purpose in making a certain class of people conscious of such a thing as a symphonic ensemble. It was obvious that a large number had never been in the auditorium before. Anyway, they saw some movie stars." The critics seemed unable to accept Gershwin's musical origins.

Harold Arlen, long one of Gershwin's Tin Pan Alley colleagues, described Gershwin during his California year to Joe Morella and Edward Z. Epstein, authors of *Paulette: The Adventurous Life of Paulette Goddard:* "During the last year George was very often unhappy and uneasy. Lots of people were writing well—Rodgers, Porter, others—and, of course, George liked to be kingpin. I felt that something was wrong with him one day when after a lot of us played the piano, George said to me, 'No, you don't. I'm not going to follow you.' I was shocked with surprise. Since we were always together in one bunch trying to help one another, there was little show of jealousy. When he acted that way, I felt uneasy. I knew something was wrong with him, and I thought it was Hollywooditis." Arlen was not alone in his diagnosis. Everyone else appears to have decided it was the turnabout in George's career that made him behave in the peculiar ways that he did. They refused to consider that such a shift in fortune could have been accompanied by a slow-growing tumor.

Once, while driving with Mueller, Gershwin reached behind his valet, opened the car door and tried to push Mueller out. When one considers such bizarre behavior as this in combination with his almost falling off a podium, suffering excruciating headaches and smelling burning rubber, which, even in 1937, was known to be a symptom of a brain tumor, it is difficult to understand why nobody could see how ill he was. Perhaps the fact that he continued to write excellent songs for Hollywood films led people to believe he had to be well, whatever they saw him do.

The late songs were as good as any he ever wrote. For *Shall We Dance*, they include "I've Got Beginner's Luck," "The Last Laugh," "They Can't Take That Away from Me." The score also included "Shall We Dance," "Slap That Bass," "Let's Call the Whole Thing Off," and a delicate instrumental number called "Walking the Dog," which was used to accompany Rogers and Astaire as they strode with their dogs on the deck of a ship.

Among the songs he wrote for *A Damsel in Distress* were "Things Are Looking Up," "Nice Work If You Can Get It," "A Foggy Day," and "The Jolly Tar and the Milkmaid."

Levant writes: "When they were confronted with a situation in [that film] that permitted it, they produced a work in the madrigal style—'The Jolly Tar and the Milkmaid'—so deceptively authentic that most of those who heard it accepted it as seventeenth-century English." Gershwin was unhappy with his professional life on the West Coast. On Broadway he was constantly consulted throughout the work on the production when the matter at hand was in any way related to the score. But in Hollywood those who wrote the songs were expected to disappear once they handed them in.

In April Gershwin was still going to concerts. June Levant remembers one on April 14 sponsored by the Los Angeles Federal Music Project. It included works by Schoenberg, Webern, Adolph Weiss, Gerald Strang, and a first performance of a piece called *Nocturne* by Levant. Gershwin was there. His date for the evening was British screen actress Benita Hume, who married Ronald Colman the following year. June recalls George laughing that night, looking secure and successful. She also remembers Levant saying he was relieved when George had only good things to say about her husband's composition. On April 20 Gershwin wrote to Mabel: "I am lying on a chaise longue with a new gadget, which I have just bought, on my head. You would probably scream with laughter if you could see me. The machine is a new invention put out by the Crosley Radio Company and has been recommended by several people out here as a positive grower of hair. It's an entirely new principle and you know me for new principles."

Paul Mueller remembers telling Gershwin every time he put it on that it was a "crazy" idea, that it was giving continuous electrical shocks to the brain. "I told him I had been an engineer in Berlin, that I thought the helmet was bad for him, but I was unable to convince him to stop using it." Whether Mueller was right or not, he persisted in warning Gershwin against it and Gershwin continued to use it. In fact he had it on almost all of the time, and told friends the machine actually lessened his pain.

In *Fate Keeps on Happening*, Anita Loos, one of Goddard's closest friends, wrote, "Now, at a time when he was so near the end of his short life, George fell in love. He used to follow Paulette everywhere; he came to life in her presence as he had never done before." When the affair was at its most intense, Gershwin instructed Mueller to pull his furnishings out of storage because he intended to marry Goddard and set up house with her in Hollywood.

"But George was not at all well," Loos went on. "He was beset by headaches of alarming intensity. At that time Freud's psychoanalysis had come into vogue, bruited about by people who understood it least. Among the first to be enticed by Freudian theories were George's kin. So they sent him to a Hollywood analyst who theorized that George's headaches were caused by his guilty love for the wife of a friend, Charlie Chaplin."

In a May 19 letter to Mabel, George addressed a question she had asked about a gossip column item regarding Gershwin and Goddard: "I met Miss Goddard a couple of months ago and found her the most interesting personality I've come across since arriving in Hollywood. You would be crazy about meeting her as she has one of the most alert minds you could possibly imagine. On the other hand, she is married to the 'famous Charlie' and under such circumstances, I am not allowing myself to become too involved."

June Levant says that it was not only Goddard's alert mind that attracted George. She says Oscar told her Goddard used to wear loose fitting shorts with nothing underneath and, sitting across from Gershwin at his pool, made him wild. Mueller says he drove Gershwin and Goddard to a Palm Springs resort for a weekend. On the way back Gershwin told him to adjust the rear view mirror so it would not reflect what was happening in the back seat.

"One day," Loos continued, "at a gathering around the Gershwin swimming pool in Beverly Hills, George had a sudden excruciating headache that made him scream in agony. Paralyzed with fright, none of the family was capable of action. Up to that time Paulette had never meddled in their personal affairs but now she took over. She phoned Charlie and asked what should be done." There follows one of the dozens of accounts of someone calling the "one" doctor who should have been called sooner.

Gershwin may have ended the affair with Paulette Goddard after Mueller told him that he had heard that Goddard was having another affair with a Mexican envoy. Frankie Godowsky confirms Mueller's account, saying "in some ways George was very conventional."

But Lois Granato, Goddard's secretary, suggests the end was not as simple as this: "Paulette used to say, 'The story is so horrible. Nobody should ever talk about it. Everyone felt the problem was in George's mind. They knew George was in love with me and blamed me for George's peculiar behavior. I tried to visit George several times at home but the family refused to let me in. They would not even tell George I was at the door. They treated him terribly, controlling what he did and who he saw.' "

Edward Jablonski included the following incident in *Gershwin: A Biography*, published in 1987. "On one occasion, he suffered a dizzy spell while leaving the Brown Derby restaurant and fell to the sidewalk. One member of the party was not impressed. 'Leave him there,' she snapped, 'all he wants is attention.' " Although the author did not identify the person, friends and family say it was Leonore.

Jablonski continues, "There were periods of impaired coordination; his playing was poor; he dropped utensils on the table; he spilled water; he fell on the stairs. These inexplicable occurrences upset his sister-in-law. Once, after spilling food, he was asked to leave the table. Ira helped him upstairs to his room. For a moment their eyes met at the doorway. 'I'll never forget that look,' Ira later told a friend, 'as long as I live.' "

. . .

During Gershwin's short life, he went from a seemingly self-assured young man to a terribly ill, altogether beaten one whose weaknesses allowed those who had envied him to treat him in ways ranging from nonchalance to abuse. Critic Alexander Woollcott, in a memoir published in 1946, told this anecdote about the youthful George: "Sometimes the sheer candor of Gershwin's self-examination more than ruffled his colleagues. Sometimes it maddened them. There was the instance of the rift with Harry Ruby, himself no mean songwriter but even so, of course, no Gershwin. They were playing ball together at Gershwin's country place one summer when the game grew so rough that Gershwin withdrew. His hands, he explained, were too valuable to be thus risked.

" 'Say,' said Ruby, 'what about *my* hands?'

" 'Well,' said Gershwin, 'it's not the same thing.'

"Over this disconcerting reply Ruby brooded in silence for a long time, and in the process developed a reluctance to visit his erstwhile crony. Indeed, they did not see each other again for two years. When they did meet, it was by chance on the boardwalk of Atlantic City. Gershwin was overjoyed at the reunion. Where had good old Ruby been keeping himself? What was the matter anyway? Had he, Gershwin, said anything, done anything, to offend? After a moment's meditation, and seeing that candor seemed *de rigueur*, Ruby decided to tell him, and did so, relating the forgotten incident just as I have told it to you. 'And then,' he wound up, 'you said, 'It's not the same thing.'

"Gershwin received this in silence, took the story into the council-chambers of his heart, examined it, and then replied, 'Well, it isn't.' "

That insensitivity, the "kingpin" attitude Arlen describes, was also in evidence in what Gershwin said to Levant when they traveled together to Pittsburgh to prepare for a concert: "We took a late train for the overnight trip," Levant writes, "sharing a drawing room. A lengthy discussion of music occupied us for an hour or so, and I was actually in the midst of answering one of his questions when he calmly removed his clothes and eased himself into the lower berth with the proprietary air befitting a member of one of Lundberg's America's Sixty Families.

"There was nothing left for me to do but undress and attempt to finish my sentence as I did. George, however, resumed the thread of his discourse, and I suggested perhaps it was difficult for him to sleep on a train and would he like one of my sleeping pills—with the air of a man offering a friend an after-dinner mint.

"I adjusted myself to the inconvenience of the upper berth, reflecting on the artistic-economic progression by which Paderewski has a private car, Gershwin a drawing room and Levant a sleepless night. At this moment my light must have disturbed George's doze, for he opened his eyes, looked up at me and said drowsily: 'Upper berth—lower berth. That's the difference between talent and genius.' "

Woollcott writes that he thinks George was correct: his hands were more valuable than Ruby's. And many would say Gershwin was right in assessing he had genius and Levant only talent. Still, his attitude was bound to offend those around him, and no amount of psychoanalysis could undermine this kind of arrogance. The grandiose Gershwin is the portrait that has come down in history. As recently as March 1992, the *Hollywood Reporter* published the following:

> It is generally conceded that George Gershwin was a musical genius, and no one was more convinced of this than George himself. He once attended a concert featuring a pianist from Spain. When the concert was over, Gershwin's friend said, "Isn't he great, George?" "He's a genius," Gershwin said. "A Spanish Gershwin."
>
> Pianist Oscar Levant, a well-known wit and a good friend of George Gershwin, once asked the composer, "If you had it to do all over, George, would you fall in love with yourself again?"

. . .

What caused the transformation of the man and undermined the Gershwin revealed here was failure: critics panning the concert works, bad box-office receipts for the Broadway shows, empty rows of seats at Lewisohn Stadium when he performed there. The failure appears to have led him to send unconscious messages to everyone around to help bring him down. After Leonore, the most notorious of these people may have been Samuel Goldwyn.

The last professional project of the composer's life was the movie *The Goldwyn Follies*. In *A Smattering of Ignorance*, Levant writes of the moment when the film was finished: "The producer summoned George to a conference one afternoon and insisted that the performance of the music must be given in the presence of his full staff of loyal, well-paid amanuenses (stooges). Being with justice suspicious of his own opinion, Goldwyn augmented it with an a cappella choir of enthusiasts. The experience of thus submitting his work for the approbation of a dummy panel, whose opinion was as predictable as the result of a Jersey City election, humiliated George."

In *Goldwyn: A Biography*, A. Scott Berg writes that Goldwyn had attracted Gershwin to the film by assuring him that George Balanchine, the most celebrated new figure in the dance world, would choreograph a sequence to new music by Gershwin. Gershwin had planned to compose a piece for this purpose, but when the symptoms of the tumor began to interfere, the idea shifted to the creation of a ballet to *An American in Paris*. Vera Zorina was to be the dancer. "George Gershwin jangled Goldwyn's nerves the most. The composer always seemed tired and dizzy. Goldwyn heard that he had been secretly keeping late nights with former Goldwyn girl Paulette Goddard. Still, Gershwin showed up at his office on the lot to labor over two songs, 'Our Love Is Here to Stay,' and 'Love Walked In.' Ira's lyrics were necessarily generic because there was still not enough of a script to demand more specific sentiments. At this point Goldwyn told Gershwin only that he wanted 'hit songs you can whistle, just like Irving Berlin wrote.' " Reacting to the remark, Gershwin told Sam Behrman, "I had to live for this—to hear

Sam Goldwyn say, 'Why can't you write hits, like Irving Berlin?' "

Berg continues: "One morning in late June 1937, George complained of a headache so severe that his brother had to phone him in sick. When this news reached the head office, Goldwyn ordered him off the payroll until his return."

Gershwin accepted the demeaning conditions and even gave Goldwyn the rights to *An American in Paris* for nothing. Gershwin is reported to have felt such guilt at not being able to produce as he always did—on schedule—for Goldwyn that he offered the producer this major work as a gift. (Goldwyn didn't use *An American in Paris* in the *Goldwyn Follies.* It wasn't until 1951, when Arthur Freed produced the movie *An American in Paris* with Vincente Minnelli directing, that the score was used.) Ten years earlier, he had given George White a similar gift, but under altogether different circumstances.

Nanette Kutner, who started to work as his secretary in 1926, later wrote: "That year [1927] the *Scandals* utilized his *Rhapsody.* He asked nothing for this, yet was grateful when given an opening night box." Gershwin probably asked nothing for this because Margaret Manners, the mother of his year-old son, was dancing a solo role.

Hermes Pan, a renowned Hollywood choreographer, tells this story about how he inadvertently insulted Gershwin in much the same way that Goldwyn and Berlin insulted him—with an assault on the quality of his work. "When I was assigned to *Shall We Dance,* I had the sheet music for the score, but I hadn't heard it yet. I went on the rehearsal stage, and there was this man at the piano. I said, 'Hello, I'm the dance director for this picture. . . . Would you mind playing this? I've got to start rehearsing it tomorrow.' He said, 'Well certainly.' He started to go. I said, 'Gee, that's like a march—can you play it a little slower? 'He said, 'Oh, sure.' But it got worse. I said, 'Well, that's like a funeral march.' He tried it different ways, but nothing worked for me. 'You know something?' I said. 'Gershwin or no Gershwin, I think this stinks.' After trying it a few more times, I finally said, 'Well, excuse me, but there's a meeting I have to go to. I'll see you later.' After I'd been in the meeting for about five minutes the rehearsal pianist came in. Everybody stood up and said, 'Mr. Gershwin!' Oh, I practically went through the floor. Finally, after everybody had gone, I said, 'Mr. Gershwin, as you know, I'm embarrassed and very sorry I said what I did.' And he said, 'You know something? You might just be right.' That's how nice he was. George Gershwin was just a very modest person. He would go along with anything you suggested."

Minnelli, in *I Remember It Well*, tells this story that took place about the same time: "Two of the songs—'Our Love Is Here to Stay' and 'Love Walked In'—were nearly completed when I invited George to join me and a couple of girls about town for Saturday dinner. He arrived in his usual high spirits. 'This is George Gershwin,' I told the girls. They stared blankly back. Neither had ever heard of him. George pretended not to notice."

In her 1991 book, *Ginger: My Story*, Rogers tells an interesting tale. During the filming of *Shall We Dance*, she went out with Gershwin a few times. One day he brought her into an art-supply store to get something for himself. A paint set caught her eye. Then she waited for him outside. When he came out he handed her a wrapped package saying, 'Dear girl, this is for you.' "

Rogers writes that she did not open the package until after Gershwin died. Then she discovered not only the set she had coveted in the store but a self-portrait he had enclosed with it. "On the reverse side of the 5 x 7 art store receipt," Rogers says, "was a colorful self-portrait George had drawn with these pastels, and he had put his initials GG in the lower right hand corner. And to think I never thanked him for it. What an empty feeling I had for not acknowledging his wonderful drawing, which he must have known I would treasure, as indeed I do."

Written in the spring of 1937, the lyrics for the title song of the Astaire-Rogers movie are morose; dancing is the antidote for despair.

Life is short; we're growing older.
  Don't you be an also-ran.

On June 20 Gershwin entered Cedars of Lebanon Hospital, where his troubles were diagnosed as symptoms of "hysteria." During that examination, among the many things Gershwin told the doctors was that, four months before, he had suffered from insomnia "when he was in love." That information appears on the Discharge Summary prepared by Carl Rand, the operating surgeon, for Gabriel Segall, the attending physician.

In early July, Sam Behrman was looking forward to the Los Angeles opening of his play *Amphitryon 38* starring Alfred Lunt and Lynn Fontanne. Behrman writes of arriving on the West Coast and dining with Levant and screenwriter Sonya Levien. "We went over to the Gershwins'. Lee and Ira greeted us. George was upstairs. Lee told us he knew we were coming and would be down presently. We waited in the living room. George came downstairs accompanied by a male nurse. I stared at him. It was not the George we all knew. He was very pale. The light had gone from his eyes. He seemed old. He greeted me mirthlessly. His handshake was limp, the spring had gone out of his walk. He came to a sofa near where I was sitting and lay down on it. He tried to adjust his head against the pillows. The nurse hovered over him.

"I asked him if he felt pain. 'Behind my eyes,' he said, and repeated it: 'Behind my eyes.' I knelt beside him on the sofa and put my hand under his head. I asked him if he felt like playing the piano. He shook his head. It was the first such refusal I'd ever heard from him. . . .

"There was silence. He spoke of the *Porgy* tour, which had not been successful. I asked him whether he would come to my opening Monday night. He shook his head slowly. He moved his head around on the pillow. I took my hand away. He looked at me with lusterless eyes. I had a sinking feeling: he is no longer one of us. He turned to the nurse and said he'd like to go back to his room. The nurse got him up. They went upstairs.

"When he had gone I looked at Leonore. 'How long has he been this way?' I asked.

" 'For several weeks. He seems worse tonight. Maybe it's seeing you—reminds him of the past.'

" 'Didn't you tell me he has trouble eating?' Oscar asked Leonore.

" 'Yes,' said Lee, 'he doesn't seem to be able to manage his food. I have to cut it for him.'

"We sat for a time not speaking. Oscar, Sonya and I rose to go. I asked Lee whether I should hold the seats for them Monday night. She said certainly, that it would be a diversion for them."

A couple of days later, Behrman called Ira, who told him they had spoken to Dr. Simmel, George's West Coast psychoanalyst, who agreed that it would be "wise to separate George from his family." On January 25, 1990, Paul Mueller attributed the decision to Ira and Leonore: "They couldn't wait to get rid of him," Mueller said.

By then Gershwin had already been moved to Harburg's house with Paul Levy as his nurse. Some time during these last weeks, George called his mother at 3 A.M. She reminded him of the time and asked what on earth he was calling for at such an hour. He said he had not realized it was so late because of the time difference. Then she chastised him for making the call at all, because of the money it cost. She said Morris would have disapproved.

On June 14, Julia Van Norman wrote, "When I tune in on your spirit lately, there seems to be quite a lot of static. Something is proving troublous, I'm afraid. Anyway, all does not seem quite serene." A week later Van Norman learned that George had been admitted to Cedars of Lebanon. Immediately she wrote him an anguished letter and almost as immediately he replied with a telegram: "Thanks for your letter. Home from hospital. Feeling somewhat better. Don't worry. Expect to be well in a week or so." On July 1 Van Norman answered: "That was the nicest telegram I ever received. Knowing you are better and out of the hospital—well, you can't know how different everything looks to me. . . . I had no real warning of what had befallen you except this. I dreamt you sent me a letter and I simply could not decipher it. It looked as if your coordination had gone haywire. Judging from your handwriting, something was terribly wrong with your nervous system. I never did find out what was in the letter. But I did wake up thinking something was wrong with George. Now you are moving away from the thing, thank God."

The Levants visited George at Harburg's house. In 1991 June Levant spoke about it: "When we arrived, George came downstairs in his pajamas and dressing gown. The nurse was behind him on the stairs but did not follow him into the living room. Mueller was not there. George went to the piano and played while Oscar sang Crown. Then Oscar stayed at the piano and George came over, put his arm around me, and looked deeply into my eyes. It was a beseeching look, an expression that touched me as little else ever has. I felt so uncomfortable. Oscar was very jealous about me so I never told him about it, even after George died. But I have been haunted by that look on his face all of my life.

"After that we went by the house. Lee said, 'He doesn't have a chance. He's not going to make it.' I was stunned, shocked by this. Ira was not there at the time."

Walter Winchell, the Broadway columnist, ran an item noting the seriousness of George's condition. Leonore wired Frankie in Venice not to believe Winchell, that she must definitely not come home. Several days later, when Frankie was in Vienna, she received another wire saying George was dead.

On July 10 Alan ran away from home. He remembers feeling suddenly distraught and deciding to hitchhike to Montana, where he had some friends. The next day, in the passenger seat of a trailer truck, the driver began to weep and told the eleven-year-old at his side that he had just learned from a radio report that George Gershwin, "a great man" died. Alan says he asked to be let out but has no recall of what happened after that.

Kay Swift was attending a concert that Sunday afternoon with her daughter. Suddenly, in the midst of the performance, she stood up and said, "George is gone."

On Friday evening, July 9, Gershwin lapsed into a coma at the Harburg house with Paul Levy and Paul Mueller present.

He was taken to Cedars of Lebanon Hospital. Although an effort was made to bring in Dr. Walter E. Dandy, a leading neurosurgeon affiliated with Johns Hopkins Hospital in Baltimore, he was on a yacht in Chesapeake Bay and could not have arrived in time to make any difference.

The surgery was performed by Dr. Carl Rand, a local neurosurgeon, with Dr. Walter Ziskind, a neurologist, and Dr. Howard Naffziger, a San Francisco neurosurgeon, in attendance. Kate Wolpin remembers Ira calling her, asking if she knew where Rose was, because he was going to ask her to fly out right away. Rose was playing poker somewhere in the Rockaways and when Ira did reach her, she said she would not come out, that there was nothing for her to do.

George Pallay stationed himself ten feet away from the operating room and then served as a liaison between the physicians and the family. In a two-part report prepared for Dr. Gabriel Segall, the attending physician, Dr. Carl Rand describes the examination that took place on June 20, when Gershwin was discharged from the hospital with a diagnosis of hysteria, and then, in the second part, the surgery itself. Dr. Rand writes that "a cystic tumor seemed evident," that when they went through the thick cyst wall they found what "was thought to be a mural nodule," and that they removed as much as they could by electric cautery.

The surgery lasted five hours. The last paragraph of the report includes the following: "Patient's post-operative condition was poor and he was given a blood transfusion. . . . Hyperthermia developed and he passed away at about 11:00 a.m. on July 11, 1937."

Jablonski's 1987 biography quotes Dr. Dandy as saying, "I do not see what more could have been done for Mr. Gershwin. It was just one of those fulminant tumors. There are not many tumors that are removable, and it would be my impression that although the tumor in large part might have been extirpated and he would have recovered for a little while, it would have recurred very quickly since the whole thing fulminated so suddenly."

But several neurosurgeons who have read the operative report and seen photographs of the slides of the tumor state that this was not a glioblastoma, as Dandy implied, but a cystic astrocytoma that turned malignant. It is the slow-growing cystic astrocytoma, not the fast-growing glioblastoma, that contains a mural nodule.

Dr. Raj Murali, acting chairman of the department of neurosurgery at St. Vincent's Hospital in New York, and Dr. Robert Miller, neurosurgeon and faculty member of Yale Medical School, reviewed the discharge summary report, which included the operative note. They also studied the postoperative photomicrographs of the biopsy specimen. In March 1992, Dr. Murali wrote, "As the duration of symptoms is about three years, I would presume that this tumor started as a low-grade astrocytoma in the temporal lobe presenting with temporal lobe seizures as characterized by the olfactory aura. The tumor most probably then underwent a more malignant transformation. The rapid final deterioration was probably due to cyst formation."

Dr. Miller concurs with Dr. Murali on the diagnosis. He goes on to suggest that the reason that a neurosurgeon such as Harvey Cushing of Boston or Walter E. Dandy of Johns Hopkins Medical School or Carl W. Rand, Cushing's student, then in Los Angeles, had not been consulted before Gershwin went into the final coma lay in the close ties between psychiatry and neurology at that time. "Newly formed in 1934, there was a combined Board of Neurology *and* Psychiatry," Miller says.

When Gershwin's headaches worsened in the spring of 1937, he called Zilboorg, who suggested he consult Dr. Ernest Simmel, another psychoanalyst. "When Gershwin went to Simmel," Miller says, "he should have gone to a neurosurgeon. But many psychiatrists were not prone to think surgically at that time.

"From all that we know," Miller continues, "it appears that

the situation could have had a different ending if the diagnosis had been made earlier. If the mural nodule had been excised before malignant change, Gershwin may not have gone into an irreversible neurologic state."

Even taking into account what Dr. Miller says about many psychiatrists and neurologists being unaware of advances in neurosurgery at the time, it is difficult to understand why Ira and Leonore did so little when George's symptoms worsened in such an alarming way. One would have expected them to seek out a great neurosurgeon. That was Behrman's recommendation. But they did not act on it. On the contrary, the last weeks saw virtually no action at all.

In *Musical Stages*, an autobiography, Richard Rodgers quotes from a letter he wrote to his wife, Dorothy, on July 12, the day after Gershwin died:

"The town is in a daze and nobody talks about anything but George's death. There seems to be a certain amount of mystery as to the reason no diagnosis was made until the night before the operation, but since we don't know the details, it isn't possible to have an opinion. It's just awful."

In California, on that very same day, the day after his brother's death, Ira appeared in court with papers that had been prepared by the law firm then known as O'Melveny, Tullers & Myers. He was there to try to secure control and management of George's estate by applying for appointment as its "special administrator." Four days later, on July 16, Rose Gershwin filed papers in New York opposing Ira, claiming her right to be the estate's sole administrator. In an affidavit she stated:

"I have made a diligent search and inquiry for a will of my said deceased son, but I find none and I remember clearly that my son told me several months ago that he never made a will and that everything belonging to him, upon his decease, would go to me."

In all of the accounts presented by family and friends of George's last months, there is no suggestion that George ever considered his own death, or, if at any moment he did, could have planned for it in the cool-headed manner Rose articulated. In a separate petition Emanuel Alexander, Rose Gershwin's attorney, declared that his client be given what she asked without having to appear in court. "Mrs. Gershwin," Alexander wrote, "is at present in a weak physical state of health due to the shock which she sustained as a result of the sudden death of her famous son who was so dear and attached to her."

Rose Gershwin won. In the New York *Times*, the gross estate was listed at $430,841; the net $341,089. The valuations of specific pieces listed as part of the residuary estate were: *Rhapsody in Blue*, $20,125; *An American in Paris*, $5,000; *Of Thee I Sing*, $4,000; Concerto in F, $1,750; *Porgy and Bess*, $250.

After attending to the legal matters, Ira and Lee came back to New York on the plane that carried George's body. Ira came out of the aircraft sobbing. Irene Gallagher was driven up to the plane where, she recalls, "Lee pushed me away. She came up to me and just pushed me away."

Vera Brodsky Lawrence, a musicologist who was then a professional pianist, was giving a concert at Juilliard the night before the funeral. Lawrence says that Frances Gershwin Godowsky's father-in-law, the pianist Leopold Godowsky, was there and asked, "Will I see you at the celebration?" Lawrence characterized the question as "a most caustic remark." Obviously there were musicians who did not mourn Gershwin's death.

It rained on July 15, the day of the funeral at Temple Emanu-El on Sixty-fifth Street and Fifth Avenue. The New York *Times* reported: "Until regular police lines were formed, cutting off the east side of the avenue from Sixty-fourth to Sixty-fifth streets, three policemen who stood in the doorway of the temple were forced to link arms and brace themselves against the pressure of the crowd that sought to push its way in." The services were conducted by Dr. Nathan A. Perilman. Dr. Stephen S. Wise, rabbi of the Free Synagogue, spoke in praise of the thirty-eight-year-old composer. "The ceremonies opened with a processional," the *Times* continued, "based on Bach's 'Aria for a Suite for Strings.' . . . Then Dr. Perilman read the 90th and 102nd Psalms. Ossip Giskin played a cello solo, Schumann's 'Traumerie.' Then came Dr. Wise's eulogy; Beethoven's . . . Opus 130, played by the Perole Quartette; a prayer by Dr. Perilman and a recessional, Handel's 'Largo' by the quartette and organ."

Al Simon, who had served as assistant rehearsal pianist for *Of Thee I Sing*, attended the funeral. Speaking from a nursing home in 1989, Simon said, "The funeral had an atmosphere George would have hated. It was somber. The music was dour, too." No Gershwin tune was played. Mayor Fiorello La Guardia headed the pallbearers. Among the 3,500 people who crowded into the temple that day were former mayor Jimmy Walker and Kern, Porter, Jolson, Chaplin, Whiteman, Rogers, the Astaires, the Goldwyns, the George S. Kaufmans, Tucker, Shilkret, Knopf, Harris, Edward Warburg, Kay Swift, and Kitty Carlisle.

There was a simultaneous service at the B'nai B'rith Temple in Hollywood. Alan was excluded from all services, as were the Schneiders. The Gershwins fired Mueller, he says, without giving him enough money to get back to the East Coast.

Julia Van Norman began writing letters to herself in George's hand. Then she wrote one to Ira in George's hand asking for all her letters back. Ira returned them. When Mueller arrived in New York, he visited the Van Normans in the Bronx. Julia showed Mueller the telegram Gershwin sent after the June 20 hospitalization. Mueller was stunned that Gershwin, at that time in excruciating pain, could have managed to get the telegram off. Horace says Mueller spoke in such detail about the illness and death that the meeting "probably hastened Julia's entrance into a mental hospital." In 1992, Julia Van Norman was still hospitalized.

In 1939 Kay Swift married Faye Hubbard, a cowboy she met when they both worked at the New York World's Fair that year.

A few years later she wrote *Who Could Ask for Anything More?*, a witty book about her new life. That marriage ended in divorce. In 1992 Swift was living in New York.

With some help from Vernon Duke, Ira completed those songs for the *Goldwyn Follies* that were unfinished when his brother died. In "Our Love Is Here to Stay," a lyric Ira wrote after George died, he seems to be dealing with the connection between his brother and himself, rather than with the connection of his brother and a woman, or that of his brother and dancing and death. "Together we're going a long, long way" turns out to have been prescient. The songs of George and Ira Gershwin have maintained their popularity, as Ira suggests with the reference to the Rockies or Gibraltar.

Ira died in 1983. Friends say he was depressed the last ten years. Michael Feinstein, who worked closely with him at the end, told an interviewer in 1992 that Ira kept saying from his bed that he had lived a "terrible life." Feinstein added that there were "so many emotional issues that he hadn't dealt with. . . . When we don't deal with those things, eventually they atrophy inside of us."

After George died, Leonore entered psychoanalysis. A close relative says she did it to help her deal with the problem of being held accountable by so many of the composer's friends and colleagues. Leonore died in August 1991, at the age of ninety.

In 1938, Schoenberg contributed the following to Armitage's collection of essays:

> Many musicians do not consider George Gershwin a serious composer. But they should understand that, serious or not, he is a composer, that is, a man who lives in music and expresses everything, serious or not, sound or superficial, by means of music, because it is his native language. There are a number of composers, serious (as they believe) or not (as I know), who learned to add notes together. But they are only serious on account of a perfect lack of humor and soul.
>
> It seems to me that this difference alone is sufficient to jus-

tify calling the one a composer, but the other none. . . . I do not speak here as a musical theorist nor am I a critic, and hence I am not forced to say whether history will consider Gershwin a kind of Johann Strauss or Debussy, Offenbach or Brahms, Lehár or Puccini.

But I know he is an artist and a composer; he expressed musical ideas; and they were new, as is the way in which he expressed them.

CODA

The totally organized scores of the first generation post-Schoenberg serialists—Milton Babbitt and those who followed him—set the tone for the music that dominated composition in the decades following World War II. But something was lost when that happened. What it was can best be described by quoting Levant from his *Memoirs of an Amnesiac:* "I sometimes used to lunch at the Schoenbergs' in Brentwood. . . . Once he was humming an unhummable theme with unnegotiable leaps between intervals which were in his usual atonal style. He turned to his wife and asked, 'What is that?'

"She hesitated, stammered, and helplessly admitted that she couldn't identify it.

" 'That is the main theme from the piece I dedicated to you,' he explained sternly.

"That was quite a responsibility. The piece can not be hummed unless you're a freak. But Mrs. Schoenberg was embarrassed."

Much as he may have tried, Gershwin could not have adapted to the Schoenberg aesthetic. Irrepressible melody is what he made. His songs and concert works have, in fact, remained so popular that, in 1990, Warner Music paid the Gershwin estate $200,000,000 for the Gershwin catalog.

INDEX

INDEX

PHOTO CREDITS

AP/Wide World Photos: 24, 43, 56, 69
Collection of the author: 3
Carousel/International Museum of Photography at George Eastman House: 2
Culver Pictures: 22, 28, 37, 51, 54, 61
Courtesy Stanley Dance/Frank Driggs Collection: 12
Nancy Bloomer Duessen: 18, 42, 73
Frank Driggs Collection: 5, 6, 7, 8, 9, 10, 11, 14, 15, 16, 19, 23, 27, 38, 39, 40, 44, 46, 48, 49, 50, 52, 53, 58, 59, 60, 62, 64, 65, 70
Alan Gershwin: 4
Judy Gershwin: 36
Gershwin Archives/Library of Congress: 66, 71
The Estate of George Gershwin: 63 bottom
Robert Gilbert: 72
Anne Grossman: 13, 45
Victor Hammer Galleries: 63 top
Bill Harris: 26
© Al Hirschfeld/Margo Feiden Galleries: 1
Museum of the City of New York Theatre Archives: 32, 33, 34, 35, 57, 67
The New York Times: 20
Laura Pallay: 41
Rodgers and Hammerstein Archives/Lincoln Center Library: 21
Ann Ronell Archives: 25, 31
Mrs. Joseph Schillinger: 47
© Sibley Music Library/Eastman School of Music: 17
Mr. and Mrs. Alexander Smallens, Jr.: 55
U.S. Patent Office: 68
Katharine Weber: 29
Courtesy of Katharine Weber/Museum of the City of New York Theatre Archives: 30